DEATHS

FIELDING – Rev. Richard, on July 5th suddenly at home. Beloved husband of Janet and devoted father of Michael and Jean. Funeral July 16th. Family flowers only.

FLOWER – Miss Georgina luly 4th after a l...

When Richard died Janet not only lost her husband, she lost her job, her position in the community, his income and their home.

We have been trying to help her put her life together again.

The Corporation of the Sons of the Clergy was established 300 years ago, in Cromwell's time, to give support to clergy and their families in times of crisis.

We give cash grants to clergy and their dependants for a variety of reasons – to elderly retired clergymen or widows, for instance, who find heating or repair bills more than they can manage, for school uniforms, to provide books for ordinands in training, to help divorced clergy and their wives at the painful period of separation.

It isn't enough, of course. No cash grant can take the place of a loving husband, a father to see the children through the difficult years of adolescence, a leader in the parish, a breadwinner, a priest. But it is something; among other things it is a reminder that people care.

With your help we could do more. Please help us – in whatever way you can – with a legacy, a covenant or a donation.

Corporation of the Sons of the Clergy

1 Dean Trench Street, London SW1P 3HB.   Tel: 0171–799 3696.

Charity 207736

CHURCH PULPIT
YEAR BOOK

A Complete set of Expository Outlines for the Sundays of the Year, also for Saints' Days & Special Occasions

1997

CHANSITOR PUBLICATIONS

Published 1996 by Chansitor Publications,
a wholly owned imprint of Hymns
Ancient and Modern Limited, St Mary's
Works, St Mary's Plain, Norwich,
Norfolk, NR3 3BH

ISBN 1-85175-117-3

Typeset by Rowland Phototypesetting Limited,
Bury St Edmunds, Suffolk
Printed in Great Britain by
St Edmundsbury Press Limited, Bury St Edmunds, Suffolk

Preface

The Millennium

The Millennium Commission has allocated over two million pounds towards illuminating some four hundred churches. On the last stroke of midnight, as the new century is born, bells will peal out and church towers will light up! The *Church Floodlighting Trust* hopes that this will be a way of reminding people throughout the country that the Millennium marks the birth of Jesus.

The mainstream Churches have more in mind: the Millennium is seen as perhaps the greatest opportunity that we Christians will ever have, to exalt the Name of Jesus – with due respect of course for other Faiths. The Millennium can convey to this country what following the Lord could mean for the welfare of all in our society.

Some would like the Millennium to have the features of the Old Testament Jubilee (see Leviticus 25) At Jubilee time, burdens of debt and slavery were lifted, giving people in debt and slaves the chance to start again. What some Christians would like to see happen is for the West, with all its riches, to cancel out Third World debt. What a Jubilee! What a Millennium!

The *Church Pulpit Year Book* is dedicated, as ever, to the parish clergy, to NSMs and Readers, trusting that the material offered will be of help Sunday by Sunday, on Festivals and weekday occasions. If you are using the book for the first time you are welcomed; please note that comments and suggestions are gladly received, also possible contributions for future editions.

Francis Stephens
Editor

CHANSITOR PUBLICATIONS

Preliminary Note

For each Sunday of the year, two sermons are provided. The *first* is for the main Service, assumed to be the Eucharist, and at which the Readings will be from the ASB – simply because of the wider range over the Holy Scriptures compared with the older Book.

However, where possible links are provided with the BCP, and in any case the Indexes of *Subjects* and of *Texts*, at the back of the book, can be consulted to find an outline that suits or can be adapted. The *second sermon* is nominally for use at Evensong Prayer, and has a text usually from the ASB EP Readings; but freedom is taken to deal with other subjects from time to time.

For Saints' Days and special occasions *one* outline is provided, to be used at the Eucharist or Evensong as desired. In any case the Editor hopes the users of the book will feel free to adapt and alter, to suit the needs of individual churches or congregations.

A few additions and alterations to the Calendar have been taken from *The Promise of His Glory* and various prayers, as also from the companion volume *Lent, Holy Week and Easter. Patterns for Worship* is also recommended for its variety of prayers and its creative suggestions for worship.

Comments and suggestions are always welcome and should be addressed to The Editor, as also sermon material for future editions.

Acknowledgements: The Editor gratefully acknowledges permission from the Central Board of Finance of the Church of England to reproduce material from *The Alternative Service Book 1980; Lent, Holy week and Easter; The Promise of His Glory*, and *Patterns for Worship*. Thanks are due also to many other sources, from individuals and schools of thought, for help and material for this publication. The Editor trusts that the use of material will be forgivingly regarded as a small aid to the advancement of the Kingdom. Special thanks are due to Mrs Roberta Berke, the Revd Philip Buckler, the Right Revd Graham Dow, the Revd Canon John Inge, the Revd Tom Devonshire Jones, the Revd John Ovenden, the Revd Michael Payne, the Revd Canon Phillip Roberts, the Revd John Slater, the Revd John Stott, the Revd Dr John Thewlis, and the Revd Joanna Yates, for their contributions and help. Also the Revd J. W. Hunwicke (Compiler: *Order for Eucharist & Divine Office*, Church Union) for his assistance.

CONTENTS

For Indexes of Texts and Subjects, please see end of book. The ASB readings are for Year 1, changing to Year 2 on October 26 1997.

xi

SERMONS FOR SAINTS' DAYS AND SPECIAL OCCASIONS
1996

1997

Now many more can benefit from the healing power of St.Luke's

St Luke's is special!

We are a small, acute hospital in central London. For over 100 years we have looked after Anglican clergy and their families, missionaries from abroad and other full-time church workers.

Most of the work has been paid for by contributions from lay people, and 150 of Britain's top consultants give their services free. No charges of any kind are made to the clergy patients.

But now, many more people can benefit! St Luke's and Western Provident Association have set up a scheme which allows you, if you are an Anglican churchgoer on the electoral roll, to have independent treatment at St Luke's (or an appropriate hospital) at very reduced fees.

And that's not all! Apart from the WPA scheme, St Luke's offers outpatient psychiatric support, a Couple Counselling Service, courses on Stress Management, and LukeLine - a telephone service anyone can use, which gives free, expert and *completely* confidential advice on health problems and where help is available anywhere in the UK. If you'd like to know more about the services St Luke's offers, ring us on 0171-388 4954, or write to the Hospital Administrator at the address below.

And if you would like to join the family of supporters of St Luke's, you will be made very welcome. For example, £250 sponsors a patient for a day, £350 a surgical operation.But we are glad of *any* donation, covenant or legacy, no matter how small.Whichever option you choose, there couldn't be a better way of saying – "Thank you!".

St.Luke's

HOSPITAL FOR THE CLERGY

Caring for those who care for others

14 Fitzroy Square, London W1P 6AH. Tel: 0171-388 4954. Fax: 0171-383 4812

First Sunday in Advent *Fourth Sunday before Christmas* 1 December 1996 **'Look Forward!'**

'You, my friends, are not in the dark; you are all children of light, children of day.' 1 Thessalonians 5,5 (ASB NT Reading) or 'The night is far spent, the day is at hand; let us therefore cast off the works of darkness, and let us put on the armour of light.' Romans 13.12 (BCP Epistle)

Good News!

Advent is indeed a time of good news, when the 'Coming of the Kingdom' is to be proclaimed, and we are 'earnestly to look forward' to that 'salvation that is nearer than when we first believed' (Romans 13.11). Yet – surprisingly perhaps – Advent is something of a newcomer to the Christian Calendar. The historians tell us that it was not known at all until the fifth century, and even by the seventh century it was by no means universally accepted or observed. In those days Advent was a period of six Sundays, like Lent, and like Lent it was a penitential time. Later, six was reduced to five and eventually to the four usual Sundays that we have now; though in our new C. of E. book 'The Promise of His Glory', three Sundays are added on at the beginning to emphasize the theme of 'The Kingdom'.

So what are we particularly remembering and celebrating in Advent?

During the weeks before Jesus' birth, the only people awaiting the arrival of the Lord – apart perhaps from the three Wise Men whom we will be thinking of later at Epiphany – will have been Mary and Joseph, and their immediate family and friends; no one else. And we may fairly doubt whether – notwithstanding the words of the Angel to Mary at the Annunciation, and to Joseph – they yet fully recognized the implications of the coming birth.

Would they have seen the period as a time of penitence? Surely not; it would most certainly have been a period of preparation. Mary, like all expectant mothers, would have been sewing or knitting garments; Joseph would have been getting a crib or cot ready. And both would have been looking forward with joy and anticipatio.., while preparing for that complete change in their lives which the birth of any baby into a family of any kind inevitably brings.

Preparation for a new child may, of course, involve clearing out unwanted junk, to make physical room for the new baby; and the prospect of a new person sharing house and life may mean the making of emotional and spiritual space also. If this is the equivalent in our inner lives of penitence, so be it; but do think of this whole Advent period as one of *preparation* – which means looking forward – rather than *penitence* – which tends to mean looking back.

So let us, with Mary and Joseph, look forward to, and prepare as best we may, for the coming of the Child. On the one hand, you and I cannot prepare as if we knew nothing of what happened in the life of that child, nor of what his followers came to believe that child to be. On the other hand, we can be prepared for surprises such as a new child may provide, especially this Child, in our lives and in our thinking. Indeed, we may find that this is not only a 'God of Surprises' but a Surprising God.

Light and Dark

I can remember, as a very small boy, being carried on the shoulders of my father, through the darkness of the sleeping countryside. Above were the twinkling stars; one or two small windows could be seen, but otherwise all was totally dark. Then suddenly a startling and beautiful shaft of intense light pierced the darkness; what a beautiful sight it was, stretching from the ground below right up into the sky above, probing and searching. It was, of course, a searchlight; to me something entirely new – I can see it in my mind's eye to this day.

As we wait for, or rather, as we remember the waiting for, the birth of the baby who will be called Jesus, Emmanuel, God with us – we need to remember and to ponder that he will be like that light, piercing the dark, probing the blackness of the night. We are not to run away from the darkness; we ought not to be afraid of the darkness, whether around us or within each of us. But at the same time we are not to pretend that it does not exist. At Evensong each day those who come to church hear the lovely old Collect which begins 'Lighten our darkness Lord, we pray' (or 'we beseech thee, O Lord'). In that prayer we are acknowledging the darkness and looking for, asking for, light; just as in Advent we acknowledge the darkness and look forward to the coming of the Light into our lives.

The True Light

Rather more than eighty years ago, Edward Grey, Foreign Secretary of this country, spoke at the beginning of August 1914 some remarkable and prophetic words – 'The lights are going out all over Europe, and will not be lit again during our lifetime.' Can any of us, if we look back over the history of Europe, let alone the world, since that time, dare to claim that the lights have yet gone on again? Our world, wherever we look, is indeed in great darkness still. That is not to say that there are not – and have not been – pinpricks, and more than pinpricks, of light, of hope, of joy in the lives of each one of us and in all the nations. Surely there have, and thank god for such glimpses and flashes, but in a general sense there remains confusion and much darkness in our world.

I do not want to seem unduly pessimistic, unduly depressing, but as on this first Sunday in Advent, we look towards the light that is coming and make our preparations for it, let us not pretend. However unsatisfactory our language, however impossible it may be to express what we feel, we believe it was because of the spiritual darkness of the world, the darkness around and within each one of us, that God sent his Son. As St John puts it, 'That was the true light that was coming into the world . . . In him was life, and the life was the light of men.' Let us look forward hopefully, joyfully, enthusiastically to the birth of the light, to the coming of light into our world and ourselves; and just as Mary and Joseph were at this time preparing for a great change in their lives, such that those lives would never be the same again, let us prepare for – and be ready to accept – a change in our lives. We are not, let us be clear, passively to await the Birth; we are to prepare for it. Here is our Advent call.

AN ADVENT PRAYER

O Lord our God
make us watchful and keep us faithful
as we await the coming of your Son our Lord;
that, when he shall appear,
he may find us not sleeping in sin,
but active in his service and joyful in his praise:
for the glory of your holy name.

– Gelasian (Promise of His Glory)

Advent Sunday *Second Sermon*
The Four Last Things – 1. Death

(The eschatological themes of Advent, summarized under the title of 'The Four Last Things – Death, Judgement, Heaven and Hell' – are given readings and prayers in 'The Promise of His Glory' pp 102–111, from which our texts are taken. Please feel free to use other material as preferred)

Old Testament Reading: Job 19, 21–27; Psalm 27, 1–10, 16–end. New Testament: Romans 8.31–39.

'Who shall separate us from the love of Christ? Shall tribulation, or distress or persecution, or famine, or nakedness, or peril, or sword?' Romans 8,35.

Our Immortality

No question has ever so sorely tried and perplexed the mind and heart of humans as this: 'Shall we know and love our friends in a future life, after death, or will everything be swallowed up as a drop of water in a mighty ocean? Will we in some way retain our individuality, our personality on the "other side", or do we simply disappear, black-out, fade away in the vast depths of the universe – that universe which is being revealed, more and more, as enormous and strange beyond our understanding?'

How we search for light, how dark it all remains; yet more and more we seem to be forced round to the conclusion that scientists, of all people, seem to be putting forward: as J. S. Haldane put it, 'The conclusion forced upon me, in the course of a life devoted to natural science, is that the universe . . . is a spiritual universe in which spiritual values count for everything.' Or as Sir James Jeans wrote, 'The universe begins to look more like a great thought than a great machine.' A view to which in our own time Dr Stephen Hawking seems to agree; so it appears that the worlds of religion and of science are closer than ever, and the old material theories of life are discredited. What does this mean?

Simply this: that the real values of life are to be measured by spiritual scales, by standards that are not material. The things that matter, the measures of our life, are not what we possess; but how we have lived, and how far we have shown trust, goodness, love, towards our fellow human beings.

Trust

The teaching of Christ is full of the key word – trust. Trust in his Father, who is our Father; trust in the Father's good purpose for every living creature, for the entire created world. 'Let not your hearts be troubled, neither let them be afraid.' With learning to trust, goes another important task. We are to learn to lose our self, our self-willed, spurious identity – but only in order to find our true identity and our true self. The 'art of dying' as it has been called, is basically learning to trust.

For what we fear in death is really the loss of that self-built identity, that shaky castle we have erected as a fortress and defence. If we can cast it aside – or at least begin to do so – then much of the terror of death will be seen to vanish. If we can find meaning in our world, discover that suffering does not mean abandonment, grief can be shared, sorrow can become a stepping-stone to a truer grasp of reality, then it can become possible to bear not just the thought of our own death, but the knowledge of the pain of others. Can we not school ourselves to a better approach than that of morbid fear, of pain and dissolution, by looking calmly and putting what must happen – to all of us – into the context of faith and trust.

Surety

Yes, there was One who made things unseen his choice, who refused to live for the things that we all too often count as true riches, true success, abundance of possessions, great reputation and the rest. He carried his choice to the most supreme test of all, the death upon the cross. The world laughed at him, mocked him, saw him die in pain and failure. But the vindication came; upon the third day he was raised from the dead. Righteousness was vindicated; love was triumphant. It is to the resurrection of the Lord that we must come in the end for the certainty that goodness and truth are the only things of real worth, and that love is the sovereign and supreme key to life.

> Grant us, Lord,
> the wisdom and the grace to use rightly
> the time left to us here on earth.
> Lead us to repent of the evil we have done
> and the good we have not done;
> strengthen us to follow the steps of your Son,

in the way that leads to the fullness of eternal life;
through Jesus Christ our Lord.

(PHG)

Second Sunday in Advent *Third Sunday before Christmas* 8 December 1996 **The Book of Hope**

'Through the comfort of your holy Word, we may embrace and for ever hold fast the hope of everlasting life, which you have given us in our Saviour Jesus Christ' – The Collect for today.

Hope

One keynote of this season of Advent rings out, brief but clear, the call of hope: the hope spelt out in the Bible of the coming of Christ! 'Come, Lord Jesus,' is the prayerful call of the Church, 'Come, Lord Jesus, come quickly!' In our hymns and prayers this cry goes up to stir us from our complacency, our weariness in the dark dull days of winter, and to revitalize us with the promise and the hope in the Gospel. A hope and a promise indeed that runs through the whole of our Bible – 'Hear, and you shall have life' says Isaiah in the Old Testament, 'God's word shall prevail' – then St Paul urges us to continue in the truths we were taught and 'spread the Word, for the sake of Jesus our King who is coming to rule!'

We are never to let weariness overtake us, never to think that nothing is worth while; instead we are to recover the assurance, the inspiration, the joy and the hope given to us in the Gospel.

Moral Values

In contrast with the paganism of the ancient world, Christianity burst in with hope as a moral value. When St Paul is describing the heathen world of those days, he writes of its deadness, of its darkness, and of its despair. It abandoned itself to the sexual urges without care for law or hope – there were no moral values to hold to in life, no call to make response to what was pure and good, when the very gods themselves were examples of immorality, lust and hatred.

6

Even the Hebrew people had largely neglected or forgotten their own Law; so when John the Baptist roused them with the call that the Kingdom of heaven was at hand, they flocked to the banks of the river Jordan to be released from their sins in order to be worthy of entering a new life. The promise of Jesus was of another order than paganism and of a higher value than that of John the Baptist. Jesus cleansed with fire and the Holy Spirit, and gave to the penitent the hope of more than mere ceremonial cleanness; he pointed to the possible affinity, even union, with the nature of God himself. And he opened a new vista of hope for the perfection of the entire nature of humanity, by which we should become pure in heart, and so transformed as to be assured of life in fellowship with our Creator through all eternity.

Searching

Christ gives hope a heavenly value; heaven in the New Testament is the place of reality; earthly life is the shadow. The things that *are* are the heavenly things; faith makes them facts to us here and now, and hope gives us assurance. All the long discipline of the Hebrew people was meant to purify them from the love of things earthly, and to win their hearts' affection for those things that are above. And these things Christ teaches us to value most; he set no value on earthly possessions except as a means of promoting the coming of the Kingdom. He taught us to set our store on goodness, truth, beauty, love. Where these were valued and counted as 'pearls of great price', then we would enter into an inheritance incorruptible and undefiled, which would never fade away.

How true it is that much of our present unrest and futile searching for joy and peace, security and love, is due to the widespread loss of any belief in a future life at all; all is so dim and uncertain that we rush for the eager acquirement of the good things of this world, in order to ensure our having 'a good time' in the here and now. It seems too obvious, does it not, to point out that the possession of these things has never yet secured that much-anticipated time. For the more we seek and the more we live, for them, the more selfish, the more quarrelsome, the more unhappy we become – and the further off is the golden time of human satisfaction.

Heavenly Values

The heavenly things bring no sorrow nor distress with them. We do not quarrel with the possession of love and truth and unselfishness, for no one loses by sharing them with others. No, for the more we give them away the more we gain ourselves, and the richer and stronger becomes the Kingdom which engenders them. If only the human race could take this to heart, the whole face of this world in which we live, this tiny space capsule with its fragile crew and even more fragile structure, would be changed for the better.

Our Christian hope lays hold on the things that by their very nature are not corruptible and are unchangeable. It gives us a treasure in the heavens, where neither moth nor rust corrupts, and where thieves cannot break through and steal. Death cannot rob us of it; rather, death opens the door through which we may enter into fuller possession of eternal treasure, stored up for us in the realm of our heavenly Father.

In Christ, the Risen Lord of life and death, we have gained our immortality, and learned the meaning of hope, here and in the world to come. Christ gives us a true measure of things here and things there, and assures us of the abiding security of love, goodness, beauty and truth. Such can never die, and their partakers must needs endure for evermore.

Our Advent

And now to bring it all into relation with our Advent belief and expectation – all our hope is centred in the Person of our Incarnate Lord. He is our hope, the hope of glory; and he brings us the assurance that what he has begun, he will most certainly also complete and accomplish. Our Christianity is not a religion which tells us the story of a time long past; it looks to the future, and we trust the future and wait expectant for it.

The Bible leaves us with an unfinished story. The King has gone on a far journey, but he has not left us; he will come and claim the kingdom as his own by right. The great fact that stands out is that Christianity – because it is the faith that gives the eternal values to this life of ours, is the religion both of the present time and of the future; and because Christianity is Christ, Christ is the outstanding figure of the Christian hope. That hope centres on a coming day when the real shall become the actual, and the world will receive that Kingdom which can never be shaken, nor lost, nor overcome. To that hope, the Advent hope of the world, let us hold fast.

> O God,
> by whose command the order of time runs its course,
> forgive our impatience,
> perfect our faith,
> and, while we wait for the fulfilment of your promises,
> grant us to hold firmly to our hopes,
> because of your words and your teachings,
> through Jesus Christ our Lord.
>
> (PHG)

Advent 2   *Second Sermon*
The Four Last Things – 2. Judgement

(See note at the beginning of the Second Sermon for Advent Sunday)
Old Testament Reading: Wisdom 3.9–11, Psalm: 130. New Testament: Matthew 25.31–end.
'We must all appear before the judgement seat of Christ, so that each one may receive good or evil, according to what he has done in the body'
2 Cor. 5,10

The Christian Life

Our Christian life may be considered as one of continuous warfare against ignorance, greed and folly, moral blindness, deliberate sin and evil. We need to take our part in the battle as if its outcome depended entirely upon our own efforts; and yet we need to remember that the End will be the coming again of Christ, the Prince of Peace, and his Reign as Lord, and his reign over the earth. With the idea of the Day of the Lord, there is the parallel idea with it that the Son of Man will be the judge of all humanity. Hence in the New Testament and in the Creeds there is the statement that Christ will 'come again with glory to judge both the quick and the dead'. This certainly is the expectation of St Paul and of the New Testament writers generally; although St John tells us that the judgement is associated with Christ's first coming:

9

'And this is the judgement, that the light has come into the world, and men loved darkness rather than light, because their deeds were evil' – John 3.19

Again, there is an equalling of the gift of the Holy Spirit with the Second Coming of Christ. (John 7.39) Such sayings as these have encouraged some believers to see the judgement in terms of the working of human history, and in the general evolutionary development of the world, perhaps as laid out by Teilhard de Chardin and others.

The New Testament

The New Testament clearly means, however, by the Second Coming and the great Judgement Day, nothing less than the end of history, with a visible manifestation of Christ upon this earth. This will mean a demonstration of the Lord's eternal victory in the salvation of those who have faith in him, and the destruction of those who persist in rebellion. To what extent such statements demand a literal interpretation is a matter for legitimate difference of opinion in our approach to the Scriptures. What is clear and cannot be dismissed is that judgement is certain in the long run; we cannot have moral and spiritual values without it. Once again Advent calls us to look on life, particularly our personal life, from the eternal aspect.

The relation between God and the soul is a personal matter. We matter to God; his judgement will be personal, since he has given to each one of us an immortal soul, and the welfare of that soul is of importance to both God and ourselves. This surely means that God has a purpose for us – and for the world in which he has set us. We must decide now – 'Choose life!' is the Bible call. 'To meet Christ, we must be like Christ. And to be like Christ we must be in Christ, clothed with his righteousness, invested with his new nature.' (Bp. Gore)

A PRAYER FOR SELF-JUDGEMENT

Almighty God,
we must all appear
before the judgement seat of your Son.
Keep us steadfast and faithful
in his service,

and enable us so to judge ourselves
in this life,
that we may not be condemned
on the day of his appearing;
for his tender mercy's sake. Amen.
                                    (PHG)

Third Sunday in Advent   *Second Sunday before*
Christmas   15 December   **The Forerunner**
'John said, "I am as Isaiah prophesied: 'A voice that cries in the wilder-
ness, Make a straight way for the Lord!'" John 1,23 (ASB Gospel)

A Prophet – and More than a Prophet

John was accepted by the people as a prophet, as did the Lord
himself, but Christ identified John as not just a prophet, but as
the prophet with a special task – that of being the 'Forerunner of
the Messiah', so identified by the ancient prophet Malachi. These
words of Malachi were generally accepted as making one of the
essential marks of Messianic prophecy. Certainly John it was who
aroused the people from their lethargy. His preaching stirred
the national consciousness, making the nation eager, expectant
and open-eyed. What were the outstanding features of John's
character?

Courage

As John looked ahead to the Kingdom, whose advent he proclaimed, his eye was clear and his mind unclouded. He was a
visionary in the best sense, and at the same time he was intensely
practical. The word of the Living God came to him, and he
answered the call to be Messiah's herald. He pursued his ministry
with the great vision of the Advent before him. In preaching, a
dominant note was that of sheer practicality, sheer plain speaking,
as we can see in the answers he gave to those who inquired of
him.

Humility

John realized the importance of his task, but remained wonderfully humble. His ministry was stamped with the marks of severity and sternness: the spirit of the wild and desolate wilderness seemed to have entered his soul. We know that severity and humility are not always united in any one soul; it has been rightly said that sternness is 'the sister of pride, more often than of lowliness'. Yet, for all his austerity, John was humble. The very success of his mission made the people ask whether he could be Messiah – but he answered without compromise: 'I am not the Christ.' Severe in the presence of evil and vice, stern also in the presence of Herod and the evils of his court, John was humble as a child in the presence of him who was to come.

Limitations

From passages in the Gospels, we learn that John may have had incomplete views of the mission of the Jesus whom he heralded. Even so, he glorified the Lord. He looked for a Messiah whose fan was in his hand (Luke 3.17) and what John foresaw was true; Jesus came to separate the wheat from the chaff. Yet, it was equally true that Christ would neither strive nor cry; a bruised reed he would not break, and smoking flax he would not quench. These aspects of the message of the Messiah were only dimly seen by John, and they perplexed him as he pondered over them in his prison – so soon to glorify God by his martyrdom.

We, too, surely have imperfect views of God; our small human minds cannot really comprehend the greatness and the vast perspective of the Creator and Ruler of the universe. Yet, if we strive to be like John the Baptist, and cultivate those characteristics of which we have been thinking, we also may glorify God and enjoy him for ever.

OUR MODEL

Let Christ be your model
For every word and deed
Moving or standing,
seated, eating,
silent or speaking.
Study him

and you will grow in his love.

Let this be your wisdom,
This your meditation,
*   This your study.*
To have him always in mind
*   to move you to imitation*
*   to win you to his love.*

– Archbishop Goodier

Advent 3   *Second Sermon*
The Four Last Things – 3. Heaven
(See note at the beginning of the Second Sermon for Advent Sunday)
Old Testament Reading: Daniel 12.1–3; Psalm 16. New Testament:
Mark 12.18–27
'In my Father's house are many rooms.' John 14.2.

Heaven
From the earliest times, heaven was identified with the place where God dwells. As Jehovah was seen as a sky-god, to be with God is therefore to be in heaven, both for later Judaism and for Christianity. The Christian conviction concerning the life after death however was never a mere borrowing or extension of the ideas of the rabbinic teachers; the Christian hope had an altogether new centre and ground: the Resurrection of Jesus Christ. 'Being raised with Christ' is the new view of life after death, in contrast with both the mere pagan and Old Testament conception of it as something ghostly and unreal. 'Flesh and blood cannot inherit the kingdom of God' (1 Cor. 15,50) says St Paul. Nevertheless, at our resurrection we shall possess what in the world of spirit corresponds to our bodies in the material world – means of expression, identification, recognition and so on. The life to come will not be ghostly and insubstantial, as in the pagan view, but there will be a redemption of the physical order as well as of the spiritual, in opposition to the common Greek view that matter is in itself evil and irredeemable.

Here and Now

The very fact that Christ has ascended 'far above the heavens' suggests that space itself has been transcended; we know today how our earth is a tiny planet set towards the edge of an enormous galaxy, which is itself merely one amidst hundreds or even thousands of other galaxies. The distances, the numbers, the differences are so difficult to even begin to grasp, that our human minds give up. Perhaps the most comforting and helpful of texts from the Bible are our Lord's own words:

'Let not your hearts be troubled; believe in God, believe also in me. In my Father's house are many rooms; if it were not so, I would have told you. I go to prepare a place for you.' (John 14.2)

These words surely imply that we will have space, time and means to become, perhaps, what we had never been able to become on earth. There will be the opportunity for us to develop skills and aims that were ideals and hopes crushed or kept down by circumstances – poverty, illness, the need to work like slaves to support a family or a dependent relative, the lack of encouragement, the lack of teachers or leaders, the physical stranglehold of some dire disease or the results of some unfortunate accident which forced disablement upon us. Here in a new life would be the chance to develop, to grow, to expand into areas of skill and experience that our life on earth denied the time, the energy, even the opportunity to reach before.

A New Hope

The Christian view of life after death is based upon a new hope and a new ground. It is based upon the resurrection of Jesus Christ, not on mere speculation, nor on philosophic thinking, nor on apocalyptic visions, or theological speculation. Alas, later theology began to map out the future life with a precision that is far from being Biblical. Souls were held to be in a state of suspended animation, as it were, until the Day of Resurrection, when they would rise with their reborn bodies – as Stanley Spencer depicts in his great but misleading paintings. On the other hand, the doctrine of Purgatory (which contains in itself the great truth that spiritual growth and change may not be confined to this life) became a rigidly classified system, repulsive to logic and to Christian love alike. Now, thank God, it has become an almost totally abandoned theory, except perhaps in remote and primitive corners of the Roman obedience.

The Triumph
Christ was representative humanity; in him the human race triumphed, in principle, over death. Those who are 'in Christ' partake of the New Humanity (2 Cor. 5,17; 1 Peter 1,3). At Baptism we die with Christ and are raised to share in his risen life. 'Henceforth we are alive unto God in Christ Jesus' (Romans 6,11). 'We walk by faith, not by sight' (2 Cor. 5,7) Our assurance of eternal life, the life of Heaven, comes from the work of the Holy Spirit within us; that Spirit who is the agent by whom we come to faith, and whose presence is the assurance of that Christ in whom we have believed, until after our physical death we shall see him as he is.

> *Father, you made us in your image*
> *and your Son accepted death for our salvation.*
> *Help us to keep our watch in prayer at all times.*
> *May we be free from sin*
> *when we leave this world,*
> *and rejoice in peace with you for ever;*
> *through Jesus Christ our lord. Amen.*
>
> (PHG)

Fourth Sunday in Advent *Sunday next before Christmas* 22 December **The Light**
And Mary said, 'Behold I am the handmaid of the Lord; let it be to me according to your word.' Luke 1.38 (ASB Gospel)

The Birth is near
Today is the fourth and final Sunday in Advent. We may recall the words of that well-known hymn:

> *Nearer and nearer draws the time,*
> *The time that shall surely be,*
> *When the earth shall be filled with the glory of God*
> *As the waters cover the sea.*
>
> (NEH 495; A&M Rev. 271)

Now clearly the writer of those words was looking ahead, looking to the future, looking to the wider consummation of God's work and God's glory in the world; but it is also true that for Mary, and for us, 'nearer and nearer draws the time' – the time of a birth which will both herald the dawn of a new age, and will disclose or reveal the glory of God in a new way – a new light, a new light of glory, will have come into the world.

At this moment of the Church's year, the light that is Christ is in the darkness of the womb; but just as Mary's full time has almost come – that moment when the new baby, the new life is delivered into our world, so we can at last begin to see light at the end of our tunnel, light on the edge of the horizon, piercing the darkness.

Mary

Mary's labour, Mary's work to bring the child into the world, has yet to be accomplished. We may remember how that child, grown to full stature, will later point to the sorrow of a woman in travail, but go on the say that when the child is born she will remember no longer the pain, for joy that a child has been born into the world. We, like Mary, can surely now begin to look beyond that labour to the joy that will follow; in our darkness we can look towards the light, just as that child comes to the point of being delivered from darkness into the world's light.

But neither Mary nor we are to ignore the risks; birth, whether physical or spiritual is a risk, as of course we may well say that each moment of life is. It is not only presidents and kings who are 'but one heartbeat from eternity' – but every birth is, and in Mary's time more certainly was, a risky business – risky for the baby, risky for the mother.

God

God sent his Son as we are told and as we believe. For many there is still a residue of the feeling that the Bible story is somewhat too close to ancient fables of the Greek and Roman gods; Zeus and other classic deities, who descended from Mount Olympus and begot children down here upon earthly women. It is an old picture or myth embedded in the folk-tales of long ago. Jesus himself will say 'God is spirit, and those who worship him must worship in spirit and in truth' – fables and myths are to be seen for what they are, attempts of our ancestors to come to terms with the mysteries of the world and of human life, to describe the indescribable and explain the inexplicable. Yet the conception and birth of Jesus represents an emptying of God, a giving of himself by God, the accepting of the risks of the placing of himself at the mercy of his own creation. Firmly we believe that Jesus, the Second Person of the Holy Trinity, God from God, Light from Light, was born for us and for our salvation, the salvation of the whole world. Suppose the Child had died at the childbirth; suppose Herod's soldiers had caught up with Mary and Joseph, in that shocking massacre of the infants, the innocents. No doubt God's infinite powers and resources would in some other way have brought about the redemption of our world – but what a risk, what a gamble in the truest sense, our Creator was taking.

Our Share

In becoming Christians, in pinning our hopes and our faith in Christ, we too take a risk, each one of us. We are scorned by many, we are often made to feel 'odd', perhaps old-fashioned, fuddy-duddy, and even guilty for standing aside from the standards and customs of the world where they conflict with our faith. There may be scorn, we may expect attempts to trip us up, metaphorically if not in some practical sense. Let us take the risk of going to the stable this Christmas tide; let the light from the stable and from the Child in the manger, draw us to join with the shepherds and the Wise Men. God has taken a risk, and we should be ready to respond by ourselves also taking a risk.

The humility of that stable can speak to each of us, and can touch each one of us; the shepherds left their sheep – irresponsible the farmer might say, and probably did. The Wise Men doubtless had many important things to look to in their lives in their far country, but they were prepared to ignore all that, to leave their problems and do the only important thing, namely, to follow their star and find the king, even in a stable. Yes indeed, sometimes there are more important things in life than what others tell you that you should be doing.

The Light

The light is coming, let us come to the light. If we will but do just that, then we shall share and rejoice at those 'Tidings of great Joy' the angels announce, and on Wednesday next, Christmas Day, find we need no longer be afraid, but filled with power and hope, joy and light, strength and new life.

Advent 4 *Second Sermon*
The Four Last Things – 4. Hell

(See note at the beginning of the Second Sermon for Advent Sunday)
Old Testament Reading: Proverbs 15.3–11; Psalm: 14. New Testament Reading: Matthew 5.29 & 30.
'If your hand causes you to sin, cut it off; it is better for you to enter into life maimed, than with two hands to go to hell.' Mark 9,43.

What does the Bible tell us?
The New Testament gives a somewhat ambiguous picture. In the Revelation of St John, chapter 20, vv. 11–14, we read that those whose names were not written in the book of life are thrown into the 'lake of fire, the second death'. If all this is symbolical, we do find the phrase 'eternal punishment' in Matthew 25, v. 46, used by Jesus himself, according to the evangelist. The author of the Letter to the Hebrews certainly warns us not to fall away from the gospel, or 'how shall we escape if we neglect so great a salvation'? (2.1–3) but this is not hell-fire. St Paul is more vehement in 2 Thessalonians, suggesting that the ultimate fate of those who refuse God's offer of salvation may be annihilation rather than eternal punishment (2.8–10). Where 'Gehenna' is spoken of, note that this is the name for the refuse dump outside Jerusalem, where ever-burning fires consumed the rubbish and filth of the city – a place of cleansing rather than destruction or unending torment.

Images
It was no doubt inevitable that the images of fire, worm, and grinding of teeth which we find in the New Testament should have been understood in a literal sense by later ages. Christians were chiefly marked off from purveyors of other religions in the ancient world, by their emphasis on the importance of moral choice. We find St Augustine devoting much space in his 'City of God' to proving that the fire of hell is something physical or semi-physical. Till very recently the fear of hell was considered a

perfectly respectable inducement towards conversion; the weakening of belief in the verbal inspiration of the Bible has meant that 'hell-fire' has largely disappeared from theology.

So if the New Testament language about hell is symbolic, of what is it symbolic? Most modern theologians would say that 'hell means separation from God'. It is not a punishment which God inflicts; it is what we do to ourselves.

In This Life

It follows therefore that hell (like heaven) begins in this life; see John 3.36. Throughout our whole period of life on earth we are moving either towards life or towards death, and judgment is in that sense already begun the moment we are born. But as long as we are on earth the process is reversible. The implication would seem to be that final loss, rather than eternal punishment, is the fate of those who ultimately refuse.

Let us be clear that the one important point to hold on to is, that whether in this life or in the next, God as revealed in our Lord Jesus Christ, is the ultimate norm by which we human creatures will be judged; so let us be resolved to live life in his light, putting our trust in him. The cross and Passion show the reality of God's forgiveness, and the brutal cost to Christ, who, sinless himself, suffered the penalty of the worst sinner in society, the cruel death upon the cross. The Cross and Passion awake the penitence for our own sins and errors, and hence bring us to our knees, where we may in the mercy of God, receive his forgiveness in Christ our Lord.

A PRAYER

Grant us, Lord,
the wisdom and the grace to use rightly
the time left to us here on earth.
Lead us to repent of our sins,
the evil we have done and the good we have not done;
strengthen us to follow in the steps of your Son,
in the way that leads us to the fullness of eternal life;
through Jesus Christ our Lord.

(ASB)

Christmas Day   Wednesday 25 December
At Midnight or Early Day   **Welcome!**

'Glory to God in the highest and peace on earth, goodwill towards men.'
Luke 2,14 (Gospel, BCP & ASB) or, 'Unto us a Child is born, unto us
a Son is given!' Isaiah 9,6 (O.T. Lesson, ASB)

Welcome to you all

Welcome to you all, on this joyful night! We are all full of joy in
the thought of this great festival. Our family gatherings, our holi-
day, our parties together, sharing the good things of life one with
another, our Christmas presents, our decorations and Christmas
trees – all express the happiness we share, because of the birth in
a stable of a Child. A special Child! If we are sometimes more
occupied with the good cheer, and the presents, and the jollity,
than with remembering the origins of all this joy and happiness,
here in church our minds must go back to Bethlehem. 'O come let
us adore him!' – 'Hark the herald angels sing!' 'Away in a manger!'
– everything in our familiar hymns and music, in sacred words
and prayers, reminds us, stirs us up, to dwell upon the glorious
truth of the coming of Jesus, Son of God, into our human life here
on earth, coming to share our birth and growth, our sorrows and
pains, our happinesses and joys, our work and our hopes.

Peace on Earth

Yet, what a world to come into – so much sadness, so much
violence, so much bitterness and hatred. War in so many places
still, the threat of violence and brutality in so many countries, and
in our own land here the bombs, and the savagery just below the
surface, violence often not under the surface, but out in the open
in all its brutality. And the poverty, the homelessness, of so many.

   We each have a duty to contribute in however small a way,
towards peace, towards goodwill, towards stability, towards justice and concord amongst peoples and between one another. Let
us do our obvious duty, to make the best and not the worst of
troubles; to lift up, rather than add yet more weight to the common
burden to be borne. Christmas brings out our good nature; do not
let that good nature disappear all too quickly when the festival is
over! Be ready to help, whenever and wherever possible; do not
add needless weight to the common burden, but add your voice

and your assistance wherever you can, to assist and to cheerfully take whatever part you may be able to take, in building up not pulling down.

Joy

We who have in our hearts the joy which cannot be taken away from us, the joy, that is, of the Presence of the Lord Jesus, with us here and now, shall we allow ourselves to grieve that Lord, if we live as if without belief in the power of his Spirit, or without confidence in his Love and his changeless purpose? If we want peace, we must practise the first principles, not just for this Christmas, when good temper and cheerful good nature are easy to display; but still more in refusal to take offence, in suppressing selfish vanity, in happily taking our share in hardship, in dropping our little squabbles, our so easy grumbles, our cynical talk and gossip and nagging.

Jesus comes to each one of us this Christmas and puts to us a searching question: Are you doing all you can to promote harmony, love and caring; and to prevent misunderstandings, angers, crossness, depression? If you are, then Christ will be with you, Christ will be supporting you with his grace and his power. Let the New Year be open to his power, the power that can transform not just your life and your actions, but transform you, yourself.

> May the joy of the angels,
> the eagerness of the shepherds,
> the obedience of Mary and Joseph,
> and the peace of the Christ Child
> be with you and those you love,
> this Christmas and evermore.
>   (PHG)

Christmas Day   Wednesday
25 December   Christmas Joy

To us a Child is born, to us a Son is given: and his name will be called the Prince of Peace.' Isaiah 9.6 or, 'Since God has loved us so much, we too should love one another.' 1 John 4.11. (ASB N.T. Lessons) or 'The

Word was made flesh, and dwelt among us, and we beheld his glory'
(BCP Gospel)

Full of Joy!

A very joyful Christmas to you all – a Christmas full of joy! I can wish you joy, and you can wish each other joy, only because of the words of the angel – 'Fear not, I bring you tidings of great joy, which shall be for you and for all people; for to you is born this day a Saviour, who is Christ the Lord.' Without those words and all that those words imply, the Christmas greetings we pass to each other – perhaps sometimes rather glibly – those greetings are hollow indeed.

During Advent we have been considering the spiritual darkness within each one of us, in more or less degree, and in the world around us, darkness heavy and all too clearly threatening. But we also have been thinking of light coming into us and into the world; and now Jesus has been born, the baby so long awaited has arrived. Light has come into the world, beating down the darkness, and we can learn again how Christ is the light of each one of us, of every person of every race, of every colour and of every ancestry, who is born into this world. As Isaiah wrote, 'The people who walked in darkness have seen a great light.'

Christmas Glory!

The very first words we hear about the new-born Christ are spoken to those in darkness, to the shepherds watching their flocks by night. As they sit there, the glory of the Lord shines round about them – again, we have the contrast of darkness and light. Our favourite carol 'While shepherds watched their flocks by night' has them 'all seated on the ground'; doubtless shepherds do sit around from time to time, watching their sheep, but although St Luke makes no reference to them sitting down, the idea is surely an image of what so many of us, even in our busy lives, do so much of the time. Spiritually speaking, at least, we sit idly around; and though the story is written as if the shepherds made their own decision to go over to Bethlehem, we can well imagine them hearing the Angel's voice within them, urging them as we are urged here and now – 'Move! Get up and on your feet, go to Bethlehem right now, go! and see what has happened! Don't just sit here on the hillside, get up and go!'

The Glory of God

To come into, or to be in, the Presence of the Glory of God may be – surely must be – for most of us something to be feared, or at least apprehensive. Why? Because we know how far we are from that tremendous state of Love to which each one of us is called by our God, the God who *is* love. We know all too well that we shy away from God, we avoid God, we try to ignore God, in the hope that in some way or other we can be rid of him and the embarrassment he causes to us. As we read elsewhere, 'his love is too high for us', we cannot attain to it; we know our weakness and our inability, and we are afraid. Like Adam and Eve in the Garden of Eden story, we know that we have sinned and we are afraid. In this materialistic and hedonistic age, perhaps we dare not call it sin – 'sin' is a politically incorrect word, no doubt. We may deny sin, we may deny that we sin, but we cannot deny, living towards the end of this 20th century, awaiting the Millennium, that we live in an age of dis-ease. Yes, we have uneasy feelings that are all around us – and within us – things are not as they should be. Only to read our newspapers or watch our TV, makes it very clear that there is something very wrong with society here and throughout the world. The times are full of danger, violence seems to have a free run, brutality and cruelty is the staple of our literature, our films, our TV; and fills our papers.

The Child

The birth of the Child speaks of love in a world full of hate, of humility in a world full of pride, of true life in a world where death in so many terrifying shapes, too often seems to hold all power. As we come, if we will come, to the presence of the Child there in the stable, we can dare to acknowledge – in the presence of his vulnerability and his weakness – our own weakness and vulnerability which we too often cover up, which we are too ashamed to allow to show; and we can drop the tensions of busy lives, drop the worries and anxieties (all the worries, anxieties and strains of keeping up with the Joneses) of succeeding in the way our world thinks of success. All these things, and so many others, will become irrelevant in the presence of this Child, the sign and symbol of another kind of life – a life of co-operation rather than bitter competition, of peace rather than war, of love rather than hate, of give rather than grab. To pray for our enemies rather than hating and cursing them, of understanding and forgiving. If we look at that Christ Child in the stable, and go on to remember – as we must – that Child grown into a Man, and that Man hanging upon the cross, yet able to say 'Father, forgive them, for they know not what they do' – the way of eternal Love is the Way of the Cross. So today we can have joy indeed, because that birth of the Saviour encompasses also his death and his resurrection, through which that gift of joy eternal, which we call salvation, is established for us and for all the world.

Persevere

May we persevere in believing and in seeking, in listening and in putting into action, the love of the new-born Child, born for us and for all this world of ours; and may you, this Christmas and through the New Year, have that joy and that inner peace, which I am persuaded that Jesus Christ alone can give.

> *Our courteous Lord does not want his servants to despair, even if they fall, frequently and grievously. Our falling does not stop his loving us. Peace and and love are always at work in us, but we are not always in peace and love.*

> *The Lady Julian of Norwich*

Sunday after Christmas Day
29 December   The People of God

'God's love for us was revealed when God sent his only Son into the world so that we could have life through him.' 1 John 4.9 (ASB Introductory Sentence)

The People of God

God is the reason for our being gathered together, here Sunday by Sunday, year by year. We are the People of God – a proud and loving claim. And yet we are led astray from this wonderful fact by our embarrassment about the Church. The Church's lack of success in our time is bound to be puzzling and hard to accept. We should like it better if the Church were popular, successful, influential and vigorous.

God is God

Precisely because this is our situation, we need to remind ourselves of the One who has called us together. God is God – and nothing we can do can add to that. Nothing we can do can subtract from it. So, we cannot manipulate him. He is not an angry parent to be placated by flattery. And he will go on calling people to his purpose. Tempted to bewail our situation, we sympathize with the Psalmist: 'Lord God of Hosts, how long?' (Ps. 80.4). But the best of the psalms which express this sort of feeling go on to express hope. Hope – perhaps the hardest Christian virtue today. It is even said that hope has emigrated from the Churches. It sometimes seems to have left us altogether. Understandably perhaps, in a century which has witnessed greater horrors and greater dislocations than any other in this Millennium. But the same century has also produced people who could hope in the darkness. Such was the German Jew who wrote on the walls of his concentration camp:

> *I believe in the sun even when it is not shining;*
> *I believe in love even when I cannot feel it;*
> *I believe in God, even when he is silent.*

Abandoned

The Church is becoming more invisible in our time. Bewitched by the past, we feel, as a Church, that perhaps we have been abandoned. All that we can do is to hold on to what we have got. Any true experience of God includes the feeling of loss and separation. Jesus' cry of dereliction on the Cross shows us, warns us, that when he took upon himself the sins of the world, he felt abandoned by God. The saints, too, experience something of this. St John of the Cross described the agony of the 'Dark Night of the Soul'. It is almost as if the darkness, the sense of being utterly alone, is a necessary stage that we must pass through. As Jesus says, trying to prepare the disciples for his death,

You will be sorrowful, but your sorrow will turn to joy. (John 16.20)

Hope, then, can be simply expressed. Hope is the hope that our sorrow will be turned into joy. To us humans there is a difference

25

in these things, the difference between joy and sorrow. Hope is the hope that for the Lord there is no difference; everything that comes from him is a good and perfect gift.

To you, Lord, is entrusted all that we have and are – our salvation, our vocation, our daily work, our families, our life and our death. So at the end, Lord, our prayer is the sum of all desire and of all prayer. Take and receive, Lord, my whole freedom, my memory, my understanding and my whole will, all that I have and possess. From you it came, Lord, and to you I offer it again. All is yours; dispose of it entirely according to your will. Give me only your love and your grace, for that is enough.

Karl Rahner

Invisible?

If we find it hard sometimes to hope for the Church in such terms, there are, we might suggest, plenty of Biblical precedents for the Church's invisibility. Israel, as a nation faithful to God, was reduced to a faithful remnant – and finally to one man, who ended his days on a cross, outside the city and reviled by his countrymen. Yet that achieved what nothing else could.

Though invisible, we are to be the salt that gives flavour to the whole. We are to be the leaven in the lump – hidden we may be, from many, but nevertheless co-operating with God. But if we are to be invisible and not simply to disappear, we need to drink deeply of the water of prayer. If our hope is to grow, then our love for our Lord needs to grow too. If we are to see our way ahead, then we need to sit under his word, and learn from it.

Finally, we have to learn to entrust to the Lord all that we are, and all that we have. We may well say with Dag Hammerskjold, the 'Man for Peace', who wrote in his book of verse *Markings* this prayer:

> *Keep me in thy love*
> *As thou wouldest that all should be kept in mine.*
> *May everything in this my being*
> *Be directed to thy glory*
> *And may I never despair.*
> *For I am under thy hand,*
> *And in thee is all power and all goodness.*

Christmas 1 *Second Sermon* 29 December
St Thomas Becket, Archbishop of Canterbury, Martyr

'I will raise up for myself a faithful priest, who shall do according to what is in my heart and in my mind, says the Lord.' 1 Samuel 2.35
('The Cloud of Witnesses')

A Changed Man

Thomas Becket was born in London in 1118; his mother has been thought to have been an Arab, a Saracen, but this is disputed. He was undoubtedly a brilliant scholar and a remarkably strong-willed and intelligent man; making the Church his career, he rose rapidly, studied in Paris, was ordained deacon in 1154 and nominated Archdeacon of Canterbury. The King, Henry II, made him Lord Chancellor in the next year, and as a bosom friend of the king his future seemed assured. Vigorous, hot-tempered, fond of field sports, popular, magnificent, he was advanced to the primatial see of Canterbury in 1162; the world seemed to be at his feet.

But as archbishop, Thomas abandoned all luxury, and in his own words 'from being a proud vain man, a patron of play-actors, and follower of hounds' he became 'a shepherd of souls'. He abandoned luxury and opposed the encroachments of the king on the rights of the Church and the liberties of the clergy. For seven years the disputes went on, becoming more and more difficult and violent; he went into exile, then returned to England on December 1st 1170. King Henry in a fit of rage, let fall the imprudent words before his knights 'Will no one rid me of this pestilent priest!'

Four of the knights rode to Canterbury, and in the evening of December 29th murdered the archbishop in a side chapel of his cathedral. It was in defence of the Church, and its ideals and jurisdiction that he was killed; his last words were: 'I die willingly for the Name of Jesus, and in defence of his Church.' The ordinary people treated him as a martyr at once, and he was canonized formally three years later by the Pope (1173).

St Thomas' shrine made Canterbury one of the most important and famous cities in Christendom, and to it came people of all ranks and qualities, the sick and the sad, the rich and the poor,

kings, nobility and peasants. The shrine was stripped of its valuable ornaments, and the relics of the Saint taken away and burnt,
under Henry VIII. The stained glass – or most of it – depicting
the miracles taking place at the Shrine, remained however, down
the years to our own time. A modern version of the Shrine was
commissioned from Sir Ninian Comper, but never built; however,
devotion to St Thomas has grown again, and is now centred on
the 'Altar of the Sword's Point' marking the spot where St Thomas
was murdered.

'A martyrdom is always the design of God, for his love of men,
to warn them and to lead them, to bring them back to his ways.
It is never the design of man; for the true martyr is he who has
become the instrument of God, who has lost his will in the will
of God, and who no longer desires anything for himself, not
even the glory of being a martyr.'   (Murder in the Cathedral)

*Collect: Preserve your Church, O Lord, from the hands of evil men;
and as your holy martyr Thomas died in her defence, give her always
the protection of faithful leaders, who shall guard her freedom and
guide your people in the way of holiness: through Jesus Christ our
Lord.*   *(Cloud of Witnesses)*

Second Sunday after Christmas 5 January 1997
The Holy Family

*'As Jesus grew up he advanced in wisdom and in favour with God and
man.' Luke 2.52 (ASB Gospel) or, 'His name was called Jesus, which
was so called by the angel before he was conceived in the womb.' Luke
2.21 (BCP Gospel)*

Jesus
The New Year begins for us as Christians, with the holy name
'Jesus'. This name given to our Saviour is the same as 'Joshua' in
its meaning – 'The Deliverer' or 'The Saviour'. We can say that
for us as Christians, this name is a summary of the Gospel; the
good tidings, 'god spel' in Old English. Our faith calls us to be
conformed to our Saviour in thought, in word, and in deed, and

to spread that Gospel that he himself preached and taught. We are to strive to have the mind of Christ – 'Have this mind in you, which was also in Christ Jesus' says St Paul (Phil. 2.5). We are to imitate him whose words were spirit and life; as he himself said 'The words I have spoken to you are spirit and are life' (John 6.63). We are to lead others to understand the words of truth, of holiness, of hope. And we are called to be like the Lord, who went about 'doing good' – not mere negative goodness, but positive action in his name and for his sake. We are called to continue his work on earth, to speak his words through personal witness, and above all to allow all our thinking and all our actions to be controlled by his thoughts, his teaching, his example, as we seek to follow him this year and all our lives.

(If the New Year has already been observed with a Watch-night Service or similar, the above may be omitted)

The Family

There are many fables – dating from mediaeval times – about the childhood of Jesus, and they tell astonishing stories – how he made little clay birds and threw them in the air, when they took wing and flew away, for instance – but in the New Testament there are only two short sentences: 'The child grew and became strong, filled with wisdom; and the favour of God was upon him.' Luke 2.40; and 'Jesus increased in wisdom and in stature, and in favour with God and man.' Luke again, 2.52. Both are terse enough to sound almost like school reports, but they do give us a picture of a boy developing physically, mentally and spiritually, and popular with those who knew him.

The Boyhood

We may be sure that Jesus lived the life of an ordinary, healthy, well brought up boy. In those days education was held in considerable esteem; there were schools in all the towns, and the local rabbi would hold classes in the synagogue in villages. Jesus would have attended school like any other boy, learned passages of Scripture and been instructed in the Faith. We note, for instance, how the passages he quotes in the Wilderness come from the section of Deuteronomy which Jewish children learned at their first catechism. And we must remember that the interpretation of these or other Bible passages would be both taught and discussed in the schools. It seems clear that Jesus had already learned enough in the local synagogues in Nazareth, to look forward eagerly to meeting the scholars of the capital and 'both listening to them and putting questions' as St Luke tells us. It was not that he was lost in Jerusalem, on the occasion of the first Passover pilgrimage that he had been allowed to join, having reached the age of twelve; no, the Temple and the teachers there were for him the great object of his devotion. For him, the Temple was not just 'God's House', it was 'My Father's House', and his loyalty to his Father was greater than that to his family. How surprising, then, that Joseph and Mary should not know where to find him! But addressing God as one's own 'Father' made little sense to ordinary people, and even his parents 'did not understand what he meant.' (v.50)

Preparation

We may wonder if some of the scholars to whom Jesus listened, and of whom he made his enquiries, eventually were amongst those who joined in his condemnation twenty or so years later. They were sincere teachers and learned in the Scriptures; not all were so tied by devotion to the great men of the past and their commentaries, as to be unable to adapt their vision to some new aspect, nor so fanatical as to condemn. They too were about the Father's business, though unable to take the step into the new that the life of Jesus meant.

We can be sure that Jesus persevered in the thinking which prepared him for the fulfilment of 'his Father's business' even though it eventually led him to the Cross. Like Jesus, we can ask questions and give answers, and in our prayers and thoughts cry, as St Paul tells us, 'Abba! Father!' and bear witness that we are children of God (Romans 8.16,17) if we share his sufferings in our own small way, so that we may eventually share his splendour, having shared his endurance.

Christmas 2   *Second Sermon*   Spirit of Truth

'God is spirit, and those who worship must worship in spirit and in truth.' John 4,24 (ASB EP)

Unconventional

It was a very unconventional thing that our Lord was doing on that hot day by the roadside. In fact it was two unconventional things: first, to talk to a woman openly and publicly; and secondly, for a Jew to have any dealings at all with a Samaritan. The bitterness of Northern Ireland between the Prods and the Papes; the bitterness between the blacks and the whites, which still erupt in riots and brutality in the USA; the brutality between nations and tribes in Africa – all these have similarities to the ancient distrust and hatred of Jew and Samaritan. Yet is was in these unpromising circumstances that Jesus made a tremendous disclosure at Jacob's well. First he had begun by talking to the woman about her personal religion, and about her personal morality. And she did what people very often do when they find themselves pressed with awkward questions – she diverted the talk to the matter of religious controversy; a much safer ground.

It's much the same today. If one is trying to present the personal significance of religion to someone, very often they will say, 'What about the Nonconformists? What about the Roman Catholics? How about the Toronto Blessing?' All much safer ground.

So with the woman – she tried to divert Our Lord: 'Our fathers worshipped in this mountain; but you Jews say God can only be worshipped in Jerusalem.' And Jesus is not annoyed, he does not despise the woman – he never despises anyone. Indeed to her he gives a momentous declaration: 'The time approaches when real worshippers will worship the Father in spirit and in truth. Such are the worshippers that God wants; God is spirit, and those who worship him must worship in spirit and in truth.'

This was what the prophets had said; Malachi for example said, 'In every place incense shall be offered to my Name, and a pure offering.' Not only in Jerusalem but in every place. So St Peter came to see. 'Every nation that works righteousness shall be accepted of him.' Particularist religion has come to an end.

Revelation

The woman is astonished; she picks up the prophecy that the Lord has made and interprets it as meaning the Messiah. 'I know that Messiah (that is Christ) is coming; when he comes he will tell us everything,' she says. Christ's response is to declare himself that very Messiah – an astonishing revelation, at which the woman is so surprised that she puts down her water-jar and hurries back to the town, where she spreads her message: 'Come and see . . . !' We are told (v. 30) that many believed, and after hearing Christ, make their declaration of faith (v. 42) 'We have heard him ourselves; and we know that this is in truth the Saviour of the world.'

The religion which is the expression of the Lord's Being, and of his relation to us, is universal, for all peoples in all places at all times – catholic indeed. There is no preference for any particular place, not Jerusalem nor Samaria, not Rome nor Constantinople nor Canterbury. It is a religion of the equal worth of every single human soul, because each soul is capable of 'sonship' and of receiving the fullest possible recognition. Everywhere, in every place, wherever there is a human soul capable of God, and desiring God. He has made us to worship him; he is our Father, and the worship he asks of us is the worship that only those can render who recognize who they are, and what God is.

The Epiphany of Our Lord   Monday 6 January
The Light of the World

'Arise, shine, Jerusalem, for your light has come, and the glory of the Lord has risen upon you.' Isaiah 60,1 (ASB Introductory Sentence)

The King

The Wise Men from the East followed the light, the light of the star which had suddenly and surprisingly appeared in the firmament of heaven. Its message for them was sufficiently strong, sufficiently urgent, for them to take to the roads to find this new King. 'Where is he who has been born king of the Jews?' was their enquiry when they reached Jerusalem. No wonder Herod was surprised and worried – after all, he *was* the king, recognized by the Roman Empire, and any successor to the throne would – or should – be from his own family. We know what followed, as soon as the Wise Men left; a 'task force' as we would call it today, was sent post haste to Bethlehem, and all the male children of two years old or under were brutally put to death. Here was something far worse than the dreadful massacre at Dunblane; for Bethlehem, the message of the Wise Men was one of death.

The King Rejected

The Hebrew people as a whole rejected Jesus as the promised Messiah; this was not the sort of Messiah they expected or wanted.

> 'They all were looking for a King
> To slay their foes and raise them high:
> Thou cam'st a little baby thing
> That made a woman cry.'
> *(George Macdonald)*

His own disciples made the mistake of thinking in terms of nationalism. Nathanael denied that 'anything good could come out of Nazareth' but went on to accept Jesus as Messiah – 'Rabbi, you are the Son of God; you are the King of Israel.' (John 1,49) It took a long, long time for the hopes and longings of the apostles to change; even after the Resurrection, so little had they learnt of the truth, that they were still asking, 'Lord, will you at this time restore the kingdom to Israel?' (Acts 1.6) – His kingdom is worldwide; in Christ there is neither Jew nor Gentile for 'he is our peace, who has made us both one . . . making peace, . . . reconciling us to God through the cross' (Ephesians 2.14 ff).

The King of all Humanity

Christ's kingdom is universal, then, and he is indeed the universal King. The gospel of the kingdom is as big and broad as humanity itself. 'Jesus Christ is Lord of all' declares St Peter (Acts 10.36) Lord of all because he died for all; and since he died for all he has the right to claim the allegiance of all.

Clearly the title the Wise Men applied to Jesus is inadequate – he is not only King of the Jews, but he is also the King of all nations and of all peoples. But the Magi did prefigure that fact; they were themselves Gentiles from western lands (they saw the star 'in the east') and their homage was the prefiguring of multitudes thereafter, over all the world, from every nation and every people, including ourselves here today.

Adventure with the King

Every Christian has his or her daily tasks to accomplish; many of them of course humdrum without any exciting experiences. But, always, there is an underlying movement of the Spirit which we know as an inspiration – a burning fire which occasionally bursts forth into a warm glow of consolation, or even a flame of colour and heat. We as Christians, like the Wise Men, are always searching for the King. They found him in a place unexpected, and with no signs of royalty. This is true also for us. We find the King in our fellow human beings, in our family, in our work. We find him in the Scriptures and in the Church.

We have a spiritual adventure which lasts as long as our life itself lasts. The Wise Men had their star as an indication of God's guiding providence; we have more than a star – we have the scriptures to reflect upon, and to draw out the meaning of them for our lives. We have the Church, with the sacraments which bring the holy Presence of the Lord our King to our very selves. With Christ, our daily lives can be rich and colourful. Think of that magnificent wall-painting by the artist Benozzo Gozzoli, in the little chapel of the Medici Palace in Florence; here is a sumptuous picture of the cavalcade of the Magi, displaying beautiful finery and gorgeous costumes as they make their way through a smiling landscape to reach the Madonna and Child, with Joseph close at hand. Picturesque and colourful, this painting shows life as a journey of joy, of grace, charm and gaiety, which can lift us from the greyness and dullness that sometimes seems so overpowering, and point to the glowing colours of Christ's rule of righteousness and peace, stretching far and wide over the earth and bringing joy, peace and prosperity to all humanity.

> *Kings shall fall down before him,*
> *And gold and incense bring;*
> *All nations shall adore him,*
> *His praise all people sing;*
> *To him shall prayer unceasing*
> *And daily vows ascend;*
> *His kingdom still increasing,*
> *A kingdom without end.*

> *James Montgomery (EH 45, NEH 55)*

First Sunday of Epiphany: The Baptism of Christ   12 January   'My Son, my Beloved!'

He saw the Spirit of God descending, like a dove, to alight upon him; and a voice from heaven was heard, saying, 'This is my Son, my Beloved, on whom my favour rests.' Matthew 3.17 (ASB Gospel)

Jesus and the Spirit

Here today, as we commemorate the beginning of the public life and mission of Christ our Lord, we are told of the Spirit manifesting himself, symbolized by the dove hovering over the newly-baptized Christ. There is something very beautiful and inspiring about the relationship of Christ and the Spirit. Both the Annunciation and the Baptism of Our Lord recall that time when the Spirit moved over a barren world, making it rich and fertile by his presence and power.

'The earth was without form, and void, and darkness was upon the face of the deep; and the Spirit of God was moving over the face of the waters' (Genesis 1.1).

Mary at the Annunciation was made fruitful through the work of the Spirit, so that her cousin could cry out, 'Blessed are you among women, and blessed is the fruit of your womb!' (Luke 1.42) Then the Spirit at the beginning of Christ's public ministry moves over a world that had become a wilderness through sin; and makes it, through Christ, once again rich and fertile with grace.

After his baptism, the Spirit led Jesus into the wilderness for forty days of fasting and prayer; in that wilderness the Lord was to be put to the test by Satan, and – triumphant – would emerge to lead the new People of God into the Promised Land of his Kingdom.

The Guide

This same Spirit, down the ages, has been and still is, the guide and protector of the Mystical Body of Christ, the Church, just as the Spirit was guide and protector of the Christ of Palestine, moving through the villages and treading along the dusty roads. More, we and all Christians are all under his influence and guidance, if we will but take it. With Christ we were baptized with water and the Spirit; immersed with Christ, we died to ourselves, and are buried in the cleansing waters to rise to new life. Indeed, is not this the mystic transformation of the whole human race? United with Christ, our sinful humanity stands in the healing waters to be made holy, to be redeemed, by him who is all-holy and our Redeemer.

> Almighty God,
> who anointed Jesus at his Baptism with the Holy Spirit
> and revealed him as your beloved Son:
> give to us who are born of water and Spirit,
> the will to surrender ourselves to your service,
> that we may rejoice to be called your children;
> through Jesus Christ our Lord.
>
> *(PHG Collect of the Day, p. 355)*

First Sunday of Epiphany *Second Sermon*
'The Spirit of the Lord'

'He who is mightier than I is coming ... He will baptize you with the Holy Spirit and with fire.' Luke 3.16 (PHG EP)

Baptism and the Holy Spirit

The heavenly Father refers to Jesus at his baptism as 'the beloved Son, with whom I am well pleased'. What pleased the Father most in Jesus was the love he showed, the love which develops and issues in obedience. That is what God expects in us also; and it is only the Spirit that can make it possible. It is said that when the famous composer Verdi produced a rather shoddy opera in Florence, the enthusiastic yet undiscriminating audience went into quite unwarranted raptures, and cheered the composer to the echo. But Verdi paid little heed. He raised his eyes to the box where sat the genius Rossini. Rossini sat in stony silence, altogether unimpressed. For Verdi, that was the opinion which mattered most. Unless he satisfied the maestro, the cheers of the crowd meant nothing.

Approval

As Christians we aim to please. It is not the applause of men and women we seek, but the approval of God. To gain that approval we need the mark of love, the love of one another as children of one Father, brothers and sisters together. Does God see this love, unmistakably, in us? Or do we have to confess that all too often it is conspicuous by its absence?

Love, divine love, for God and for our fellow human beings, with an entire dependence on the Holy Spirit – these are the essentials. Notice too that they are interrelated. We need both aspects; for it is only as we depend on the Spirit that we can show the love needed, for the Christian's love *is* 'the love of the Spirit'.

Display

There are two areas where this love of the Spirit needs to be displayed. The first is in the Church itself. It is here that the love we send out is to be tested, for if we cannot love our fellow Christians, we shall find it hard indeed to love the rest of the humans we meet, live alongside, deal with day by day and from time to time. Yet, too often it is within the Church that our love breaks down. Frederick William Faber, the hymnwriter, used to say that religious people are an unkind lot. Sometimes that is all too sadly true; within a local congregation there can be unseemly divisions, often, alas, over small and in the greater view, unseemly matters. And relations between Christians of different communions, though improved and improving quite astonishingly, are by no means as yet, always what they should be. It is more important that we should love our friends in other denominations than that we should necessarily find a formula to bring us into an organic union. Indeed, it is only as we learn to love 'in the Spirit' that the Spirit will open the way to closer unity.

The World

The other area for the Spirit's love to be shown is, of course, the world. The world is where our Christian love is to be supremely manifested. The Church is the body of Christ, in which his love for a fallen race and a sick society is to be expressed. 'Unless we love our brother (or sister) whom we have seen,' says St John, 'we cannot love God whom we have not seen.' It is the love of the Spirit which is lacking in so much service today; we have plenty of philanthropic do-gooders and protesters and power-people, but what we need is love – selfless, sacrificial Christian love. And it is only the Holy Spirit who can give us it.

One last word: it is this. The love of the Spirit excludes love of self. The Christian loves his fellow-Christians and his neighbours in the world we live in; we may even manage to love our enemies. But we do not love ourselves; we have died to self and to all its demands. This is what happens when we are indeed filled with the Spirit.

Let us pray with Charles Wesley:

> *In me thy Spirit dwells;*
> *In me thy mercies move;*
> *So shall the fervour of my zeal*
> *Be the pure flame of Love.*

Second Sunday of Epiphany
19 January   'Speak for yourself!'

'You shall go to whatever people I send you, and say whatever I tell you to say.' Jeremiah 1.7 (ASB OT Reading)

The Call

The voice of God came to Paul suddenly, unexpectedly. He was bitterly opposed to the false heresy of Christ, as he would certainly have put it; and he was very active in persecuting those obnoxious heretics who claimed to be following what they said Christ had taught. With startling suddenness, he underwent a great change, became one of Christ's most devoted disciples, and so remained for the rest of his life.

And what a life! A quite unimpressive little man, compared with the physically strong Peter, for instance, muscular and fit through his years of fishing and boating. Paul was also frequently ill, as we know from his description of his 'thorn in the flesh' (2. Cor. 12,7) and the illness that 'utterly, unbearably crushed' (1.8,9) him from time to time. Yet while God's grace had to work hard to convert Simon of Galilee into Peter the Rock, it seems that God acted with blinding – literally! – speed to make the persecutor of the Christians into the great lover of Christ.

What about us?

In the first place, we must make ourselves aware of the claim our Lord has upon us, as well as upon famous men and women like the Saints, to say nothing of so many, many other good and precious people who have influenced events and lives and even countries, to small or great effect in their times. Each man or woman became aware in some way of Christ's claim upon him or her, and responded. If we ourselves have not acknowledged that claim, and have not fully or even partially responded to it, we must think more deeply, pray more carefully, and make our response now, in this present time.

Changes

Not only must we remember that Christ calls lesser as well as greater men and women to change their lives, we must remember that within the life of each one of us – however good we may be, or trust that we are – there are always some things, even of a lesser nature or importance, that need changing, too. They are what seem the petty faults of trifling ill-temper, idleness, careless and unkind talk, lack of respect or care for the lives and ways of living of others, the pushful way of trying to always be right, or just at the centre of things, and so on.

Joy in Change

Sudden surprises can bring joy or sorrow to our lives, depending on what they are. What a joyful surprise it was to the early Christians, when they found that St Paul was on their side instead of being an enemy still, full of fire and anger.

For all of us, widely different as we are, far apart from one another in age, outlook, abilities and occupations; but for all there are ways of serving God and of being useful to the Church and to our neighbours. For some the ways are great, for many they are small – but important all the same. The first step towards helping in any way, and carrying out any task, is to realize that opportunities are there; there is work to do, there are people who need our help, the Church can always use our time and energy.

God wants us all to give him what we can, and to serve his cause in this world about us, here and now, to the best of our abilities and powers.

Second Sunday of Epiphany   *Second Sermon*
The Call

'The first thing Andrew did was to find his brother Simon. He said to him, 'We have found the Messiah (which is the Hebrew for "Christ") And he brought him to Jesus.' John 1.41 (ASB EP)

Brothers

Surprising it is, how often there are surprises in the Bible. Things are quite different from what we might expect; people behave differently from what we are used to; events don't turn out as we might expect.

Take our Gospel reading. Bethany was a small place on the bank of the River Jordan, so small and unimportant that it had been forgotten even by the time it was being looked for, by the scholar and historian Origen, at the beginning of the third century A.D. But this is the village where the incidents in our gospel for today took place – incidents which were to have extremely important effects upon the mission and the life of Our Lord, and effects which influenced or even took over, the life and whole outlook of his Body, the Church.

Peter

Firstly, here it was that Peter was brought to Jesus – in fact it was here that 'Simon son of John' was renamed 'Cephas', that is 'Peter', the 'Rock', by Jesus himself. At this very early point in his mission to the world, Jesus saw that here, in this bluff fisherman, was the man to be his second-in-command, the organizer and leader of the band of apostles – as yet not completed nor formed – who would take on and spread about his message and his teaching. More, they would be the basis of the Christian Church – and of them all, Peter was to have the most important place. Today, it is the successor to Peter who is certainly the best-known Christian leader, and it is to him, under Christ, that vast numbers of Christians throughout the world look for leadership, instruction, teaching and discipline.

However much we, in the Anglican Communion, may regret aspects of Papal teaching and Roman discipline, seeing these as sad degeneration from the pure and primitive days of Peter the Apostle and the Lord himself, yet there is no denying the historical

40

basis in our Lord's own words to Peter. In our New Testament reading today we see that other pillar of the Church, St Paul, making it his important business to see and meet Cephas, and stay with him for a fortnight, discussing the matters of the Kingdom, we may be sure, and how the infant Church should proceed in doing the work of its Master.

Nathanael

Nathanael is a figure about whom little is known. He is not in any list of the Twelve, and in fact it is not said that he became a disciple. His initial doubt – 'Can anything good come from Nazareth?' – soon becomes recognition of One who is not only Rabbi (Teacher) but astonishingly, 'Son of God' and 'King of Israel'. An even more astonishing statement comes from Jesus in response to Nathanael's words of acclamation and recognition: 'You shall see heaven wide open, and God's angels ascending and descending upon the Son of Man!'

Jesus refers to himself obliquely in a number of places as 'The Son of Man' – he seems to prefer this title or identification, suggesting a figure whose destiny was to be played out both on earth and in heaven, as he makes clear here in an oblique reference to Jacob's dream vision (Genesis 28.12) of the ladder set up between earth and heaven, with the angels of God going up and down upon it. When Nathanael saw Jesus, it was surely to him the true Israelite vision of Israel in heaven with his true counterpart on earth. Jesus was a figure whose destiny was to be played out both on earth and in heaven.

Ninth Sunday before Easter
(Septuagesima)   27 January (Education Sunday)
Education & Religion

'The people were astounded at the teachings of Jesus: for he taught them with authority.' Matthew 7.28,29 (ASB Postcommunion Sentence)

Problems, Problems . . .

To talk about education is not easy, especially where pretty well everyone hearing what is being said, will have been through some form of formal education; and if you have either suffered or benefited, you will have preconceived ideas. The greatest educational-ist was, of course, our Lord, and it is his doctrine that we try to carry forward in our Church Schools today. In the Schools the seeds of all knowledge and thought are, we hope, sown in the minds of the children. It is an awesome and yet wonderful task and opportunity.

'Give me the Child'

'Give me the child 'til he's seven and I will show you the man' said Rousseau; and with all our children of both sexes there is indeed a strong possibility of opening doors and windows that will affect lives for ever. It is with the young that values can be planted in our youth – values that as the children grow them-selves, they may reject or mould to themselves; but at least with Religious Education lessons, the values have a chance of being nurtured.

The Bible is a beautiful masterpiece of poetry – the stories of the Old Testament are wildly exciting – Daniel and the Lions, Jonah and the Whale, Noah and the Ark; the desperate deeds of Samson; and while the New Testament teaches us the facts of Christ's life and teaching, teaching that our culture is based upon, I believe strongly it is every child's right to be exposed to Christian basics. The children should be taught the stories of the Bible, for they will then have a more comprehensive understanding of what Christianity is.

Knowledge and Respect

I appreciate that many people disagree with me over this, but I personally feel strongly about it. I understand all the arguments as to why the Daily Assembly has been abolished in some schools, and why Religious Education no longer exists as such. Our multi-ethnic society makes it necessary and right that we should be truly aware of our neighbours, learn about their beliefs, and respect their customs and festivals. Yet I see no reason why our culture and our faith should vanish, while we accommodate the cultures and faiths of others. The religions of Muslims and Hindus have a definite and welcome place in our society, as we have welcomed the Hebrew faith, and the teachings of the Buddha and of the Prophet have much to offer us intellectually, but alongside the teaching of Christ and his Church. This is why we keep the Daily Assembly at our Parish School. It is a most important part of our

School Day, for here we meet as a family, and the stories the children are told by either myself or the Deputy, usually will have a moral base that refers generally to the world in which we all live. In our Assembly we try to capture a sense of belonging, for we all belong to one another, we all share the same air and the same world and we must learn to be appreciative of others and always helpful.

Schools and Church
Church Schools do not try to take over or replace the work and the role of the Church, but we should all be walking together. Here in this parish the relationship between Church and School is excellent; the clergy take Assembly once a week and the children are well aware of their vocation and the role they have in life. The children like and respect the clergy and know that their work is to promote the teaching of the Church and Bible about God our Father and Jesus Christ our Lord. There is a general atmosphere of love and care when they are around.

Ethos
The ethos of the Church School is very important to me; and it means far more than a weekly RE lesson. I believe one of our tasks is to make children aware that they are more than a mind and a body. They need to be aware of the spiritual side of life, which is so important for a deeper understanding of the universe. I have a slogan on my wall for staff, as a reminder of what we are here for. 'Have you made your children THINK today?'

We have many different nationalities in our school – Japanese, Bangladeshi, Greek, West Indian, Polish and others. We are not an elitist school, to pick and choose our pupils. Everyone is welcome to work with us, for on earth we are one family, and the greater the understanding between peoples and nations the sooner the world will behave like one family. The education we offer is to make the children think, question and explore; to begin to equip them with skills, both physical and mental, that they will need later on. We try to give them a feeling for one another – a feeling that is not measured by success alone but by genuine love and respect.

(Copies of the Education Sunday Leaflet 1997 can be had from the Promotions Secretary, National Society, Church House, Great Smith Street, Westminster, London SW1P 3NZ)

Ninth Sunday before Easter   *Second Sermon*
Change

'He began to teach by the lake-side. The crowd that gathered round him was so large that he had to get into a boat on the lake, and there he sat, with the whole crowd on the beach right down to the water's edge.'
St Mark 4.1 (ASB EP)

The Lakeside
Mark, Matthew and Luke all record how Jesus gave this story, and Mark and Matthew tell us that he would not have been able to have been heard, if he had not entered the boat, and been pushed out from the shore. Circumstances had changed – in the early days Jesus preached to the Sabbath-day congregations in the local synagogues; but now he is reported as speaking in the open air, often at a distance from any town or village. What brought about this change? Because of the rift that was opening between Jesus and the official Hebrew Church, the synagogues were reluctant to invite him any more; and in some areas local officials would have forbidden his speaking in the villages.

All the same, our Lord attracted crowds whatever the authorities might say; and often the crowds were too big to be accommodated indoors. Christ of all people was not swayed by popularity, but he must have felt some satisfaction because people were coming to listen to his message in large numbers, and he must have hoped that a fair proportion of them might be influenced by his words.

Communication Then and Now
Almost the only way of influencing large numbers of people in New Testament times would have been through open-air meetings, whether for political or religious purposes. Today, of course, while such meetings still have a part to play, it is radio, television and the Press with news and advertisements that really get 'the message' over, whatever it may be.

What would Jesus do, if he were proclaiming his message in our times today? We may be sure that he would have retained the personal touch, by which he won so many people – like Peter, and his other disciples, and figures like the Centurion or Nicodemus – but we can be sure that he would have adapted himself to modern ways of communication to reach the mass of the people.

There was a fine attempt, for instance, to bring the Bible to the ordinary people of the day, in a strikingly illustrated version entitled 'The Bible for Today'. The illustrations in fact, were a most important part of getting over the message; most were pictures of life today and the common backgrounds of today – the town, the village, the busy city streets with gigantic buildings, or the country with farmland and little towns springing up here and there. Equally, the people were shown looking with hope and fear to the giants of their times; ambition and pride, outrages which shock the moral sense, brutality and by contrast care and love. Whether we look in the Bible or our newspapers or our TV screens, we see the signs of the age, and the spirit of the times, of our own times, of all times.

Updating the Parable

Jesus, we may be sure, would now make changes in his parables; he took care that they were topical and understood in the New Testament times, and he would do the same today.

What would have happened to the Parable of the Sower? Today less and less people know anything much about country life and country ways; the reason is simply that far fewer people are involved in farming and know something of agricultural methods. The farmer of today would find the details of the parable irrelevant to their ways of sowing and reaping – machinery has taken the place of handwork, for instance. Less seed is wasted because the ground is properly broken up; weeds are kept at bay with the use of chemical sprays, and so the corn is less likely to be choked. But the parable still points out how easy it can be to close our ears to God's call to us, and how easy it can be to allow worldly concerns and interests to crowd our religion out of life, let alone the lack of staying power to continue in the way of life we have decided to adopt, following in the footsteps of Christ.

Still the Lord's Call
The teller of the story, and the lessons it is his purpose to convey, remain the same. Since Jesus preached on the shore of the lake, times have changed, and the way people live has altered out of all comparison. Yet his message remains the same, and his warnings are still valid, and we can take our lives and alter our ways so that we conform to the ideals, and the hopes, that Jesus put before his audiences so long ago, two thousand years of the world's history. And still we can find our hope and our salvation in him, the Saviour of all Humanity down the ages.

The Presentation of Christ in the Temple
2 February (Sexagesima Sunday)   The Promise

'Guided by the Spirit, Simeon came into the Temple, and when the parents brought in the child Jesus to do for him what was customary under the Law, he took him in his arms, praised God, and said, "This day, Master, thou givest thy servant his discharge in peace; now is thy promise fulfilled."' Luke 2,27–29

Nunc Dimittis
Consider first the scene: The young mother and her child fulfilling the requirements of the Law. She, the pure Virgin, humbly submitting herself to the ritual purification. He, the great High Priest who eternally makes intercession for us, being redeemed from the obligations of priestly service in the Temple. All done quietly and unostentatiously – merely a small domestic ceremony amidst the perpetual bustle and flurry of the normal Temple routine of sacrifice and prayer.

It was as common and unexceptional a scene as a Sunday afternoon Baptism in an English parish church; doubtless few of the worshippers were even aware of it happening, until an elderly white-bearded man pushed his way towards the child's mother, and asked if he might hold the baby. With the child cradled in his arms, the old man blessed his God, and poured forth his praise for 'A light to enlighten the pagans, and the glory of the people of Israel.'

The Messiah

Simeon was not one of the Temple priests; St Luke describes him simply as 'upright' and 'devout'. As we in our time are glad to see in our churches and cathedrals, day by day, faithful older men and women, who come in to pray and praise God, so in the great Temple of Jerusalem, men like Simeon and women like Anna would be around. But Simeon had a particular devotion – as St Luke makes clear, he was one who 'looked forward to Israel's comforting'. The phrase is strange to our ears, but familiar to any devout Jew of his day. He was waiting patiently for the promised Coming of the Messiah.

The Sentry

He was not alone; in a sense, all Israel was waiting for the Messiah; and whenever someone claimed to be the long-awaited Lord's Anointed, there were always those ready to believe their claims and to follow them, even sometimes to die for them. But with Simeon, it was different. Day after day he continued to watch in the Temple, like a sentry on guard duty, waiting for the signal that he knew would one day appear. His patience was at last rewarded, and as St Luke tells us, inspired by the Holy Spirit he saw that the child this mother carried was not just another Jewish kiddie brought to undergo the ritual requirements of the Law, but the Chosen One of Israel coming into his own Temple.

At last, his patience had been rewarded – and with what a reward! Simeon could leave his post and die contented, for he had cradled the Lord's Anointed in his arms, and had seen God in the eyes of a child.

'Now, Master, you can let your servant go in peace, just as you promised.'

The Lesson

The lesson Simeon teaches us is one we all need to learn. He did nothing spectacular, made no mark on his contemporaries, wrote no books; he just quietly got on with his job of waiting, day after day, certain that God would be faithful to his promises.

For us, 'depart in peace' has come to have overtones of prayers for the departed. No, Simeon was not praying for death; he was simply claiming his just discharge after long years of faithful service. Now, if death came, he could face it peacefully and without fear, because he had already seen his salvation.

Instinctively, the mind goes forward in time to the opening words of St John's first letter – words that might well have been Simeon's as he gazed at the Child, who was also his Saviour:

'That which has existed since the beginning,
which we have heard, and which we have seen with our own eyes,
that we have watched, and touched with our hands:
the Word who is life – that life was made visible.
We saw it and we are giving you our testimony,
telling you of the eternal life, which was with the Father,
and has been made visible to us.'

(1 John 1.1–2)

Jesus, the eternal Word of the Father, made flesh in the body of Mary, was his salvation; eternal life was to be found in him.

The Light
But this is no private consolation to be hugged to himself for fear that others would snatch it from him. That was the sin of the Jews as a whole, for they could only think of the revelation between God and themselves as a sign of favouritism. That was not Simeon's view: 'A light this child shall be, not only for me, but for the pagans, and the glory of your people Israel.'

To the Gentiles who sat in darkness, this Child is to be a light; and here we catch an echo of Isaiah:

'It is not enough for you to be my servant,
to restore the tribes of Jacob,
and bring back the survivors of Israel;
I will make you the Light of the nations
so that my salvation will reach the ends of the earth.'

(Isaiah 49.6)

The Presentation of Christ in the Temple
Second Sermon (Sexagesima)   Healing

'A woman, whose little daughter was possessed by an unclean spirit, heard of him, and came and fell down at his feet. Now the woman was a Greek, a Syrophoenician by birth. And she begged him to cast the demon out of her daughter.' Mark 7.25 (ASB EP)

Christ's Healings

The Lord's works of healing flowed out from his unfailing and all-prevailing compassion. We might go so far as to say that his compassion was a vital element in his Gospel of God's love and grace. Jesus could not but help, whenever human suffering – of the body or of the mind – was presented to him. We must not think that his mighty works of healing were done with the simple aim of authenticating his mission, even though some of them clearly pointed to that end. He fulfilled the prophecy that he would hear our griefs and carry our sorrows (Isaiah, 53.4). All who were in need – lepers, paralytics, deaf, dumb, diseased, mentally deranged – as well as the sin-sick – were his loved brothers and sisters. He shrank from none; he set the first and greatest example of a life governed and guided by a passion for humanity.

Pity

The mother of the afflicted child, whose healing she sought at Christ's hands, had clearly heard of the Saviour's compassion and his powers. She was aware that she was a foreigner, no Jew, and could not claim anything on the basis of race. She made no claim, nor did she make any pretence of a claim, other than that which every one of God's children can make – namely, to the Divine compassion. We are all finally dependent on God's mercy.

It is the best of all claims and it is one which will always evoke a response. The divine mercy includes interest, pity, sympathy, compassion – and a willing desire to help. Good men – sometimes even bad men – feel compassion for their fellows; a good – even a not-so-good – parent will be considerate towards the children. God is always merciful towards his creatures. The mother of this afflicted child claimed God's universal mercy as the basis of her request: 'Sir! have pity on me, Son of David; my daughter is tormented by a devil' (Matt. 15.22).

A Sharp Answer

Jesus replies to her with a strangely sharp and bitter answer; his mission, he says, is to the children of Israel and not to heathen 'dogs', the typical Jewish term of contempt, for those outside the Covenant.

Do we perhaps see here another side of Jesus, hardly mentioned in the Gospels – Jesus the Jew, with something of the exclusiveness that then, and still sometimes today, can mark the Hebrew nature? Or are we seeing a tired Lord, seeking just a little respite from the constant pressures of the crowds and the questioners, the seekers and the sick? Note that the Evangelist tells us that 'he entered a house, and would not have anyone know it' so that he could snatch a little time of rest and recuperation. 'But he could not be hid,' we are told. And here comes this unfortunate woman, with her begging and praying, just when he is relaxing in a badly-needed few minutes of peace and quiet.

It may be, as Bernard Shaw wrote about this episode, that 'she melted the Jewishness out of Jesus'. Or we may prefer to think that, although he replied to her request as any Jew would be expected to, yet he was hoping that the woman would reach out beyond the barriers of race and creed. There is no record of his tone of voice, nor of the encouraging smile he doubtless gave. Reach out, she certainly did; she struck a humorous note, she took his sharp reply as a peg on which to hang an amusing answer. She amused him with her wit and keenness of mind.

Laughter, the Healer

We cannot doubt but that Jesus had a keen sense of humour. Consider his parables: if we did not know them so well and associate them with the solemn atmosphere of the church, we would, for sure, burst out laughing at the story of the Two Carpenters – the one with a speck of sawdust in his eye, the other with a whole plank! Or the joke of the Camel and the Eye of the Needle – the hairy great camel, all legs and long neck, trying to get through the eye of a needle!

While the crowd enjoyed these jokes, and laughed, for sure the Teacher also joined in.

Laughter is said to be a great healer; often a conflict or argument can be resolved by laughter, tension broken with a joke. Let us remember how faith brings healing, and how laughter can change our attitudes and melt away stiffness and fears.

Seventh Sunday before Easter (*Quinquagesima; Sunday next before Lent*)
9 February   Compassion

'It is not the healthy that need a doctor, but the sick.' Mark 2.17 *(ASB Gospel)*

The Changing Picture of God

In the Old Testament, the picture presented to us of God is so often one that we find difficult to accept or understand; the Lord appears as not merely a 'jealous' God, but one with many of the attributes of the savage chieftains of primitive times. He has something of the unpredictability of Nature; he sends plagues and destruction upon the people, the tribes of the earth. It is only gradually that we see the evolving of the ideals of mercy, pity, love and forgiveness that make up the picture of the loving, caring Father that Jesus teaches us about.

However, in the teachings of the prophet Hosea we find clearly expressed the ideals of love, of hope, and of forgiveness that play so vital a part in the preaching and the life of Christ.

Hosea

The story of the life of Hosea is a strange one. His wife proves unfaithful, and bears children in her unfaithfulness; symbolic of the unfaithful relationship of the nation of Israel to their Lord. Depravity leads to despair and decay, with punishment descending upon the unrepentant nation – 'Your iniquity was the cause of your downfall'. And yet God is merciful and loving, turns away his wrath, and in the beautiful passage we heard just now, will be like dew watering plants so that they may revive, and grow, and be lovely. God will not let Israel go – as the hymn has it, 'O love that will not let me go . . .'

Here is an appropriate motto we can adopt for Lent; let us try to learn its meaning in the weeks ahead.

Philemon

From the New Testament, we have today a very short Epistle, St Paul's letter to Philemon.

This is one of the few personal letters from the Apostle to be preserved, maybe the only *really* personal one. In it Paul deals with a personal problem, how to cope with a runaway slave. This man, named Onesimus, which means 'helpful', had come into contact with Paul when the apostle was a prisoner in Rome, and had obviously proved helpful indeed. It may well be that Onesimus was able to read and write, and acted as Paul's secretary – we must remember that Paul had 'the care of all the churches', and the letters preserved in our Bibles represent only a small fraction of what must have been sent out. (Ancient Rome had an excellent postal system all over the Empire, secure and rapid; and we know that many administrators, politicians and authors, used assistants – often slaves – who could take dictation in shorthand and then produce 'fair copies'.) By coincidence, Paul knew the slave's master, Philemon, who lived at Colossae, and had been converted to Christianity by the Apostle. It is possible also that Paul had baptized Onesimus ('my child, Onesimus, whose father I have become . . .') perhaps in Rome. At any rate, Paul is sending Onesimus back to his master – but his 'covering letter' is saying that the slave is now a changed man, and what a useful assistant he is – so, broadly hinting that Philemon will let Onesimus stay with Paul. Paul even offers to pay any costs that may have been involved (v. 18,19) but makes it clear that he (Paul) wants some return (v. 20) and is confident of Philemon's obedience (v. 21).

How did St Paul's letter succeed?

We are not told in the New Testament, but anyone listening to the letter and its pleading can hardly imagine Philemon saying 'No'; and then we have the intriguing fact that some fifty years after all this, a famous bishop, Ignatius, was being taken to Rome to be martyred; on his path – his triumph, we may say – he wrote to the Christians of the places he passed, and to Ephesus he gives congratulations on the good reports he has heard of their bishop. Who is this bishop? His name is Onesimus – almost certainly the runaway slave who assisted St Paul with his correspondence.

And is it not very likely – almost certain – that the letters of St Paul we now have in our Bibles, or most of them, are due to the industry and care of Onesimus? He it was, scholars believe, who gathered up the Apostle's letters in the form of drafts and copies perhaps, and as a kind of guarantee added this little letter concerning himself.

The Apostle's compassion, therefore, had the effect of not only bringing a runaway back to his master, but also of bringing a soul back to the Lord and Master of All; and through the action of that one-time runaway slave, giving us the benefit of the invaluable and wonderful letters of St Paul to inspire and teach us. After the Apostle's martyrdom, it does seem that a certain disregard of his teaching took possession of the infant Christian world; it was the glory of Onesimus to assist in the recovery and reinstatement of Paul and his epistles in the main stream of Christian theology, to the benefit of us all.

PRAYER

> *O God of all the nations of the earth,*
> *remember those who though created in your image,*
> *are ignorant of your love;*
> *and in fulfilment of the sacrifice of your Son,*
> *may the prayers and labours of the Church,*
> *deliver them from false faith or unbelief,*
> *and bring them to worship you;*
> *through him who is the resurrection*
> *and the life of all who trust in you,*
> *Jesus Christ our Lord.*
>
> *(LHWE p. 92)*

Sunday next before Lent *Second Sermon*
Mistakes
'*Let him who is without sin, cast the first stone.*' John 8.7 *(EP ASB)*

A Mixed Manuscript
It can be very irritating for an author, having written a large number of pages, and arranged them in the right order, to then find that one page has 'gone missing' and in some mysterious way is lost. Of course, with a word-processor this won't happen too often, nor with taped scripts – but even these are sometimes at fault. However clever we do become, somehow mistakes do still occur.

Somehow or other the writer of this story about Jesus and the woman taken in adultery, managed to get his manuscript mixed up. It became separated from the volume, or scroll, it was intended for. The copyists were baffled; but one took matters into his own hands and placed the story in St John's Gospel, immediately after the words,

'You judge by worldly standards; I pass judgement upon no man, but if I do judge, my judgement is true, for it is not I alone that judge, but I and my Father who sent me.' (John 8.15, 16)

Archbishop Temple described him as a genius for so doing, for our Lord's words about judgement make a splendid introduction to the story, and drive home what it teaches.

Conscience

When Jesus said, 'Let him who is faultless cast the first stone', the woman's accusers slipped away, one by one. Here some copies of the manuscript have the words 'convicted by their consciences'. We do not know whether these words were in the original and were carelessly left out, or whether some copyist put them in to make the point clearer, but they emphasize something that is important; Jesus directed the crowd to look – not at the woman's sin, but at the hidden sins in their own lives, and at the evil in their own hearts.

Oh yes, we are all very quick to notice what other people do wrong, to spot their faults, and sometimes just too quick to talk about them. Do we look into our own hearts and lives as carefully, and put our faults and sins into the clear light of God's vision?

No Condoning

The copyists made mistakes, no doubt; but do we make a mistake when we read or hear this story? Many people like to think that Jesus is condoning the woman's sin by his merciful attitude. This is quite untrue; by his merciful attitude our Lord did not condone her sin in any way, nor condone the sins of others. As he told her to go, he warned her – and we do not know how stern his voice may have been for his words: 'Go, and sin no more.' If we do not hear that note of warning in his voice, and apply it to ourselves, we misread the story and misjudge our Lord. The true aim of justice is not punishment for its own sake, but the discouragement of wrongdoing and the reform and renewal of the wrongdoer. This should be our attitude to our fellow men and women.

Ash Wednesday *The First Day of Lent*
12 February **The Enemy Within**

'Where do these wars and battles between yourselves first start? Isn't it precisely in the desires fighting inside your own selves?' James 4.1 (An ASB NT Reading)

Conflict and Holiness

The anguished query of St James speaks to us of our own internal conflicts, which are actually inimical to holiness. We are sometimes, indeed, the 'household divided against itself' (Matt. 12.25) as Jesus told his accusers, or like St Paul 'I do not do the good I want, but the evil I do not want' (Romans 7.19). Paul was certainly aware of the problem, and his theme would be echoed by the insights of psychology in our own century. They would warn us that the danger can be even more acute when – as all too often – we are not really *aware* that we are at war within ourselves. Depth psychology speaks of the conflict between aims and ideals consciously held, and the unconscious wishes and fears at variance with them which occur in us all.

Oh, you may say, what a lot of introspection when there is plenty of evil out there, of just the sort which Jesus was addressing, when he healed the blind and dumb and dealt with Satan's power.

True, but could it be that there is conflict in the world between nations because there is conflict within nations; and that there is conflict within nations because there is conflict between people, and there is conflict between people because there is conflict within people.

As Jesus so often did, we need to start right there. 'It is what comes out of a person that defiles that person' (Matt. 15.18) and we might add, defiles the world. If we want to become holy this Lent, we could do worse than look at the hidden conflicts within.

Awareness and Projection

We are so often not aware of conflicts eating away at our souls, since if we were we could not bear it. 'Mankind cannot bear very much reality' wrote T. S. Eliot, and how right he was. Yes, we repress our guilts and fears, our angers and our feelings of inadequacy. And what is worse, we project them onto others. The driver of the car emerging too fast from a side road and hitting a car which has right of way on the main road, will leap out in fury and scream, 'What a heck of a speed you were tearing up the tarmac at, you dangerous so-and-so!' The effects of projection on a larger scale can be very, very disastrous: the Nazis projected their repressed guilt and inferiority on the Jews, and made them the scapegoats for German misfortunes. We may well ask the men of violence of the IRA and of Hammas what their real anger is about, deep down; and we see enough of the horrors of Serbia and of Rwanda to know that religion and nationalism can be covers for the working out of internal conflicts with appalling results.

Be clear however; none of us is immune – we all escape from our guilts and fears and inadequacies, those parts of ourselves we do not care to acknowledge, by repressing them and projecting them onto others.

Opening Up

How much of our aggression, our self-righteousness, our impatience with others, is driven by projection? Our repressed fears and guilts, angers and inadequacies condemn us to fruitless conflicts with others. If we are to become holy, we need to be at peace with ourselves. Only if we are at peace with ourselves can we be engaged in truly constructive conflict, which has really to do with gospel truth and not our own hang-ups.

How can we tackle the things which are not even part of our conscious selves? Only by opening up ourselves to God. By exposing ourselves to that perfect love which casts out fear. It is the Cross which expresses once and for all, in its fullness the complete acceptance of the love of God; and if we are able to feel that full acceptance we shall be able to begin to integrate those parts of ourselves which are repressed, and so find freedom from the conflicts which bind us and which hold us down.

In God's presence and love we are given the means and strength to dig deeper and face the conflict; this is the first step to becoming truly whole and truly holy. The alternative of playing safe and living in the shadows will never bring us to the glorious liberty of the children of God, which is our inheritance. Don't settle for half-living!

Come out of the Shadows

It was Karl Jung's splendid clue, that we experience God as we become aware of our whole personality influencing our conscious mind; we need to open ourselves to God and hear the self we really are emerging out of our shadow selves, our pretended selves, our counterfeit selves. We can discover, under the shadow of God's wing, our projections of our fears, guilts and inadequacies onto others. At root, our repressions are driven by fear; and it is only the perfect love of God which can drive out fear, the love we can see in the cross. In that love we can be able to bring the dark side of ourselves into the light; and awareness can lead to repentance for the harm we have done in projecting that dark side onto others. Repentance can lead to forgiveness; forgiveness can lead to healing and to holiness; holiness means wholeness and freedom, as it has always meant.

May we approach the Cross this Lent and find the perfect love of God which casts out fear. May we find resolutions to the conflicts which bind us down, and be set free to experience the glorious liberty of the children of God. May we find holiness – holiness and freedom.

J.I.

First Sunday in Lent   16 February   The Desert

'Jesus was led up by the Spirit into the wilderness, to be tempted by the devil. And he fasted forty days and forty nights, and afterwards he was hungry.' Matt. 4,1 (ASB Gospel) 'As chastened, and not killed: as sorrowful, yet always rejoicing: as poor, yet making many rich; as having nothing, and yet possessing all things.' 2 Corinthians 6.9 (BCP Epistle)

The First Lent

The very first Lent was kept in the desert, the wilderness. Jesus spent forty days out there, alone, with little in the way of food, and drink, little in the way of shelter, little in the way of comfort; much in the way of hardship, much in the way of privation, much in the way of temptation. It is in memory of those forty critical days of our Lord's life that we keep our Lent; because of his privations we have our little bits of fasting, we give up some of the things we like, we make rather larger contributions to whatever good causes we favour, and above all we try to put ourselves in a closer rapport, a closer touch, with God our Father, while trying to emulate something of the quiet, the stillness, of the wilderness, with its utter loneliness.

We may picture in our minds the quiet atmosphere of our own countryside; but few parts of Great Britain are really lonely. There are usually some signs of humanity – fences or walls, paths and roads. In the distance a little house, perhaps with a walled garden; perhaps on the horizon a spire. We may go to remoter places, with no sign at all of the work of humanity – except maybe some faint track. Not like the desert, with its heat, its absolute loneliness, its crushing emptiness, its inhumanity and hostility.

Critical

It was a crucial time for Jesus; we picture him trying to get some little shelter beside an emaciated tree, or some relief in the shade of a rock. He was kept alive by berries and herbs which had not been scorched dry; drink was from the rare spring of brackish water. The first move of the Spirit of evil was the raising of doubts – '*If* you are the Son of God – prove it . . .' On the ground were rounded pebbles, suggesting small loaves of bread; his hunger was considerable. 'Use your power to turn these stones into bread . . . You must not perish out here from starvation.' Or more subtly, 'Use your power to provide food for the hungry . . . help the starving masses of the world . . . succour the poor . . .' Here was a tempting possibility of great appeal – but into the mind would come the text 'Man shall not live by bread alone . . .' Food is a must for life, but the true need is to be ruled and nourished and guided by the word of God. If this is accepted, all else will fall into place.

The Devil

The devil never gives up. Another thought comes into the Lord's mind: display his own faith in the power of the Father, through working some spectacular miracle. To throw himself down from the pinnacle of the Temple, trusting in God for safety – was there not a text in the Bible which promised divine protection? 'Why, yes! "He will give his angels charge of you, to guard you; on their hands they will bear you up, lest you strike your foot against a stone" '(Ps 91, 11–12). How very decisive!

But wait – is there not another text with very different implications? 'You shall not tempt the Lord your God!' (Deuteronomy 6.16) Throwing oneself down from the Temple spire would amount to distrusting God, putting God to the test, tempting *him*, if that were possible.

No, sensational miracles are not the way to win souls to God; but what is the way to save men and women? Satan has another suggestion – 'Worship me, and I will give you the world, its kingdoms and power!' Did he mean Jesus to take the popular way, be the Messiah who would liberate Israel from the Roman dominion? This seems certainly to have been the thinking of the crowds who cried 'Hosanna!' at the Lord's entry into Jerusalem on Palm Sunday. Or was it perhaps to become an ally of the power of Rome, influence the Emperor towards just and benevolent government, keeping peace throughout the world, eventually himself taking the reins and becoming king – later on the people were all too ready to pressurize him in this direction (John 6.15).

The Way of Love
There and then Jesus must have chosen the way of love, of service, of suffering, and if needful, the way of sacrifice and death. Already he must have seen at the end of the road, the shadow of a cross. And that cross would symbolize a cross in the heart of God – it has been said that there was a cross in the divine heart before ever there was a cross on Calvary. That cross symbolized the pain of human suffering, human foolishness and human pride, and the human refusal of love. St Paul found the divine and eternal life personalized in himself when he could write of Jesus as 'the son of God who loved me and gave his life for me'.

Each of us ought to be able to say the same, and begin this Lent to tread the way of love, the way of the Cross, which leads to the heart of God.

Lent 1 *Second Sermon* **Temptations**

'I acknowledge my faults: and my sin is ever before me.' Ps 51 (ASB EP)

The Sense of Sin

It is a strong and clear view of sin which the Bible puts before us, very different from the apologetic dismissal of some psychologist theologian, or the more or less complete suppression we find in modern thought.

And just as clear and definite is the Church's teaching. In almost every service confession of sin is placed in the forefront of our approach to God. And this is not the mere casual mention of it as of a venial fault, or a failure to reach an ideal standard, but as a definite and personal transgression of God's law. In the daily Offices of prayer, at the Holy Eucharist, in the Litany, in whatever form they are used, the same note runs; a note very much at variance with the all-too-light view of sin which is prevalent in our thinking today.

A True Perception

We need the convincing, convicting power of the Holy Spirit to bring us to a true perception of the nature of sin. The world and we ourselves need to realize the true point of view from which sin is to be regarded. We speak of evil, but do we mean sin? We say that sin is selfishness, but do we think that selfishness is sin? Sin is the interpretation of evil as an offence against God; a disobedience to the law and will of God; an alienation and a separation from God. It is as we seek to know God that we come to realize what sin is.

Knowledge of God

A knowledge of God must come by the teaching of the Holy Spirit through the revelation of God, which he has given us in his Son Jesus Christ. 'Of sin because they believe not on me' (John 8.24) 'He that has seen me, has seen the Father' (John 14.9) The Bible is not primarily a revelation of sin; it is a revelation of God. The revelation of sin which it contains, comes in as the obverse of the revelation of God which it gives to us.

Where there is no knowledge of a personal God there can be no conviction of sin, and no true knowledge of sin in its essential nature. This is a view that is confirmed by the whole moral sense of humanity. From this, what follows?

Why, a deep conviction of sin – what it is; and of our own personal sinfulness, wrought upon the mind and the heart by the power of the Holy Spirit.

Evidence of Life

A sense of sin, and our shame on account of it, is far from being hopeless. In fact it is evidence of true life in its very pain, of enlightenment in its shame, of nearness to God in our humiliation before this.

David was never so near to God as when he poured out his heart and soul in those imperishable words of confession and repentance which we have just recited in the 51st Psalm. Peter was never so truly Christ's disciple as when he went out into the grey morning, broken by the Master's look, and wept bitterly (Luke 22.62) It is the realization that he who is not only the Almighty God – holy, pure, and just – but the loving Father who has revealed himself and his boundless love for sinners, in the person of Jesus Christ his only son, our Lord. And he, while he makes known the purity of his character, and his hatred of sin, makes known also the love of his fatherly heart, and his tender yearning over the sinner, in that he gave his only begotten Son to be the propitiation for our sins.

The cross of Christ, it has been well said, it the measure of God's hatred of sin. And when once the Holy Spirit convicts a human being of sin, and shows what it really is, and what it is in the self, that man or woman will never make light of it, or seek to minimize it.

The Next Step

Instead, a human soul will realize the deep truth of these words: 'If we say we have no sin, we deceive ourselves, and the truth is not in us.' (1 John 1,8) And that realization will lead us to the next step: 'If we confess our sins, he is faithful and just, and will forgive our sins and cleanse us from all unrighteousness.' (1 John 1,9) 'Whoever keeps God's word, in them truly love for God is perfected' (1 John 2,5)

> *O Lord Christ,*
> *before whose judgement seat we must all appear,*

keep us steadfast and faithful in your service,
and enable us so to judge ourselves in this life,
that we may not be condemned
*   on the Day of your appearing;*
for your tender mercy's sake.

(PHG 36)

Second Sunday in Lent   23 February
Jesus Wept

'When Jesus came in sight of the city, he wept over it and said, "If only you had known, on this great day, the way that leads to peace! But no, it is hidden from your sight."' Luke 19.41 (ASB Gospel)

Destruction
Sometimes destruction is essential; for instance, to create a clearing-ground for new building. Thus the distress and degradation of slums makes way for better housing. Such destruction and demolition is clearly a good thing, for it should bring comfort, health and happiness in the place of wretchedness, overcrowding and despair. However, the old inhabitants may be so attached to their shacks or overcrowded courtyards, that they are distressed at the removal; and sometimes the new buildings prove less successful than hoped, as with many of the great 'tower blocks' built after World War 2. These are now themselves the objects of destruction, in their turn, and we can only hope that the lessons of the past have been learnt by the architects and town-planners of our own time. In Nature the decay of the old gives vitality to the new; seeds 'die' in the earth, yet bring forth the beauty of fresh plants and flowers, as the seasons move on and the earth spins on its orbit.

The Tears of Christ
The destruction of the Temple at Jerusalem was not in preparation for a new and finer building; it was the final stroke of the bitter conflict between Jewish faith and hope, and the power of the Roman Empire. The immovable object in the path of the

unstoppable force – and the object lost out. This dreadful happening was obvious to the intelligent mind with knowledge of the political and religious forces at odds – the only question was 'When?' Christ wept over the thought of it; he loved the Temple, with its traditions, its beauty and its holiness, and all it stood for; but he could see clearly the future. And his tears were equally for the blindness of the people, his own people, who were ready enough to follow some political Messiah, but not Jesus; and would suffer the terrible tragedy of their mistaken choice all too soon, in AD 70 in fact.

Not Made with Hands

But the destruction of the Temple made way for a new temple 'not made with hands'; the temple which was Christ himself, in which all people could find salvation. But first of all even this temple had its time of destruction. It lay crucified upon a cross and darkness reigned over it. But then, out of death and darkness came life and light; and a whole new world arose to restore the imbalance of the old. 'What sign do you show us?' said the Temple priests. 'Destroy this temple,' answered Christ, 'and I will raise it up again in three days.' (John 2,19)

That is what happened; he spoke of the temple of his body – and because of that new life, the destiny of the world itself became altered; mortality put on immortality. 'The very stone which the builders rejected, has become the head of the corner' (Acts 4.11)

Here is the supreme example of the greatest good arising out of ruin; for out of death came a wonderful resurrection, not only of the temple which was Christ, but of humanity's hopes for the future. 'I am come that they may have life and have it abundantly,' said the Lord. (John 10.10) We all need a kind of self-destruction; we are told that we must lose our life in order to gain it (John 16.25) We must, in other words, be ready to destroy the egoism of our nature, and in its place put on the new ego of Jesus Christ.

> *Set us free, O Lord,*
> *from the bondage of sin and fear;*
> *that in your service*
> *we may find our freedom,*
> *and in your will our peace;*
> *through Jesus Christ our Lord.*

(PHG 106)

Lent 2 *Second Sermon* The Unclean Spirit

When the unclean spirit has gone out of a man, he passes through waterless places seeking rest; and finding none, he says, 'I will return to my house from which I came.' Luke 11.24 (EP ASB)

Healing
Jesus had just performed a healing – the cleansing of an unfortunate man who was unable to speak. Whether he was completely dumb or could make some kind of stammering noises we do not know; nor whether his affliction had come upon him at some difficult time of life, or an accident, perhaps, a violent shock of some kind, or whether it was from birth. The gospels make it clear that Jesus, like most people of his time, believed in evil spirits which needed to be exorcised or cast out. Luke's report makes it clear that some of the bystanders at least assumed that to drive out, drive away, evil spirits, the exorcist had to have assistance from 'the Prince of Evil' himself, Beelzebub or Satan. Jesus is very blunt in pointing out that to expect Satan to do something good is very foolish – this would be like a kingdom divided against itself, leaving it open to attack and conquest by some other nation. Satan would not be so foolish!

And, the Lord goes on, 'What about the healings that your own people perform? Are these through the power of evil?' Exorcism was not unusual, it seems, for the learned rabbis to undertake from time to time. Surely these would be through the power of God – if not, what hypocrisy you are showing by complaining about the healings performed by Christ!

Our Responsibilities
Most of us, if we are honest in our self-knowledge, will admit to an uncleanness of spirit which needs cleansing. This is something for which we ourselves are responsible, and which we can set right by accepting God's forgiveness for the past, his will for the present, and his grace for the future.

It is only when we place ourselves in the presence of God, that we become aware of his burning holiness, and of our lack of holiness. Then we may exclaim, with the young Isaiah in the Temple, 'unhappy me, for I am a man of unclean lips, and the people among whom I live are similarly unclean' (Isaiah 6,5) Or with Peter at the Sea of Galilee, suddenly aware of the goodness of Jesus, and crying out, 'Depart from me, for I am a sinful man, O Lord' (Luke 5.8) – though this was really the last thing he wanted.

The Cure
The real cure lies in having the Holy Spirit dwelling within us. For evil and uncleanness cannot live with holiness, nor even in the desire for holiness. Jesus tells a very pointed parable about the man from whom an unclean spirit has been cast out, but who left his heart empty. So when the homeless spirit, tired of wandering in search of somewhere to settle, returns to his old abode and finds it still entenanted, he goes off and spreads the good news to his cronies. They all return together to occupy the empty heart. The message, as Jesus says, is that the final state of the man is worse than before.

PRAYER FOR TODAY

Cleanse the thoughts of our hearts
by your Holy Spirit,
that we may perfectly love you
and worthily worship you,
our Lord and God.
(George Appleton)

Third Sunday in Lent *(Fourth before Easter)*
2 March **A Hard Saying**
'Jesus put this question to his disciples, "Who do the crowds say I am?"
And they answered, "John the Baptist; others Elijah; and others say one
of the ancient prophets come back to life." "But you," he said, "who do
you say I am?"' Luke 9, 18–20 (ASB Gospel)

The Question
There is no doubt much in Christian teaching that is hard to accept. It is much easier to say with the disciples in today's Gospel, nothing – it was only Peter who spoke up, after a pregnant pause. 'The

Christ of God' he says. The others kept very quiet. Then it came as a further shock to the disciples that Jesus should abandon his work of teaching and healing in Galilee, and travel up to Jerusalem, knowing full well the imminent possibility of arrest, suffering, and a cruel death. Was this not destroying all the positive good he had been doing? Moreover, he made it clear that in deciding on the road of the cross, he was not seeking to gain earthly power and rule for himself. Very probably, this announcement was the reason for Judas' disillusionment and eventual betrayal – he certainly could not understand Jesus' choice of a shameful death rather than a throne and a kingdom.

Difficult . . .

Later, as the Christian gospel spread, the cross seemed in St Paul's words, 'a stumbling block to the Jews and foolishness to the Greeks'. Later still, in the Middle Ages, St Thomas à Kempis remarked upon 'the few lovers of the cross of Christ'. It was then difficult, for the disciples, and it is now, for us, in our time, to understand the choosing of the path of suffering and sacrifice, the way of the Cross.

But the way of the cross was a vital part of the ministry of Christ; vital because it is a showing, in the first place, that Christ entered into suffering and experienced it all; and in the second, that what he chose and did gives a new significance to suffering, through his self-sacrifice upon the cross. We know suffering is always evil, but Christ used it – and we can follow his example in our own small way – as an opportunity of self-sacrifice and self-giving. So it is that in the wider scheme of things, it can lead to good. Bearing illness and disappointments with patience and love, helps to diminish – in whatever small way – the growth of suffering in the world. It helps God's work of bringing reconciliation and gladness to the world. In Christ we are shown how we, in our small way, can use suffering creatively and bring forth from it some good.

Take up the Cross

Christ says, 'If anyone would be my disciple, let him deny himself, take up his cross and follow me.' (Matthew 16, 24) He asked his apostles, 'Are you able to drink the cup that I drink, or be baptized with the baptism with which I was baptized?' Our answer must be that in some way, we can. We must open our hearts to Christ, even though at times this will involve self-denial and personal hurt and pain.

Lent 3   *Second Sermon*   **Peter**

'Herod the king laid violent hands upon some who belonged to the church. He killed James the brother of John with the sword; and when he saw that it pleased the Jews, he proceeded to arrest Peter also'. Acts 12.1 – 3 (ASB EP)

A Galilean

When Jesus was arrested in the Garden of Gethsemane, and brought to the house of the High Priest, only two of his disciples dared to follow Jesus there. One was John, who was known to the High Priest, and seems to have been in no danger; the other was Peter, who mingled cautiously with the servants in the courtyard. His accent, and perhaps his clothes and appearance, soon revealed to the sharp eyes and ears of the women servants that he was a Galilean, perhaps a bit of a country bumpkin who stood out in the crowd. One of the girls asked him if he was not a follower of the prisoner, since Jesus had come from Galilee. Fearful of being arrested and put up beside Jesus to face the relentless questioning of the priests and elders, Peter answered, 'I do not know him.' Fear induced Peter to make a false reply. He knew Christ as well as any man knew him, and better than most. He had spent the last three years constantly in his company. His answer was a lie. But remember James, the first recorded martyr, had just been killed.

Arrested

And then Peter is taken prisoner. The military guard, like a regular Roman army guard, was divided into four squads, each of which was on duty for one of the four watches of the night; Peter was bound with chains and was sleeping between two soldiers, and there were sentries at the doors. The escape can hardly be described as just another miracle story; it has every suggestion of plain truth. Even the trance-like state Peter is said to have been in, while being led by 'the angel', seems highly probable, as does his sudden realization that he is free and alone, and the slightly comic business with the maid Rhoda who (eventually) lets him in to the house of Mary.

Faith and Courage

A moment of temporary cowardice was the cause of Peter denying our Lord. It is still a common cause of failure to witness for Jesus and to follow Jesus. Fear of unpopularity, fear of being the 'odd man (or woman) out', and other fears, hold us back. However, fear is very far from being the only cause of Christian failure. Laziness holds many people back; they will not go to the trouble involved in really serving Jesus; greed may hold back others, or they break the commandments of God for monetary gain; hatred holds back others – not hatred of God, but hatred of some of their fellow human beings – for their colour, or wealth, or political opinions. Selfishness, obstinacy, pride and other false or foolish qualities all make us act like Peter, and refuse to stand by Christ's side in time of trouble.

Help in Trouble

In spite of the fears and obstacles, that may lead us in our hearts to deny Jesus or to neglect him and his cause, there is available to us a power of great strength and great love, to help us to accept Jesus and to follow him, even in times of trouble.

Jesus had gone out of his way to warn Peter, telling him beforehand, in advance of the test that lay ahead: 'I tell you, Peter, the cock will not crow tonight before you have denied me three times' (Luke 22.34) God goes out of his way to help us all, in times of temptation and spiritual danger, for he sends us the Holy Spirit to warn, to strengthen and to guide; and to help us to know Jesus better, to understand what he wants us to do, and in all things to follow him more closely.

> *God of compassion,*
> *you have willed that the gate of mercy*
> *should always stand open for your people.*
> *Look upon us with your love,*
> *that we who strive to follow the path of your will*
> *may continue in that path to the end of our lives;*
> *through Jesus Christ our Lord.* (*PHG 104*)

Fourth Sunday in Lent *(Third Sunday before Easter)* 9 March **Transfiguration**

(For Mothering Sunday see p. 263)
'When Christ is revealed, we shall be like him; for we shall see him as he is.' 1 John 3.2 (ASB Introductory Sentence)

A Critical Time

The Transfiguration of our Lord, which we commemorate today, occurred at a very critical moment in his life. In the early days of his preaching and teaching, the people 'heard him gladly'. But his teaching made it clear that his ideas of the Messiah were not theirs, and inevitably there was a falling-off of the support that had earlier been so remarkable. The increasing strength of Jesus' conviction that the path he was treading would lead to the Cross, was discouraging to the disciples, whose spirits were dropping as the prospect was becoming every day nearer and more certain of a terrible and fatal end. 'So, if the Son must needs go down into the valley of the shadow of death, the Father's face will shine upon him for a moment, before he enters it, with a brightness and confirmation which will not be obscured. Jesus is most glorious in giving himself up for the salvation of the world.'

Rapt in Communion

The Gospels give us something of the significance and meaning of the event, to Christ himself and to the 'Chosen Three' who witnessed it. Luke tells us that the three watching disciples 'were heavy with sleep but kept awake' which suggests that the Transfiguration took place at night. He also says that it was while Jesus was praying: we may picture Jesus rapt in communion with the Father, his face glowing with love and joy in the light of the moon. The glory of his spirit shone through, and there was an aura of brilliance around his praying figure.

Mysterious Figures ...

The Old Testament looked forward to the New. In fact, the Old is fulfilled in the New. The work of the Messiah is foreshadowed in the Law and the Prophets. So it is, that in Moses and Elijah are seen the representatives of the Law and the Prophets, representatives of a past age, talking with Jesus about his Passion and his

69

Death. They prepared the way for Jesus Christ, looking forward to the coming of that greater One, with whom they now confer.

When Jesus spoke to his disciples about the death he was to die, they received his message with ill favour; Peter tried to turn him from his appointed path. In fact his friends gave voice to the Tempter's fell desires and evil hopes. The representatives of the Old Covenant knew what was the Saviour's mission, and encouraged him in it.

The Disciples
The splendours, the glory, and the light overwhelmed the three, and two remained speechless. Peter had not the gift of silence, and what he said was foolish, though well-intentioned. The whole incident shows how far the Lord was above his disciples, even though the three did rise in some measure to the occasion. It was good to be on the Mount with the Lord; the vision was not prolonged, but it was good to have seen it and shared in it. They would see Christ henceforward in a new way. They were given a visible sign that God was at work in and through Christ.

He was the one through whom God's glory and majesty were revealed, and who was to bring in God's kingly rule. Christ had been revealed as the bearer of God's revelation; now they saw him as the One whose divine glory would enable him to confront pain and overcome suffering, and triumph over them; and he would give his followers the same means of meeting the world's problems. Strengthened for the time of conflict that lay ahead, the very problems appeared differently, and their own lives were changed.

The Voice
The Divine Voice authenticated Christ and his mission. As at his baptism, here it was confirmed once again. The Father recognized the Son with joy and delight; the voice cheered the Son and taught the disciples. The joy was in the utter dedication and courage in which he was ready to face agony and even death. The words for the disciples to take to heart were: 'This is my Son, listen to him!' So, we are taught that it is not enough to worship him in his glory; we must listen to the teaching he gives, and obey his commands.

Lent 4 *Second Sermon* **'Still Small Voice'**

'The Lord is my light and my salvation; whom then shall I fear?' Ps 27.1 (ASB EP)

'He arose and fled for his life'

The prophet Elijah bravely defied the wrath of the wicked King Ahab and his angry Queen, Jezebel; but when the furious message came from the Queen: 'So may the gods do to me and more also, if I do not make your life as one of the prophets of Baal' (slain by Elijah) 'by this time tomorrow!' he made a hurried flight in great fear. Tired out, and probably in a trough of depression, such as often follows a great emotional experience, he went out into the wilderness and there, under a broom tree, prayed for death, and fell asleep.

In his sleep an angel came to him and gave him the command 'Arise and eat'. The prophet saw a cake baked on hot coals and a vessel of water. Obediently he ate and drank, and lay down again. The experience was repeated; in the morning Elijah, refreshed and his mind at ease, continues on his long journey to Mount Horeb, where God spoke to Moses, and the Covenant was made between the Chosen People and their Lord, as the Book Exodus tells us (19.3–6)

Mount Horeb

While he was there, staying in a cave, four experiences happened to the Prophet. A great wind tore at the mountain, but Elijah was unmoved – the Lord was not in the wind. Then came an earthquake which caused rocks to come hurtling down the mountainside. The Lord was not in the earthquake. Then a desert fire flared up and ran in amongst the scrub and dry foliage – again, the Lord was not there. After all the noise and fury, there came a still small voice. Elijah felt the Presence of God; he wrapped his face in his mantle and stood at the entrance to the cave – waiting. 'What are you doing here, Elijah?' said the voice. Was this a gentle reproach for the tumult at Mount Carmel and the horrible slaughter of the priests of Baal? At any rate, Elijah is sent back into danger to speak the Word of the Lord, and to find his own successor – Elisha, who will continue the work of the Lord – and a successor to the king – but that is another story.

Spiritual Refreshment

In the duties and journey of life, the Christian – like Elijah – needs a spiritual refreshment and food, otherwise the strains of the journey become too great. We pray each day 'Give us this day our daily bread'; we are asking for food not only for the body but also for the spirit. Jesus, after the feeding of the crowd in the countryside of Lake Galilee (John 6.1–14), spoke of the Bread of Life (6.32, 33); a bread coming down from heaven, which not only gives strength for the duties, difficulties and adventures of life, but nourishes the spirit for the eventual sharing of God's eternal life. In the Eucharist we are sacramentally fed with this spiritual nourishment (John 6.50, 51) The first disciples said to Jesus, 'Lord, give us this bread always.' We who are his disciples of today, pray the same prayer, repeating it trustfully, lovingly, gratefully; and remembering the Lord's promise when we may feel empty, tired or depressed, or faced with some unexpected demand or need for inner strength and moral courage.

> *Drop thy still dews of quietness,*
> *Till all our strivings cease;*
> *Take from our souls the strain and stress,*
> *And let our ordered lives confess*
> *The beauty of thy peace.*
> *John Whittier (NEH 353)*

Fifth Sunday in Lent *(Passion Sunday)*
16 March **Pilgrims All**

'Among those who went up to worship at the festival were some Greeks. These approached Philip, who came from Bethsaida in Galilee, and put this request to him, "Sir, we should like to see Jesus."' John 12.20 (ASB Gospel) or, 'He offered himself without blemish to God, a spiritual and eternal sacrifice.' Hebrews 9.14 (BCP)

Visitors

Tremendous crowds of pilgrims visit Mecca, the holy city of the Moslem world, the city of the Black Stone, every year; similar vast crowds go to Rome to greet the Pope at Easter; in the same way multitudes of pilgrims made their ways to the City of Jerusalem, to worship at the great new Temple built by Herod, especially at the time of the great festival, the Passover. Pilgrimages seem to be an almost universal custom, habit, exercise, devotion – call it what you will – amongst all the peoples and nations of humanity. Is it the desire for a change of scene; or a time for thinking about our life and its ways and means; is it maybe an urge for 'fresh woods and pastures new' (Milton's Lycidas)?

Amongst the pilgrims to the Jerusalem Temple, St John records this group of Greeks. Whether they were Greek Jews or simply Greeks we are not told, but they had heard of this new prophet, Jesus, and were anxious to see and hear him. Jesus, with his disciples, had come – like the multitudes of pious Jews from so many countries as well as Palestine itself – devout believers and faithful Hebrews.

His Last Appearance

This was to be his last public appearance in the Holy City before the Supper in the Upper Room. The events of Holy Week were surely in his mind; the horrors of the next few days were, we may say, weighing on his soul. What he says to the Greeks, to the disciples, and to those of the crowds who were no doubt eager to hear what the Prophet might say, and were pressing close, was in effect a concentrated interpretation of his coming Passion and death. The presence of the Greeks and other foreigners, Jesus was taking as a sign that his hour had come. The salvation of the whole world, of all humanity, is about to be achieved.

Glorification

That will be a glorification of humanity in the glorification of God – that is, the revelation of God's infinite goodness and mercy, in the sacrifice of Jesus Christ. 'Father, glorify your name, reveal yourself! I when I am lifted up, will draw all men to myself!'

That revelation will mean pain and horror, torture and death for himself. St John in his Gospel does not describe the tragic scene in Gethsemane – 'Let this cup pass from me' – the sweat and tears like great drops of blood – the agony of mind and heart – but shows the meaning. Can Jesus ask to be spared the pain and horror? No, because this is the essential purpose of his coming into this world of ours. His metaphor from Nature – the death of the grain of wheat is the necessary cause of the wonders of the harvest.

St Paul

We remember St Paul's great teaching of the resurrection body, which we heard this morning in the reading from Colossians. 'In baptism you were buried with him, in baptism also you were raised to life with him, through your faith in the active power of God who raised him from the dead.' What you sow in the ground must die before new life springs from it.

What is uniquely true of Christ's death and resurrection, has a general truth for us all. It is only as we give ourselves away, in the act of faith and in deeds of love and service, that we die to self, but live with the quality of eternal life. Jesus died – yes, and it was in order that he might live – live in us, live in his body upon earth, the Church.

'THOSE WHO FOLLOWED WERE AFRAID'

O Christ, you call me, and every disciple, to follow you.
You are my way to God;
You are the life of my soul,
You are my resurrection from the dead:
You are the pattern of my life.
All I have to do, is to follow,
Master and Lord.

Lent 5 *Second Sermon* **Christ Ahead**

'They were on the road, going up to Jerusalem, and Jesus was walking ahead of them; and they were amazed, and those who followed were afraid.' Mark 10.32 (EP ASB)

The Road to Jerusalem

Jesus looked ahead; he looked towards his crucifixion. He set his face to go to Jerusalem. He knew what awaited him there. He would be handed over to the foreign power. He would be maltreated, mocked, spat upon, flogged, killed. The way he must go is the Way of the Cross. In spite of all this, Jesus goes ahead. There is a strange aura, a strange light, about him as he walks on the road some way ahead of his apostles. They do not understand – how could they? – but they are aware that some deep spiritual conflict is going on, and that Jesus is battling inwardly with all the fears and terrors that the thought of a brutal death brings to an innocent victim. They are frightened.

The Lord indicates a brief halt; they sit down together, hardly daring to look at him, his face pale and drawn, his eyes deep-sunk with strain. He tells them, now, briefly and bluntly, what is going to happen.

Horrified, they sit there dumbstruck, appalled at the vision of the future so soon to be upon them.

James and John

The fishermen brothers, James and John, have been mulling over the promises that the Lord had been making at the beginning of their journey; maybe because of this, they were not, it seems, so aware of the black cloud hanging over the little band, as the others. What has caught their attention is the idea that they will all be well off, in the days to come; after all, Hebrew teaching was that riches were a sign of God's favour. Well off, and in the seats of power no doubt! for that is what Jesus was promising (vv. 29–31) In a kind of haze of innocence, the two brothers ask Jesus for specific favours in the kingdom to come; thrones, one on the Lord's right hand, the other on the left.

A Shocked Silence

A horrified silence descends upon everyone. To make such crude demands, at this time of all times ... Jesus sits for a few long moments saying nothing; then in almost a bantering tone, tells the two they don't know what they are asking ... 'Are you able to share the bitter cup I have to drink, or to be baptized with the baptism of blood that I must accept?' The brothers are beginning to see that they have made a terrible mistake, but 'We are able' ... they reply. Jesus tells them that to grant the favours they ask is not for him to grant, but at the decree of the Father. A general rumble of discontent at the twins comes from the other apostles: and Jesus goes on to pronounce bluntly that the ranks and triumphs of earthly kingdoms have no place in the world to come.

'Instead, if you want to be great you must take the role of a servant, even a slave if you want to really get on . . . The Son of Man came not to be served, but to serve – and to give his life a ransom for many.'

The rest of the journey seems to be, not surprisingly, walked in silence. Can we drink that cup?

With the benefit of hindsight and the knowledge of the servant Jesus, we ought to be ready to do so; perhaps we can reply humbly and without self-trusting: Yes Lord, but only with your aid and your grace, to enable me.

Palm Sunday *(The Sunday next before Easter)*
23 March   **'Hosanna in the highest!'**

'Hosanna to the Son of David! Blessed is he who comes in the name of the Lord! Hosanna in the highest!' Matthew 21.9 (ASB Introductory Sentence)

Glory – and Tragedy

This Sunday, which begins the most important week of the year for us – Holy Week – is a day of glory and also of impending tragedy; the two aspects are inextricably bound together. Over-shadowing the splendour and joy of the acceptance of Christ as the Messiah and the King, is the darkness of tragedy with the threat of death to come. The Hosannas of joy and greeting from the crowds will become jeers and execration; the palms held high at his entrance to the Holy City will all too soon shape themselves into crosses of pain and sorrow. Amidst the plaudits and songs of joy of the crowd, their proclaimed King rides on in sadness. The Messiah they hail is in tears as he makes his triumphant journey down from Bethany into the City.

Beauty – and Ruins

The sight of Jerusalem lying below in all its loveliness, fresh and new with the marvellous work still to be completed in some places, makes the tears well up in his eyes, because he knows that soon all that beauty will be swept aside in ruins, scattered and trodden down. Like the palms strewn in his path, it will become dust and ashes.

In that famous city, which for centuries had been the centre of worship for God's own people, he, the Holy One of God, the long-awaited King of Israel, was to meet his crucified death. It was a silent Messiah then, his countenance marked with deep sadness, who rode amid the acclamations of the multitude on that Spring day in Palestine, to meet his fate.

Sadness – and Joy

Yet, the sadness was not incompatible with joy. Christ longed for the moment of tragedy ahead. It was his 'hour' of which he had so often spoken. Joyfully he accepted his Father's edict that he must die. For, after all, this land and this city had been prepared for this very purpose. Centuries before, they had been granted to the Chosen People of God, so that – one day – the great work of salvation might be accomplished there; accomplished by a baptism of death.

Death – and Life

And that death meant life. Mark Antony, in Shakespeare's great play *Julius Caesar* looks down at the dead body of the great man, and says, 'Are all thy conquests, glories, triumphs, spoils – shrunk to this little measure?' (Act III, Sc.1) All the great power and glory of Caesar has been reduced to dust and ashes. But Mary could hold the dead Christ in her arms, and hold One who 'will rule from sea to sea, to the very ends of the earth'.

Today we make our rejoicing with our palms and our hymns, because we know that through that sacrificial death of the Lord Jesus, we have been redeemed and have the promise of eternal life with him in glory.

Palm Sunday *Second Sermon* Rejection

The tenants said to one another, 'This is the heir; come, let us kill him, and the inheritance will be ours.' Mark 12.7 (ASB EP)

'Who Authorized You?'

Jesus was walking in the Temple, we are told, the day after his triumphant entry into Jerusalem, and he was accosted by the chief priests, the scribes and the elders, who no doubt were feeling aggrieved and angry at having their privileges attacked and their power over-ridden, by someone who had no official standing and no ecclesiastical authority. When they raised this question of authority with Jesus, he responded with a double-edged reply – if they would pronounce as to the authority of John the Baptist, and say whether it was from God or from man, then he, Jesus, would tell them what *his* authority was. Not surprisingly, they were taken aback, since to denounce publicly John the Baptist as being no real prophet, would stir up great trouble for them amongst the people.

So they fell back upon 'don't know!' as their reply; giving Jesus the opportunity to refuse to answer himself. Instead, he produced one of his most pointed and stinging of parables.

The Vineyard

Jesus describes a landowner who rented out a vineyard, which he had planted and worked at, because he was going to live abroad. When he sent his agents to collect the rent, in the form of some of the fruit, they were roughly treated by the tenants and turned away. More, when he tried again later, the agents were beaten, wounded, and even killed. In the end he sent his son, thinking he would be respected; but no, worse still, he was brutally murdered.

In this grim parable, Jesus pictured how in times past, little attention was paid to the various prophets sent by God, and how some were violently attacked, or worse. The climax came when God sent his own Son, the long-awaited Messiah; but he too was hated by many, and was cruelly put to death.

And What about Us?

Here is a sad reminder to us, not only of the actual events which brought our Lord's ministry on earth to a sudden and dreadful close; but that we can all be seen as sharers in those events, alas, by the way we have rejected or ignored some of the teachings of Jesus and what he stands for. It is a mistake to see this parable as only allotting the blame to those immediately responsible for our Lord's death. The true causes are deeper and older and nearer, very near indeed – the parable asks us all, here and now, a question which in various ways and in varying words Jesus put to many, during his ministry – 'What think ye of Christ? What is your attitude to me?'

How will we answer?
It is all too easy to turn Jesus away, not by violence like the tenants in the parable, not like the Jews and the Romans to whom the parable alludes, but by our own indifference, our own love of self, or our own lack of the courage needed to follow him through the temptations and the demands and the pressures of daily life.

> *Lord Jesus Christ,*
> *alive and at large in the world,*
> *help us to follow and find you there today*
> *in the places where we work,*
> *meet people, spend money,*
> *and make plans.*
> *Take me as a disciple of your Kingdom*
> *to see through your eyes*
> *and hear the questions you are asking,*
> *to welcome all with your trust and truth,*
> *and to change the things that contradict God's love*
> *by the power of your Cross*
> *and the freedom of your Spirit.*
> *Bp John Taylor of Winchester*

Maundy Thursday   27 March
The New Covenant
'This cup is the new covenant sealed by my blood.' 1 Corinthians 11.23
(ASB NT Reading; BCP Epistle)

Authentic
'This cup is the new covenant sealed in my blood.' It is believed that the two epistles to the Corinthians were both written before the four Gospels; if this is so, and the scholars seem unanimous that it is, then the words spoken by Jesus over the bread and the cup at the Last Supper, as recorded by Paul, have a powerful claim

to authenticity. St Mark's gospel may conceivably date from about the same time as St Paul's epistles; in that gospel we read similar, perhaps more correctly remembered words, from the very lips of the Lord: 'This is my blood of the covenant.'

The 'covenant' named is hardly to be taken as a compact between human beings, as might be between Jesus and his disciples; it must surely be a covenant between God and his people. But it is surely not the Sinai Covenant, nor any other described in the Jewish histories, but a new covenant, even if Mark omits 'new' in his account.

Jeremiah

The most likely reference is to the prophecy of Jeremiah, ch. 31, verses 31–34:

> 'Behold the days are coming, says the Lord,
> when I will make a new covenant with the house of Israel and the house of Judah,
> not like the covenant which I made with their fathers
> when I took them out of the land of Egypt.
> My covenant, which they broke, though I was their husband, says the Lord.
> But this is the covenant which I will make with the house of Israel,
> after those days, says the Lord:
> I will put my law within them, and I will write it upon their hearts;
> and I will be their God, and they shall be my people.
> And no longer shall each man teach his neighbour,
> and each his brother, saying, "Know the Lord."
> For they shall all know me, from the least of them to the greatest;
> for I will forgive their iniquity, and remember their sin no more.'

In the words over the bread and wine, Jesus was implying that the time was at hand when men would no longer attempt to keep covenant with God, by obeying a code of law. God would inspire them simply to know his will, and spontaneously to carry it into effect. The prophetic words of Jesus at the Last Supper conclude his religious and moral teaching, his attack on legalism and casuistry, his demand for unconditional acts of love.

Sacrifice

The reference to blood implies that the New Covenant was to be sealed, like the old Covenant, by sacrifice; specifically, as Paul understood, by death; not the 'figurative' death of animals, but the actual death of Jesus himself.

Sacrifice, in the Jewish understanding is a means of communion with God provided by him for the benefit of men, although it is by men that the sacrificial act of immolation must be performed. 'The life of the flesh is in the blood; and I have given it for you upon the altar, to make atonement for your souls.' (Lev. 17.11). His death was foreseen as the atoning act of forgiveness that God would provide, in order to inaugurate the New Covenant, a sacrifice that requires the obedience of the Christ, to the Father's will.

This understanding of the Covenant sacrifice was to be affirmed in the great classical statements of the Atonement:

'God was in Christ reconciling the world to himself, not reckoning their trespasses against them.' (2 Cor. 5, 19)
'God so loved the world that he gave his only begotten Son.' (John 3.16)
'He who has seen me has seen the Father.' (John 14.9)

The Cross

The power of the Cross depends upon the recognition, in faith, of Jesus as identified with the divine – as Christ, Image of the Invisible, Brightness of the Glory, exact Likeness of God's Being, Word made flesh.

The disclosure of God's love for them at Calvary opens the hearts of men and women to receive the Spirit, who puts God's Law within them and writes it in their hearts, fulfilling Jeremiah's prophecy, so that they spontaneously do his will. The Kingdom is made manifest.

Good Friday 28 March The Cross

Pilate said to the Jews, 'Behold your king.' They cried out, 'Away with him, away with him, crucify him!' Pilate said to them, 'Shall I crucify your king?' John 19, 14–16 (Passion Narrative – John; 'Lent, Holy Week & Easter') or, 'They took Jesus, and led him away. And he, bearing his cross, went forth into a place called the Place of a Skull, which is called in the Hebrew, Golgotha: where they crucified him, and two others with him, on either side one, and Jesus in the midst.' John 19, 17–18 (BCP Gospel)

The Centre

The Cross is the centre of Christianity. From it radiates all the power of the Church. If the Cross had been a failure, all human life would have had no meaning, no future. It is through the Cross that all our sacramental life, with its power of salvation, stems. Through the Cross, prayer to God for mercy and forgiveness is made possible; and through it also, human nature gains the ability to survive enternally in glory. All problems concerning sin and death have their focus in the Cross. The whole history of humanity, our hopes and our future destiny, are bound up with it. Christ's self-surrender, by allowing himself to be nailed to its cruel wood, conferred freedom on all human beings. Like a knife, the Cross cut through the bonds of evil, that had fettered all mankind.

Courage

All the Gospels tell how some of the women who had followed Jesus from Galilee watched by the Cross, and did not go away until they had seen our Lord's dead body taken down from the Cross and placed in the tomb (Luke 23.55; Mark 15.40) In this they certainly showed more courage than the men folk, for only St John stayed with Mary (John 19.25, 26) and heard the moving words of the Lord, 'Woman, behold your son!' to Mary, and 'Behold, your mother!' to John. (27).

The Criminal

Whether, as has been suggested, the priests asked for the two thieves – or as seems more likely, agitators or rebels – to be executed with Jesus in order to degrade him in the eyes of the people, or, it may have been that the soldiers, happening to have two other prisoners under sentence of death, crucified all three together to save themselves time and trouble, cannot be known. Luke tells us how one of the criminals declared his faith in Jesus, saying, 'Jesus, remember me when you come to your kingdom!' What great faith he had in Jesus; many people who saw Jesus doing wonderful things did not believe in him; this man believed in someone who was being executed, like himself, as a criminal. We should not be ashamed to wish that our faith in Christ could be as strong as that of this poor wretch.

Life through Death
Christ died the death of a criminal so that all criminals might have life. We are all sinners, we are all far short of what we are intended to be. Therefore it is penitence that draws us to Jesus. It is not our achievements nor our success, but rather our sense of need, which brings us to Christ, and to reliance on his promises. Faith is an intensely personal thing, and is between persons. Our whole relationship with Jesus is relationship of love, of personal love.

Misfortune and suffering come at some time to everyone, all too often without there being any personal cause or reason. What matters is our reaction, the attitude we take. We can become insecure and bitter – 'Why has this happened to me?' The question can haunt us; we can feel we are at a crisis of our life and our condition. We can either rebel, and cry out in anger and bitterness, or we can turn in our need to Christ, and find even the blackest circumstances can bring good. Even our worst misfortunes and our worst sins can be a means of drawing near to Christ – and to be near him is what matters most of all, sinners that we are.

Christ and Us
It was at the latest time, the final hour, that the crucified criminal turned to Christ. The Lord Jesus, stretched upon the Cross, in agony of pain, suffered not only in himself, but in all suffering humanity, and in so doing gave meaning and significance to every sorrow and to all pains. For the Cross on which he suffered was not a mere temporary emblem of cruelty and punishment; it had an eternal significance. All the world was to be embraced by its shadow. Its power was universal. It was not an end – a cul-de-sac of death. Far from that – it was indeed a power for life.

The Tomb
The Gospels tell us that not far from the Cross was a tomb – a tomb in which no human body had been laid. A tomb implies death – but in this case it also implies life, because the cross is a life-giving power. Resurrection was to follow death by crucifixion – a resurrection in which we can all share. In his dying for us, the Christ who arose from the dead, drew us all into his life. From

the darkness which covered the earth, and from death upon the Cross, there came the light of a glorious all-embracing resurrection; the world gained its finest hour. The Cross can only be truly understood in the dawn light of Easter.

Triumph
The cruel and terrible failure of Good Friday will become a triumph; the love that embraced pain and death, will be seen to be immortal – a love that is as strong as ever, a love stronger than death.

> *We adore you, O Christ, and we bless you,*
> *because by your holy cross you have*
>   *redeemed the world.*
> *Father, hear our prayer and forgive us.*
> *Unstop our ears*
>   *that we may receive the gospel of the Cross.*
> *Lighten our eyes*
>   *that we may see your glory*
>   *in the face of your Son.*
> *Penetrate our minds*
>   *that your truth may make us whole.*
> *Irradiate our hearts with your love*
>   *that we may love one another for Christ's sake.*
> *Father, forgive us.*
>   *(Lent, Holy Week, Easter, p. 210)*

Easter Early Morning   30 March
The True Joy!
'Very early in the morning on the first day of the week they came to the bomb, just as the sun was rising. Alleluya!' (Mark 16.2 – ASB for use in the early morning)
(Where there is a midnight or very early celebration, LHWE provides a Vigil and a Service of Light (p. 228 and onwards), Baptism (p. 234), and Eucharist (p. 236) with sermon after the Gospel (p. 234)
'Alleluya! Christ is risen!' All: 'He is risen indeed! Alleluya!' (p. 230)

The Light

We have just taken part in what is the most joyful and the most moving of all Church services – in the darkness just before the dawn, the Resurrection of our Lord Jesus Christ is proclaimed in spoken word and dramatic symbol, with the Easter Candle, lit from the New Fire, showing forth Christ the Light of the world rising from the darkness of the grave. The joy and triumph of victory, victory over death and sin, is no fantasy. Newness of life, resurrection from the dead is not wishful thinking; it is based on reality. We see its truth in the fact that Christ rose from the dead.

Sin and death are defeated foes. This great victory is the message of our faith, our Christianity, our gospel. And our duty, our joyful task, is to ourselves spread that message to all we meet, to let others know the happiness of faith, the relief of sin removed, the joy of love, of life, of beauty, that the Risen Christ brings to all.

And in a most moving symbol of that spreading of the Good News, we each lit our little candle from the flame of the Easter Candle, and passed that flame to our neighbour, so that the darkness of the night is bit by bit removed and overborne. And bit by bit we recognize the people beside us and around us, and greet them in the faith of Christ, as the sacred Light shows us how the Gospel must be spread like those little flames, until the whole world is given the Good News, and the grace and truth of our Blessed Saviour reaches all peoples in all places. The power of the Resurrection drives us on; it compels us to go out and to win others to know and accept the Living Lord, the Risen Christ.

> Alleluya! Christ is risen!
> *All:* He is risen indeed! Alleluya!

Easter Day   30 March
The Victory of the Resurrection

'He is not here, he has been raised again, as he said he would be. Come and see the place where he was laid, then go quickly and tell his disciples.' Matthew 28.6, 7 (ASB Gospel) or, 'On the first day of the week Mary Magdalen came to the tomb early while it was still dark, and saw that the stone had been taken away from the tomb.' John 20.1 (ASB Gospel)

or, 'The first day of the week cometh Mary Magdalen early when it was yet dark, unto the sepulchre.' John 20.1 (BCP Gospel)

Never the Same Again!

Very early on a Sunday morning an event occurred that shook the world, and had fantastic and wonderful results, results that we see and rejoice in, results that altered our whole human history.

That event was, of course, the resurrection of the crucified Christ from his grave. On that morning a new civilization, a new culture, arose, and a fresh beauty, a new outlook upon life, appeared upon our earth. Christianity arose with Christ upon that Easter day; it was not just the physical body of Christ that came forth from the tomb. In a sense a new Christ was born, a Christ with a new body made up of all those united to him in his Church.

This was a new Christ who was to repeat for all time and all ages, in a mystical manner, in a spiritual sense, the history of the Christ who died on Calvary, and who rose again to life. This was a Christ who was to suffer innumerable crucifixions and as many resurrections.

Renewal

There was to be a constant Christian renewal through the ages. That word 'renewal' is a keyword at Easter. Since the Mystical Body of Christ rose with the historic Christ, it has continuously died in persecution – and each time has been renewed with fresh vigour and power.

And what is true of the Church is also true of every individual member in it. The life of every Christian is fruitful in so far as it has been crucified with Christ, buried with him and risen again with him. Every Christian is in a sense another Christ incarnate; your life with its ups and downs, its anxieties and suffering, its happinesses, should be the re-living of the sufferings and triumphs of Christ in our own small way. Because Christ came to transform our human life, to add a completely new dimension to all our human activities, to provide a spiritual adventure. With Christ in us, and we in Christ, the most hum-drum life can become something new and wonderful, an exciting spiritual experience.

The Message of Easter

Yes, Easter has some very important things for us to accept and understand. In the first place, Easter tells us not to despair but to hope; the disciples were in the depths of despair on Good Friday, but wonderful news was no further away than Easter Day. Then, Easter tells us that although the opposite often seems to be the case, good *is* stronger than evil. Jesus was on the side of good, he was the very incarnation of good, and the failure of evil and foolish men to destroy him – although they appeared to have done so – proclaim the eventual victory of good. Above all, the Easter message is the promise of life, real life, true life, beyond the grave.

The first Easter message of all was that message which the women brought to the apostles, when they came running back from the tomb: 'The tomb is empty! The body of the Lord is not there!' As Peter and John ran off to investigate what must have seemed an impossible tale, they cannot have expected what was to follow and what an astonishing story of splendour and triumph, out of past ruin and destruction and death, was to come, banishing the darkness of sin, despair and failure. Now salvation and hope and the promise of future bliss belong to all humanity, to all who affirm faith in Christ, to all those who believe in his sacrifice and celebrate his glory in his Risen Life.

PRAYER

God of truth,
we have seen with our eyes
and touched with our hands
the bread of life.
Strengthen our faith
that we may grow in love for you
and for each other;
through Jesus Christ our risen Lord.
(Patterns for Worship 52.18)

Easter Day *Second Sermon* Peace and Power

'Jesus came and stood among the disciples, and said to them, "Peace be with you!"' John 20.19 (BCP & ASB EP)

Salutation

Twice in this evening's Gospel reading, the Lord says 'Peace be with you!' to his disciples. That salutation was more than just a polite form of greeting and welcome. We should see it as an offer of grace, of that peace which they would remember their Lord speaking of, at the Last Supper. He said then, 'My peace I give you; but not as the world gives, do I give it to you.' Twice this evening he spoke the same words to his fearful, shattered followers, hiding away now, afraid of the authorities, whether of the Temple or of the Occupation Forces.

The Lord not only dispersed the fears of his followers, but also – by his very presence, and the showing of his wounds (v. 20), imparted a deep calmness of the spirit together with a profound joy.

The Spirit

We notice that according to St John's account, the giving of the Holy Spirit takes place now, on the evening of Easter Sunday, not in association with the Feast of Pentecost, as we are told by St Luke in his 'Acts of the Apostles'. In John, Jesus simply appears, despite the locked doors – perhaps this is the same Upper Room where the Last Supper was celebrated. The disciples experience him in a new way, not the same as before his crucifixion nor in the way they had seen Lazarus, after Jesus had raised him from the dead. The words of the Lord make it clear that this is the commissioning of the disciples both for preaching – 'As the Father has sent me, even so I send you' – and for the forgiving of sins – 'If you forgive the sins of any, they are forgiven; if you retain the sins of any, they are retained.' What a powerful commission this is; this experience of Jesus is going to determine how they will preach Jesus and celebrate his presence in the future.

Peace

The greeting of Jesus is a greeting of peace; a peace which is linked with the Passion and the Resurrection, a 'peace that the world cannot give'. And with this peace and with this commission, Jesus is sending the disciples just as the Father sent him. In so doing, Jesus is not only saying something important about his relationship with the Father, but he is also saying that believers share in the very life of God himself. This sharing is underlined by the gift of the Holy Spirit and the mission to forgive sins: in other words, the disciples are to continue the very work of Jesus himself, upon this earth.

Mary Magdalen
The striking and lovely story of the Magdalen at the tomb has been a favourite subject for artists down the ages. The beautiful, weeping woman with her long, dark red hair, mistaking – in her grief – the Lord for a gardener; then the amazing revelation that he, her loved one, was in fact still alive, living, breathing, talking – and declaring himself to her by the use of a particular intonation of her name, an intonation or accent which she immediately recognized as being that of her Lord. It brings to mind the striking piece of poetic prose by Henry Scott Holland, which many of us will have heard and shared in, at the funeral of some loved one. Here are a few lines:

> Death is nothing at all. I have only slipped away into the next room. I am I, and you are you. Whatever we were to each other, that we are still. Call me by my old familiar name, speak of me in that easy way which you always used. Put no difference into your tone, wear no forced air of solemnity or sorrow. Laugh as we always laughed ... Play, smile, think of me ... I am but waiting for you for an interval ... very near. All is well.

May this be a very happy and very blessed Eastertide, and may we all be joyful proofs of the truth of the Resurrection, so that many others may be led to that truth and to the Faith through us.

First Sunday after Easter (*Low Sunday*)
6 April   **The Witness of the Doubters**
'Thomas said, "My Lord and my God!" Jesus said, "Because you have seen me you have faith. Happy are they who never see me and yet have faith."' John 20, 28 & 29 (ASB Gospel) or, 'You have not seen him, yet you love him, and trust in him now.' 1 Peter 1.8 (ASB N.T. Reading)

Doubting Thomas
The apostle Thomas would not believe his friends, when they told him that the Lord had risen from the dead, and that they had actually seen him, spoken to him, been close beside him, had seen the terrible

scars and marks of the wounds, and had received his commission to take over his unfinished work of preaching and teaching.

We speak of 'Doubting Thomas', and maybe tend too easily to look down upon him as a questioner of the reality of the Lord's Resurrection. But let us be clear: it was not just Thomas who expressed doubts. The story told by the women who hurried back from the tomb on Easter morning with their strange news, was not well received by the apostles. 'Now it was Mary Magdalene, and Joanna, and Mary the mother of James, and the other women with them who told this to the apostles; but these words seemed to them an idle tale, and they did not believe them.' (Luke 24.10, 11) St Matthew writes of others who had their doubts (28.17) and Mark also (16.11 and 13).

In addition, St Paul speaks in his letters of Christians who rejected – not perhaps the Lord's Resurrection, but – the belief that there is a future life for us at all (I Corinthians 15, 12–19 and 32–34) Paul declares vehemently that belief in life after death is an essential part of our Christian faith, and so the Church has always taught.

Our Belief
The doubts felt and expressed by Thomas, and by other followers of the Lord, were dissolved. St Thomas changed his mind because Jesus appeared to him and allowed him to satisfy himself that the Lord was indeed flesh and blood. It may be that some others who were doubtful were satisfied in the same way, although the details are not given in the Gospels. St Paul lists appearances of the Risen Lord (1 Cor. 15.3–8) including an appearance to 'more than five hundred brethren . . . most of whom are still alive . . .' Others may have been convinced by what their friends – who did see Jesus – told them. But it is clear that before long there was a substantial number of people who accepted the fact that Jesus had risen from the dead. Some believed it from the start; others questioned at first but for various reasons they came to believe with certainty.

Two Good Reasons
We may well place our belief in the Resurrection on two good reasons: the first, the fact that we have been told of doubters and non-believers in the New Testament, reflects the honesty of the writers. They did not hesitate to include in their records the instances of doubters. Secondly, we have in the hesitation of

Thomas, and of other disciples when the news was first brought to them, and of men and women mentioned in St Paul's letters, evidence that the first Christians did not rush to accept the Resurrection. They treated it as a happening so strange, so far outside of human experience, that it was hard to believe. Yet, in the end, they did believe, either because of what they themselves saw and heard, and could not deny; or because the men and women who told them of their experiences, were themselves so obviously sincere that their words carried full conviction.

Later Evidence
More evidence is in Scripture, though not in the Gospels but in Acts and in the Epistles. There we get a picture of the life and work of Christians in many differing places – yet everywhere there is an eagerness to make Christ known, and of their willingness to face danger and even death, rather than deny him. This is not the attitude of men and women following a Leader who had been successful for a few years in Palestine, but had then died a criminal's death and been seen no more.

The first Christians were sure that whatever dangers and difficulties, trials and punishments they exposed themselves to in following Christ, they could do so in hope and trust, for their Leader had conquered death not only for himself, but for them too, and for all his faithful followers.

In this sense, as we live so nearly two thousand years after the events which are now in our thoughts, we too bear our witness to our belief in the Risen and Victorious Christ, if in our lives also we serve him and seek to follow in his footsteps.

Easter 1   *Second Sermon*   **Eternal Life**

'This is the will of my Father, that everyone who sees the Son and believes in him should have eternal life; and I will raise him up at the last day.'
John 6.40 (ASB EP)

Resurrection
The New Testament, written from the heart of the Church's experience, is concerned with resurrection; a resurrection that presupposes the death of the whole human being, every part of us. To

shy away from this apparent threat to our fragile independence, is to attempt to diminish the agony and the dereliction that Christ, the new Adam, faced and experienced in his own death upon the Cross.

In speaking of death, our reticence in itself bears witness to a certain truth, profound but barely understood, that death is *not* the end. Nowhere in the universe can the faithful be really 'cut away from God's hand', not even by death or the gates of Hades itself. 'Though I walk through the valley of the shadow of death, I will fear no evil: for thou art with me' (Ps. 23) Christ's replies to questions about death and life carry on the same line of teaching. 'This is the will of him who sent me, that I should lose nothing of all that he has given me.' (John 6.39) God is not the God of the dead, but the living 'for everyone who has heard and learned from the Father comes to me . . . He who believes has eternal life.' (John 6.45, 47) Again, our Lord assured his disciples that he went to 'prepare a place for them'. (John 14.2, 3) If it was not so, he would have told them.

Immortality

The Bible does not answer our questions about what 'happens' to us when the body dies. It is concerned with a much more fundamental truth which eclipses mere curiosity about what happens to us at a particular moment in our life – a moment given the clinical term 'death'. The great conclusion from the Bible is that God's faithful servants do not suffer imprisonment, or an empty existence among the shades. The fact of death cannot – in the light of Easter – prevail against the life and fellowship of God's own church. The immortality of the human being (the object of our longing, and the chief cause of our fear of death) – *this* is the gift of the living God, who conquers death.

The Gateway

The gateway to eternal life, and thus to a perspective within which our physical death is but an incident on the journey – this 'way in' is the sacrifice of self which Christ first accomplished only through his own death upon the cross, and in which he now enables Christians to follow him. And so, in Christ, the universal fact of physical decay and death becomes for humanity, as it were, the sacrament of the inward and spiritual truth that life must be wholly surrendered before it can be wholly won.

The reality of the resurrection balances and transforms the reality of death. Both realities are essential to the new life that is in Christ. The light of Christ shines through his death, and thus through the death of all who turn to him as Lord. This light is already ours, in company with all faithful souls. What we now need to do is to experience more fully what has already been given to us. Only a great Christian artist could match the mystery of this truth with words to evoke the experience of the mystery:

> We die with the dying:
> See, they depart, and we go with them.
> We are born with the dead;
> See, they return, and bring us with them.
>   T. S. Eliot

Second Sunday after Easter   13 April
A Happening on the Road

'Their eyes were opened and they recognized him.' Luke 24.31 (ASB Gospel)

The Emmaus Road

Jesus joins the two disciples on the Emmaus road. As he walks between them, so he talks. Mile after mile is covered, yet neither Cleopas nor the other (whoever that other disciple was, man or woman, we are never told) suspects who the stranger is. When the evening meal was spread and their guest became the host, then – perhaps by some familiar word or act in the blessing of the bread – 'their eyes were opened and they recognized him'. He had delayed their vision until he made himself known. St Mark in his account (16.12 & 13) tells us that 'he appeared in another form to them'. 'Another form' – to that in which they had known him in other days. The fact is stated, but the mystery is not explained.

No Longer Limited

The risen humanity of Jesus is no longer circumscribed by human limitations, nor is he dependent on ordinary food for sustenance. Being still in touch with the material universe around us all, his body possessed the capacity for eating and drinking, but he is no longer subject to physical laws. In the days of his flesh he suffered from physical exhaustion, like the rest of us; but now all is changed. For forty days he remains in Judaea and Galilee, as the Great Shepherd who will bring his flock together and confirm the faith of his followers. He appears and disappears to his friends, who are unable to read the mystery of his new life.

He ate fish and bread, and at Emmaus this was apparently a clue to his identity, for probably his companions saw the marks of the nails on those hands when lifted up in the act of blessing the food, and then knew who their companion was. But whatever change may have been produced by the Resurrection, it in no way destroyed his identity, for physically he was the same Jesus. His wounds were the recognizable proof; he showed the disciples his hands and his feet, and the wound in his side convinced Thomas.

'The Laws of Nature'

By the laws of nature, we mean simply the observed uniformities about us; Christ did not always travel by the same method as when he trudged the dusty roads of Palestine. In the earthly life 'the spirit is manifested through the body; in the life of the Risen Christ the body is manifested through the spirit' (Westcott) So the Lord had done more than come to life again. He had entered a new sphere of existence, where conditions were altered and powers enlarged, where events were not a necessity, and were perhaps altogether lifted above the 'laws of nature'. At Emmaus, a striking idea is conveyed by the word originally used for 'vanished' which points to no ordinary invisibility but rather to a dissolving into the air, as the mists in some beautiful Alpine valley roll away and vanish in the rays of the rising sun. The structure of the resurrected Body was such that it could pass through the door of the Upper Room; on Mount Olivet the Risen Lord ascends above hills and clouds, going to 'Prepare a place' for you and I, in the 'Father's House' (John 14.2).

Shall we know each other?

'With what body will they come?' 'Will personality, love, and memory be the same?' How often have we been asked, or found ourselves asking, such questions over those we love and know and long to meet again? If Jesus is the 'first-fruits' of our humanity, shall we be like him? 'Like unto his own glorious Body' cried the great Apostle, as he sees the vision of our final transfiguration when in the valley of the shadow this mortal shall put on immortality. Down in the valley we cannot see what lies beyond, but up there, in the Mount of God, we shall one day meet in the liberty of the glory of God, and we shall be like him, and see him as he is. 'I believe in the resurrection' is what we say, and what we believe in hope and endeavour; but what difference does it make to us and our life here and now? May the Living Lord so transform our characters and transfigure our lives, that our hearts may burn with love, and that we shall know 'the power of his resurrection'.

> *Heavenly Father,*
> *you have delivered us from the power of darkness,*
> *and brought us into the kingdom of your Son:*
> *grant that, as his death has recalled us to life,*
> *so his continual presence in us*
> *may raise us to eternal joy. Amen.*
>
> *(LHWE p. 239)*

Easter 2 *Second Sermon* **Grace**

'The God of all grace.' 1 Peter 5.10 (ASB EP Reading)

What is Grace?

We read in the New Testament about 'the grace of God' and 'the grace of our Lord Jesus Christ', and these expressions occur quite frequently. What exactly is the meaning of 'grace', this word used prominently and used often? In general, 'grace' means favour freely shown, more especially by a superior to an inferior. In the New Testament, it means primarily the favour and kindness of God, freely shown to humanity in the incarnate life and the atoning death of Jesus Christ.

Here is an example of stupendous favour freely given by a

superior (God almighty) to an inferior; for while we might reasonably expect some favour from God as his creation, yet sinful and
ungodly people as we are, we could in justice expect nothing but
his utmost disfavour. Nevertheless, 'God so loved the world that
he gave his only Son . . . not to condemn the world but that it
might be saved through him' (John 3.16f) Here is grace; the
redeeming activity of the divine power and love.

God's Love

Redemption, then, is the activity of the divine love; that is grace.
Grace, as St Augustine teaches, is not grace unless it is freely
given. God's love is free in that it is unmerited. He loves us freely,
regardless of our unworthiness and our sinfulness. Naturally he
wants us to be good and not bad – just as human parents want
their children to be good, if they love them, and not bad. Hence
comes God's discipline; but it comes because he loves us, not in
order that he may be able to love us.

His love is free in that it is unrestricted; it is not directed towards
his chosen people, Israel, but to all humanity, to every race, to all
the world, and in all ages.

God's Initiative

Because God is the God of all grace, the Christian Faith comes,
saying: 'This is what God has done, and still does, for you.' The
gospel is proclaimed by teaching and preaching, by sacrament and
by example – all these are 'means of grace' for they bring home
to us God's redeeming love; that love that is offered and given
freely to us, if only we will accept and receive it. Because God is
the God of all grace, he can speedily change our lives from being
little more than want, weakness and sin. By reconciliation with
God through repentance, we receive energy from him, the 'God
of all grace', with both the disposition and the power to supply
every want. His bounties and favours are as the leaves of the
forest, the waves of the sea, the stars of the sky – unnumbered
and innumerable.

Results

The Christian faith is a realistic faith. It consists of two parts –
what God does for us, and what God expects from us. First of
all, God makes us something in himself; we are 'accepted in the
Beloved'. He gives us standing before himself. That is reconcili-

ation; and the outcome of that is Christian living. What is the Christian life? First of all, *being* something in Christ; then the second part is *doing* something for Christ. As a great teacher of the Christian life used to say: 'We are saved in order to serve.'

Reconciliation on the one hand, and perseverance on the other, are but two aspects of God's loving-kindness towards his creatures. Reconciled *to* God we may be, but we need to be renewed day by day in our fellowship *with* God. Seek daily strength for daily needs; and out of his great love for us and all the world, God gives his grace – bringing life to the soul, purity to the heart, light for the mind, and power to the will.

> 'Grant us such grace that we may work Thy will
> And speak Thy words and walk before Thy face,
> Profound and calm, like waters deep and still:
> Grant us such grace.'
>
> *Christina Rossetti*

Third Sunday after Easter   20 April
'It is the Lord!'

'The disciple whom Jesus loved said to Peter, "It is the Lord!".' John 21.7 (ASB Gospel)

'Going Fishing'
Today's Gospel reading is part of an epilogue to St John's great work, perhaps an addition made later by the writer himself, perhaps by another hand. Whoever is truly responsible, the chapter is addressed to us with the question 'What is the meaning of the Resurrection for all succeeding generations of Christ's followers, now?'

It is certainly one of the most vivid of all the Gospel narratives. The apostles, seven of them, deeply depressed after the sickening events of last week, had lost all hope for their future; the wonderful story, in which they had active parts to play, had come to an end. There seemed to be nothing for them to do, but to resume their old way of life – back to the boats and the fishing. They set off, cast their nets all the night, but caught nothing.

Then, in the dim light of dawn, a stranger on the beach, in an authoritative sort of way, call to them, 'Hey, lads, caught anything?' – 'Nah, nothing doing!' He gets them to try again, and their success is remarkable indeed. John, the beloved disciple, sharper to recognize the Loved One's voice than the others, says to Peter, 'It is the Lord!' With typical impulsive reaction, Peter pulls on his peasant smock, presumably over his loincloth, and swims and wades ashore, towards that Figure.

Their breakfast is waiting; fishes on a charcoal fire, and a loaf of bread. The Lord says, 'Bring some of your catch, and we'll have breakfast.'

A Vivid Story

Certainly a straightforward and vivid story so far. But details in it suggest that the story is not told for its historical value alone, but because of the significance it has as a parable, full of symbolic elements – read the whole account when you can.

The disciples have been fishing; the other gospels put a similar scene at the beginning of Jesus' ministry, and include his famous phrase 'I will make you fishers of men.' So we may take the present narrative to represent the Church trying to fulfil its task – fishing for souls, that is, bringing men and women to the knowledge of the heavenly Father, in simple wholehearted trust. But failing – because they – we – rely on our own resources. But when we obey Christ – even when not recognizing that it is the Spirit of Christ directing us – then God's work is done.

Recognition

But we need to know who it is, who inspires us. And it is the spiritually sensitive soul who recognizes the Risen Christ. So, in St John's Easter Day narrative, it is the 'beloved disciple' who first comes to the empty tomb and recognizes its significance. But it is Peter, following behind, who leaps into the tomb and becomes the accredited witness, the chief of the Apostles. So now, the spiritually sensitive disciple recognizes the Risen Christ, but it is Peter, the man of action who does something about it. His impulsive reaction – putting his clothes on, to leap into the water! – looks like a deep need to show reverence. Perhaps it is not too farfetched to see here a psychological need such as led the priests of the Old Testament to wear special holy garments when coming into the Divine Presence, and the similar practice among all Christian ministers where the sacramental Presence of Christ is acknowledged.

The Breakfast
And reference to the Sacrament leads us on to the next point, the Lakeside Breakfast; for here again is a reference to the days before the Resurrection, the Feeding of the Five Thousand, when bread and fish were miraculously provided for the crowds. That was surely an anticipation of the Holy Communion; and a similar pattern is followed. Jesus is present with his followers at a meal. It is striking that the Eucharist is represented in early Christian art symbolized by bread and fish. Partly, no doubt, to conceal the details of the most sacred Act of the Church, but more truly in memory of the Gospel events.

But next, Christ says, 'Bring some of the fish you have caught', and this must surely symbolize that the Lord is telling us that at all the Eucharists that are to be, Holy Communion is an anticipation of the gathering, the ultimate gathering in, of all humanity into the Kingdom of God. However few may be present at our eucharistic worship, each celebration is still a meeting-point between God and all creation.

Our Christian Future
What are we specifically doing to reconcile the world to God, and to extend the Kingdom of Christ? Relying upon our own human schemes, our cleverness, our ideas of what is best, will fail. All depends upon when, like the beloved disciple, we recognize Christ in his real presence with us; and like Peter we obey him. Not our consciences, not our frustrations, but learning to wait for Christ, for his call, for his instructions, for after all, we are concerned with nothing less than the transformation of this universe into the Kingdom of God. What a call; what a destiny! May we indeed be worthy of that call.

Easter 3 *Second Sermon*
St Mark the Evangelist
'John, whose other name was Mark.' Acts 12.25 (BCP EP for St Mark)
'Barnabas took Mark with him, and sailed away to Cyprus.' Acts 15.39 (BCP)

The First

On Friday next, April 25th, the Church commemorates the writer who produced what is generally believed to be the earliest record of our Lord's life and teachings, St Mark the Evangelist, author of the Gospel printed in our Bibles after that of St Matthew and before that of St Luke. Some of us may remember the old rhyme that children were taught to say at bed-time:

> 'Matthew, Mark, Luke and John,
> Bless the bed that I lie on!'

But in spite of that, Mark is generally accepted as the author of the first gospel to be written; and certainly Matthew and Luke use pretty well the whole of Mark's material, although altering a sequence of many incidents. The experts generally seem to place Mark at around AD 65 or 70; that is, when the death of many of the companions of Jesus made it clearly necessary that as much as possible of the sayings and actions of the Lord should be recorded.

Who was Mark?

Mark is thought to have been the young man who ran away naked from the angry crowd which came with swords and clubs to arrest Jesus (Mark 14.51–52) It has also been suggested that the Last Supper took place in the house of Mary, the mother of Mark; and that the boy may have come in contact with the disciples and Jesus himself both then and on earlier occasions when the house was used as a meeting-place. St Barnabas was a cousin of Mark (Col. 4.10), and when he and Paul decided to visit Cyprus on a mission-ary tour they took the young man with them as a helper. For various reasons this turned out not to be satisfactory and he returned home. (Acts 13.13) This led to a dispute between the two leaders, for when they planned a second trip, Barnabas wanted to give Mark a second chance but Paul did not, and the two men parted company (Acts 15.36–41) Later on, it is only fair to add, Mark was forgiven by Paul, who sought his help once more (2 Tim. 4.11) 'for he is very useful in serving me'.

We know also that as well as helping Paul, Mark also worked with Peter; in his first general letter Peter mentions Mark with affection (1 Peter 5.13) in the way an older man might speak of a younger helper.

St Mark's Gospel

Tradition also has it that Mark's gospel was based largely upon the memories of Peter. There are many small details that bear this out, without being actually conclusive. That the Gospel was written at Rome seems almost certain; the great persecution under Nero took place towards the end of St Peter's life; and we can easily imagine how important it would seem to Mark and Peter and their companions to write down all they could remember of the actions and sayings of Jesus before all who knew of them at first hand, had perished. We can understand, too, that though Peter was not illiterate nor uneducated, an upbringing as a fisherman on the Lake of Galilee would hardly have been a good preparation for writing an important book in his old age; thus he would have been very glad of the help of a younger man who was better fitted for such a task. Indeed, the Gospel presents our Lord as the Strong Son of God; the Lion-like Gospel in which our Lord is seen as the One who, as a great Hero, is able to defeat evil spirits. Perhaps this was especially intended to appeal to the Roman temperament, setting forth Christ in an aspect to touch the hearts of strong men.

The Martyr

By tradition, St Mark was brutally murdered at Alexandria, where he had founded the Church; his body was laid to rest there, but about 815 his relics were removed secretly to Venice and placed in the beautiful Basilica then being built. Ever since Mark has been specially honoured as Patron of the City, and his symbol – the winged lion, resting one paw upon the Gospel of St Mark – appears everywhere, in flags, tapestries and carvings.

Fourth Sunday after Easter
27 April   Discipleship

'Jesus said to Simon Peter, "Simon, son of John, do you love me more than these?" He said to him, "Yes, Lord; you know that I love you." He said to him, "Feed my lambs."' John 21,15 (ASB Gospel)

Love is All

Not many days before this, Peter had been boasting of his value to his Master, and of the unshakeable nature of his loyalty. Then he had miserably failed in the face of danger, and showed himself false to his profession, false in his love. Christ now asks him for a renewal of his profession, offers him the opportunity to reclaim his fine ideal.

'Do you love me?' And the word the Lord uses, denotes the highest kind of love. 'Yes, Lord; you know that I love you,' is the answer; and the word for 'love' is a humbler one. With his bitter failure in mind, Peter is not making any high pretensions. His 'love' is of the humblest kind, the love that a child might offer his parent – but at least it is sincere.

Even when Deserted . . .
It had been so all through; yes, he had loved his Lord even when he deserted him and denied him – and Jesus knew that. Weakness, cowardice, selfishness – all the imperfections of our all-too-human nature – could not wholly obscure or devalue that one all-important fact. Jesus knows it; and he now rebuilds upon it. 'Feed my lambs,' he murmurs.

Love, however humble, however little allied to strength, to great gifts, to power of character – love is the one indispensable condition of fitness for the task ahead.

Yes, the Good Shepherd could commit his little ones to the care of the disciple who, for love of that Shepherd, would indeed care for the flock.

'All we need is love'
Love is the follower of Christ's supreme equipment and qualification. Oh yes, there are plenty of other sources of strength, fitness for vocation, but none so fundamental. True fellowship with Christ, our personal religion, a loyalty based on Christ as the ever-present guide and inspiration of our love. Nothing can compensate for the lack of this; no brilliant intellectual gifts, no devotion to the Church as an institution, no love of services, music, colour and ritual, delightful though these things can be in themselves. Nothing can compensate for the lack of love, care, consideration, and our personal devotion to Jesus our Lord. Unless we know our Lord face to face, and love him, we will not be able to witness for him to any real effect, in this troubled world of ours today.

'Follow Me'

We are God's instruments, we are chosen vessels to carry into action his Word, into expression into the life of a New Age to come, perhaps only a few years ahead. That a right character may be formed and kept active and alive within us, we need to take the words of Jesus home with us, in our minds and in our hearts. We are instruments in God's hands, chosen vessels to carry his Word into expression and action in the life of a new Age to come. Let us keep ever before us the knowledge of what we are, and what we are intended to be; and the words of Jesus should echo in our hearts and minds day by day: 'Follow me; feed my sheep.'

A PRAYER

> *God of truth,*
> *we have seen with our eyes*
> *and touched with our hands*
> *the bread of life.*
> *Strengthen our faith*
> *that we may grow in love for you*
> *and for each other;*
> *through Jesus Christ our Risen Lord.*
> *(Patterns for Worship 52.18)*

Easter 4   *Second Sermon*   **Faith and Truth**

'We look not to the things that are seen, but to the things that are unseen; for the things that are seen are transient, but the things that are unseen are eternal.' 2 Cor. 4.18 (ASB EP)

Faith in the Unseen

Paul speaks in language which a Greek as well as a Jew could understand. He is appealing to the underlying faith of both his converts and himself, and quotes from Psalm 116:

'I believed, and therefore will I speak; but I was sore troubled: I said in my haste, All men are liars.'

Their faith being that God, who raised Jesus from the dead, will raise them too, and place them together in his Presence. Paul seems to have reached the conclusion that the Parousia may not come until after his own death, since he has already faced death or at least the threat of death. So therefore, in the light of the coming Resurrection, temporary affliction to our outward nature is really nothing in comparison with our inward nature, and the prospect of the eternal glory in which that nature will revel.

The contrast of outward and inward man, or the seen and temporal, and the unseen and eternal would surely appeal to the Greek mind, as indeed Plato taught.

Spiritual and Mortal
If in the mortal body of the Apostle, the life of Jesus is made effective, then a spiritual life is being built up in it, which will triumph soon. The glory far beyond all comparison, outweighs the light affliction of the passing hour before the end. (Paul plays on the Hebrew word for 'glory' which is very similar to 'weighty'; no doubt the Jewish audience would appreciate the point!) In v. 15 he tells his converts that his feet are planted firmly on the earth, in spite of the lyrical style of his theological meditation: all he does is done for the converts, so the more that God's gracious unmerited love is poured out, the more may thanksgivings rise up and resound to the glory of God.

The Risen Life
Paul, as a Hellenistic Jewish Christian, is using language he hopes will appeal to both Jew and Greek, making them aware of Christ and the Risen Life by using words familiar to both groups. The touching phrase, 'an everlasting dwelling place is made ready for us in heaven' from the Proper Preface in the ASB for a funeral, takes its tone from these sentences, as does 'the promise of eternal life; for to your faithful people life is changed, not taken away.' Then, from the image of the body as a dwelling or tent, Paul turns to raiment – 'not that we would be unclothed, but that we would be further clothed.' He welcomes the thought of being 'clothed' with a heavenly body, so that what is mortal may be swallowed up in life.

Judgement

Paul's whole desire (v. 9) is to please the Lord; for everyone has, one day, to stand before the tribunal of Christ and receive his due reward or punishment for all that he has done on earth. Paul had apparently been accused by his opponents of 'getting round' people ('persuade', v. 11) Paul refuses these accusations by raising his eyes to God – 'If we are beside ourselves, it is for God' – if we are in our right mind, it is with the intention of helping you, the converts.

Above all, 'the love of Christ controls us' (v. 14) with the certainty that 'he died for all' so that they should live 'for him who died and rose again' (v. 15).

PRAYER

> Lord God,
> the protector of all who trust in you,
> without whom nothing is strong, nothing is holy,
> increase and multiply upon us your mercy,
> that you being our ruler and guide,
> we may so pass through things temporal
> that we finally lose not the things eternal.
> Grant this, heavenly Father,
> for the sake of Jesus Christ our Lord. Amen.

Fifth Sunday after Easter   (*Rogation Sunday*)
4 May   The Abundance of God's Mercy

'Hitherto have ye asked nothing in my Name: ask, and ye shall receive, that your joy may be full.' John 16.24 (BCP) or, 'When that day comes you will make your request in my name.' John 16.26 (ASB)

'Fruits of the Earth'

The origins of Rogation-tide lie in the primary importance, for our ancestors, of their farming, as indeed it is in so many parts of the world today. So prayer that God may 'give and preserve to our use the kindly fruits of the earth' as the Book of Common Prayer has it, or that 'we may employ the resources of nature to God's glory, our own well-being, and the relief of those in need', as the ASB puts it.

These petitions do raise the whole question of prayer, in its proper sense, that is, asking God to supply our needs.

There are two attitudes, we may reflect; there is a fundamentalist teaching that God will always give what we pray for hard enough (though we do think of the disappointment of children brought up in pious families, when what is hoped and prayed for does not appear after all). Or the second attitude, which we may call a reverential scepticism: Surely it is beneath God's dignity to deal with our earthly concerns! (This sometimes hides a suspicion that prayer doesn't work anyhow.)

True Prayer

Prayer in an extended sense includes much more besides petition, or asking. Of course there is gratitude – the other side of the coin – but also there are forms of mysticism, which can be more or less profound. There is the prayer of quiet, in which we try to simply remain detached from all the busy-ness of life; something specially needful in our contemporary world. The ultimate mystery of God: 'Beating up with the wings of love, against the cloud of un-knowing'.

But a warning note here: that sort of prayer is not all that different from the spiritual exercises practised in the pure Buddhist faith, which rejects belief in God as we understand it.

Our Belief

This brings up a serious question: Do we neglect prayer, in the elementary sense that is, asking God for our needs, because our belief in God is shaky? Rogation Sunday is a time for asking what may be *the* religious question of our time. The Revd Don Cupitt, Dean of Emmanuel College, Cambridge and Lecturer in the Philosophy of Religion in the University of Cambridge, wrote a book, called *Only Human*, which in effect abolished God, or as Cupitt puts it, 'Religious thought must cease to disparage this world and stop yearning for another, and basing itself on homesickness; and must no longer pretend that religious language describes invisible states of affairs in a higher world. Religious thought must bring us back to the human realm, in such a way that we see it for the first time as it really is.'

In Cupitt's view, which he shares with Buddhism, the world remains remorselessly in the grip of evil; in Christianity it is believed that some pattern in history (however inharmoniously) is being worked out, to the ultimate victory of Good.

Belief in God
Belief in God is the most reasonable and life-enhancing interpretation of our human existence. To believe that there is an eternal, perfect Being, Creator and Upholder, answers our intuition that the Universe is not self-explanatory; it must have an origin and a purpose. This is supported by our experience at its best, sometimes of his Presence, and of our need to approach Him; but above all, we find ourselves confirmed by the revelation of Jesus Christ in the Gospels and the writings about him in the New Testament. Indeed the whole Bible confirms our experience, and teaches us that although God *is* God and ultimately is in control of everything, he has implanted in the universe a degree of self-determination. Things often 'go their own way'; we often 'go our own way'. God's ultimate purpose of love depends upon this; all the miseries and disasters will be justified in the end, must be our belief, difficult though that is to accept.

Freedom
The same principle that can lead to evil and disaster is the cause of our degree of freedom, and so of our being able to co-operate with God in his goodness. In any situation, God's desire for our happiness can be supported by our own goodwill, which is expressed in two ways – prayer and action, both directed to what we, within our limitations, believe to be good. So it is our duty to pray; though remembering that prayer is no substitute for action, any more than action is for prayer, and that the field of prayer is so vast that it needs to be channelled.

The infinite patience of God is working out the achievement of his Kingdom, by love and not by arbitrary force; our prayer in its little way should reflect that infinite patience by our own perseverance.

(It may be preferred to omit the paragraph 'Our Belief' or treat it as a separate subject for discussion)

Easter 5 *Second Sermon* **Rogationtide**
'Thank the Lord for his goodness.' Ps 107 v. 8 (ASB EP)

God and Man
Leaning over a five-barred gate in the sunshine, looking over a field of green shoots, reminds us that the farmer works the land, but it is God who gives the earth, the sun, the rain – all of which contribute to the increase of the crop. At a time when nature under the hand of God is displaying her growth and glory, we think of the farmers and their work, and ask for God's blessing upon it. It should remind us of in our work, whatever it may be, we are in some way co-operating with God, and that this is what we are intended to do.

Work in the Bible
Is work a blessing or a curse? It's a fair question. Remember the doggerel put into the mouth of the old charlady, in her final words on her deathbed:

> 'Don't pity me now:
> Don't pity me never!
> I'm going to do nothing
> For ever and ever.'

We are told that, because of the evil in the world, it is the fate of humanity 'in the sweat of your face you shall eat bread'. (Gen. 3.19) Yet, this hard element in work, as all else, is redeemed by Christ. The emphasis in the Bible is that man is meant to work and that in this, he serves God and he serves his fellows. The supreme example of this is Christ, who worked for so many years in the carpenter's shop at Nazareth. We can be sure that all the work Christ did was good, and offered for God's glory, not using poor materials and not faked over to look good, but causing trouble when in use.

Slaves and Gentlemen
The Greek and Roman world was based on slavery. Cicero declared that 'No gentleman would worked for a wage' and Plato that 'No workman could be a citizen of the ideal state.' How like the colour prejudice and disrespect we see today, when some

people of differing colour are either rejected, or offered only work that 'our own people' will not undertake. The bitterness that this treatment engenders can have the most dreadful results, and is plainly against the Christian faith and the will of God our Father – Father of all races and all colours. The Christian glories in the fact that Christ was a working man, a carpenter.

As unto Thee

The Christian feels that he must do his work, carry out his job, do his part, as 'unto the Lord' and so with all his might. We may wish that we were doing something else, and how much better that would be; our work is what we can do where we are, and doing it as well as we can. That does not mean that we should not prepare ourselves if another opportunity should arise – sometimes what seems to be quite apart from our actual employment, suddenly offers an opening; we should be ready and prepared to take that opening, that chance, after carefully considering it of course. But normally our work is what we can do where we are. A nineteen-year-old girl wrote this verse:

> 'Lord of all pots and pans and things,
> Since I've no time to be
> A saint by doing lovely things
> Or watching late with Thee,
> Or dreaming in the dawnlights,
> Or storming heaven's gates –
> Make me a saint of getting meals
> And washing up the plates.
> Thou, who didst love to give men food
>   In room or by the sea,
> Accept this service that I do –
>   I do it unto Thee.'

According to the New Testament, what matters is not what our work is, but the spirit in which we do it – heartily, as unto the Lord. What matters is the care and faithfulness with which we do our work. What are we putting into our work? Do we earn our salary, our pay? Yes, we have the right to bargain to be paid more, and for better conditions, and so on. Union is strength, and trade unions are justified in pressing for better pay and conditions; but we also have the obligation to earn the pay or the salary. Fair pay for fair work – fair work for fair pay. More and more, workers and employers are getting together to discuss problems and to make their firms more efficient, and their products better value. This must be the way forward, in the difficult times of today.

Ascension Day   8 May   Great Joy!

'He led them out as far as Bethany, and blessed them with uplifted hands; and in the act of blessing he parted from them. And they returned to Jerusalem with great joy, and spent all their time in the Temple, praising God.' Luke 24.50–53

Joy

A striking feature of the description of the Ascension, is the joy which filled the heart of the disciples when Christ, their Lord and Master, withdrew from them. Departures usually involve sadness, but this departure brought great joy. 'With great joy, though this Jesus, from whom all their joy had sprung, was departed out of their sight. With joy, because Jesus had claimed his right, as the Christ, because he had shown that he had come from a Father, and had done the will of the Father, and was now to return. With joy, because Death and Hell were shown to be his Father's enemies, and he had defeated them. With joy, because being delivered from these enemies, they could serve God without fear, in holiness and righteousness all the days of their lives.' – Maurice.

Public

We recall that Christ's ministry had been in public. His crucifixion had been notoriously and cruelly public. Equally public had been his burial. The resurrection had also been public; guards were at the tomb, though they fled in terror when the great stone was wrenched away by awesome power. The Lord appeared in public several times after his Resurrection; this is particularly noticeable in the appearance at the Lakeside as told in the last chapter of the Fourth Gospel. It was natural, then, that the Ascension should take place in broad daylight. The company which was led out to the hill was not composed merely of the Eleven. There was a good number of disciples; now St Paul tells us that on one occasion, which he does not specify, Christ 'appeared to over five hundred brethren at once', and he says that most of them were alive at the time he wrote (I Cor. 15.6) We may reasonably wonder if a large number of them witnessed the Ascension.

Their hearts must have been full as he talked with them on the way. We know that their hearts were filled with joy as they returned (Luke 24.52).

Parting
As he blessed them it was that 'he parted from them'. His presence had been a blessing to them; in a blessing he left them. In his exaltation our human race was granted great honour, for we are to remember that he still carries our humanity upon him, as he makes his High Priestly intercession for us at the Throne of Grace. His accepted self-offering, an oblation accepted in the Resurrection and the Ascension, stands for all humanity and for all ages. It is for us to accept the effectuality of that offering, by our faith, obedience and love.

'The Sacrifice of Jesus is the expression in history and in time, of what is eternally true – that for all humanity there is an eternal High Priest, of whom we cay say:

> 'He pleads his passion on the Tree;
> He shows himself to God for me.'
> *Vincent Taylor*

The Sunday after Ascension Day
11 May   The Task
'The church is Christ's body, the completion of him who himself completes all things everywhere.' Ephesians 1.23 (ASB NT Reading)

The Great Task
Our Saviour's departure surprised his disciples by the reason he gave for his leaving them; it was not for 'his own good' but it was that he was leaving them for *their* good. 'It is for your own good that I am leaving you.' (St John 16.7) A number of things that Jesus said to his disciples startled them, even on occasion dis-

mayed them. Here is one of these difficult sayings; they could not see how they could be better off if Jesus left them; surely it was because of his strong presence with them, his calm personality at their side, and his wise and encouraging words, that they drew their strength to face temptation and danger. So it was most natural for them to feel that his departure, far from 'doing them good', would be for their harm.

Nevertheless, Jesus was right. His departure was for their good – and for ours, for two reasons.

The Church

The departure of Christ was the first step in setting the disciples to get to work on the great task the Lord had given them. The great task of spreading the good news, the Gospel, throughout the world, and thus bringing the Christian Church into being. While the Lord was on earth, they stayed with him, listening and learning from him. When he was gone from them, soon began the great task of carrying the Gospel with them as they dispersed to many places. There was work to be done on earth; when Jesus left his disciples, the Gospel he taught and preached began to be spread abroad, and the Church he founded, with its sacramental life, the Christian faith and the Christian way of life, put down its roots, put out its tendrils and began to bear fruit.

The Spirit

But we must not make the mistake of thinking that the spread of the Gospel was the work of the Lord's first followers, nor of the Christians who came after them down the centuries. Valiant as they were, they could not have done the work alone: it was the work of the Holy Spirit. It is that Spirit which, as he said, would give testimony of him, that has sent the Christian Faith and life into the whole of the globe, working in the hearts of men and women, filling them with love for the Lord, and with the desire themselves to proclaim him by word and deed. Like the disciples, instead of the Lord's visible presence with us, we have the voice of the Holy Spirit speaking within us, in our hearts, warning us against evil, encouraging us to do good. We are to listen for his voice, follow his guidance, and use the strength he supplies to us.

Remember how the angels said to the Apostles at the time of the Ascension, 'Men of Galilee, why do you stand looking up into heaven? This Jesus who was taken up from you into heaven, will come in the same way as you saw him go!' (Acts 1.11) There was and is work to be done on earth: and now just as then, we are not to be mere star-gazers, but are to witness, by our actions, our deeds, our love, to Christ our Lord.

> O God, most holy, loving and merciful
> let your Spirit rest upon us,
> upon the Church,
> upon the whole of humanity,
> and give us his best gifts
> of wisdom and understanding,
>   counsel and strength,
>   knowledge and godliness,
>   and the gift of your very Self
>   to dwell in our very being,
> for the sake of Jesus Christ,
> your beloved Son
> and our beloved Lord.
>
> George Appleton

Sunday after Ascension Day
Second Sermon   A Song of Victory

'Lift up your heads, O ye gates, and be ye lift up, ye everlasting doors: and the King of glory shall come in.' Ps xxiv (BCP)

A Psalm for Ascensiontide
Like all the Psalms, this Psalm was composed many hundreds of years before our Lord's Ascension took place, but such is its delight and wonder at the great deeds of God that the Church has always used it to commemorate that great triumphal final act of our Lord's life on earth.

In its origin, this psalm was to accompany the bringing of the sacred Ark into the City of Jerusalem, after the years of wandering in the wilderness when the Israelites had carried the Ark and other sacred objects through all the difficulties, trials, battles and the rest – and now, at last, as part of the thanksgiving for victory over their enemies and the foundation of the new City, the Ark was to be given its final resting-place in the magnificence of the new Temple.

Victory

The real appropriateness of this Psalm for the Ascension, is in the fact that it is a great song of victory, and the Ascension is a great sign of victory, the victory of Christ over sin and death. It was on Easter Day that Jesus was raised from the dead, and the hearts of the apostles were filled with joy; but his final and more formal triumph was forty days after Easter, at his Ascension.

In another sense, also, the Ascension is the completion of the Resurrection triumph. Those travellers with us along the road of Life, but who do not share the Faith, may ask, 'If there is life after death, shall we be any the better off for it? Will a future life be free from the perplexities, disappointments and sorrows of this present life?'

Life and Death

If the future life is not different and better, freer and happier, perhaps it might be argued, as the poet did, that it might be best if death were simply the end of all things for us:

> *'From too much love of living,*
> *From hope and fear set free,*
> *We thank with brief thanksgiving*
> *Whatever gods may be*
> *That no life lives for ever:*
> *That dead men rise up never,*
> *That even the weariest river*
> *Winds somewhere safe to sea.'*
> Swinburne

The Christian answer is in our Lord's own words to his disciples:

> *'In my Father's house are many rooms;*
> *if it were not so, would I have told you*
> *that I go to prepare a place for you?*
> *And when I go and prepare a place for you,*
> *I will come again and take you to myself,*
> *That where I am, you may be also.'*
> John 14.2–4

The Ascension, then, reminds us that when we leave this world, those who have loved Christ and tried to serve him, are only following their Master, who is waiting to receive them. And in that future life they will be in his care, and will enjoy the fullness of his love.

Pentecost (*Whit Sunday*)   18 May
The Holy Spirit

'You shall receive power when the Holy Spirit has come upon you; and you shall be my witnesses. Alleluya!' Acts 1.8 (ASB Introductory Sentence) or, 'I will pray the Father, and he shall give you another Comforter, that he may abide with you for ever, even the Spirit of truth.' John 14.15 (BCP Gospel) or, 'They were all filled with the Holy Spirit.' Acts 2,4 (BCP and ASB)

Finding Out
When a child – or for that matter, a grown-up – receives, on his or her birthday, a mysterious parcel, the sender and the contents equally mysterious and unknown, how rapidly the parcel is opened, and the gift inside brought out into the light and (hopefully) rejoiced over!

Today, when we remember and rejoice over the Holy Spirit coming to us as a gift from God, a great and special gift, we may well ask to find out more exactly, 'Who is the Holy Spirit? What does the Holy Spirit do for us and for me?'

The Holy Spirit is God
Are we as clear as we might be about the answer to the first question? Who is the Holy Spirit? Maybe some of us at least are a little confused by the old English name, 'Holy Ghost'. In olden time, 'ghost' had a different meaning from what we think of today, a sort of wandering apparition; 'Ghost' simply then meant 'Spirit', or 'soul', certainly nothing creepy or mysterious.

Our understanding is based on the teaching that the help from God is in the eternal Spirit of God, the third Person of the Blessed Trinity; and that this Spirit is in the world, present as its guide, its monitor and its judge, not merged in the world, but as proceeding from the Father who is above and beyond it all. The Athanasian

Creed, nowadays dropped from our services, makes this all much clearer, declaring that 'The Father is God, the Son is God, and the Holy Spirit is God. Yet they are not three Gods, but one God . . . The three Persons are co-eternal together and co-equal.'

The Holy Spirit is our Helper

What does the Holy Spirit do for us? What kind of gift is the Holy Spirit? Not all the gifts we receive from friends or relations are gifts of the right kind. We have all had Christmas gifts, or birthday presents, that are things we cannot use, or do not like. God does not make this kind of mistake with his gifts. All his gifts are of use to us, if we use them as he means us to.

Above all other gifts from God to us, the Holy Spirit is a present we can *use*; for what he is can be summed up in two words – he is our Helper, our Advocate.

In life, it is sometimes plain enough what is the wise and right course of action to take, and the good and right thing to do. Often, however, it is not so clear; and life seems to be getting more and more complex under today's conditions. We need guidance on many occasions, to know what God would wish us to do; and that guidance comes from the Holy Spirit.

There are times in our lives – in everyone's life – when it is hard to do what is right, when temptation is strong and difficulties are great. We need strength of character, we need courage, we need perseverance, if we are to resist evil. The help we need, when we feel weak and alone, comes from the Holy Spirit.

Whitsunday

The gift of the Holy Spirit, as given to the apostles, and down the ages to the members of the Church, to each sincere follower of Jesus Christ, is the source of strength and hope, of courage and of good counsel. Remember, we are not alone, the Spirit is always at our side; in him we have a real Person to help us, one who understands, who feels, cares and loves – and who also holds power to help us. He is the secret of hope and steadfastness; let us never hesitate to pray for grace to use to the full this rich and powerful gift, 'the Spirit of force and power'. (Isaiah 11.2)

> *O God, most holy, loving and merciful*
> *let your Spirit rest upon us*
> *upon the whole Church*

> *upon all humanity*
> *and give us his gifts*
> *of wisdom and understanding,*
> *counsel and strength,*
> *knowledge and holy fear,*
> *the gift of your very Self*
> *to dwell in us, in our very being.*
>
> G. A.

Pentecost *Second Sermon* **Power**

'The spirit of force and power' – Isaiah 11.2

Power

What a wonderfully powerful substance gunpowder must have seemed to the men – probably Chinese – who first thought it out many hundreds of years ago! How marvellous was the petrol-burning internal combustion engine, when it was first invented towards the end of the nineteenth century! Yet today we are so used to such things that we have lost our sense of wonder at them; and in any case they pale into insignificance beside later, more astonishing discoveries made in more recent years.

Use of Power

Gunpowder, petrol, dynamite, nuclear energy, all great sources of power – and all have one thing in common – they can be used in two ways: either for constructive purposes, or for destructive purposes – or more simply, for peace or for war. Explosives made easier the building of great roads and bridges, by enabling us to clear away great obstacles; but far more explosives have been used in war, cutting short millions of lives and causing untold destruction. The petrol engine used in cars and the jet engine used in planes have made the world a far easier and smaller place to live in, but are also used to power tanks, warships, bomber and fighter planes, all equipped with their own weapons of destruction.

And nowhere is the contrast more marked than in the use of nuclear power. It can be developed to make life easier for us in many ways, yet what most people know about it, is its immense power to destroy – remember Hiroshima, in war and Chernobyl, in peace. Here is one of the most useful and at the same time most destructive sources of power we have ever known, upon this fragile earth.

Power of the Spirit
Today we commemorate a very different source of power; a power for good, a power that brings peace not war, a power that far from destroying, builds and rebuilds, encourages life and growth rather than death and decay; a power that helps the small and weak, the powerless and the minorities; and above all warms and heals, enables and leads, teaches and guides.

What is this power? It is the coming of the Holy Spirit – commemorating today the descent of power upon the apostles in the upper room in Jerusalem. And not only did the Holy Spirit come to them on that special occasion, but he comes to us as well, and as powerfully as we will let him, and remains with us as long as we are willing to listen and to receive him.

'A source of great power in your lives' – that is how Jesus Christ described the Holy Spirit to his disciples, when he was preparing them in advance for the coming of the Spirit – 'You will receive power when the Holy Spirit comes upon you' (Acts 1.8)

Enrichment
The Holy Spirit uses his power in our lives for good, and through us, for the good of the world – never for evil. Secondly, His power is spiritual power, working on the human mind and the human soul, and working always in love, never in hate or distrust.

Is spiritual power of any use in the concrete, mechanical and matter-of-fact world we live in? For certain it is! On first thoughts the Spirit seems weaker than bombs, and explosives, and machines, but that is only superficial. In the real world it is far stronger, for – however ingenious they are, machines and weapons and Internet and newspapers and radio and TV – are all controlled by humans, and the Holy Spirit controls or can control the minds and the lives of all men and women who will submit to his guidance and rule.

Personal Power

How the power of the Spirit could affect for good the life of this world of ours! If only we would listen, if only we would obey his teaching, we could save this tiny planet from self-destruction; we could enrich this world for good, use our sources of power for the benefit of all and for good purposes instead of evil. Individually, we can have at our own disposal this tremendous source of spiritual strength; listen to him, and he will guide and help us in all our perplexities, and give us the power and the courage to face trouble and fight temptation, and to do what is good and right.

THE WIND OF THE SPIRIT

In every generation the Church needs to set its sails to the wind of the Spirit. The power that comes is the power of the Spirit of God, that will take us into every area of life, equip us to meet every change. We must expect, pray for, be ready for the wind of the Spirit and the fire of love, in the ever-recurring Pentecost of God's outpouring of Himself.

George Appleton

Trinity Sunday (*First after Pentecost*)
25 May   Worship

'The grace of the Lord Jesus Christ and the love of God and the fellowship of the Holy Spirit be with you all.' 2 Corinthians 13.14

Experience

How did the doctrine of the Holy Trinity come into being, we may well ask? Although it seems difficult, it is an attempt to give expression to actual facts of human experience, and it is difficult to translate experience into terms of theology. Our definitions can seem cold and hard when we compare them with the living truth. But in the words of our text, St Paul tells us what he, and those to whom he was writing, felt about God long before any need arose for any formula or statement of doctrine. St Paul was conscious of the impact of the Divine Being in a threefold way upon the life of the world.

The Love of God

When we talk about the love of God, what we mean is that the ultimate Reality behind us and all existence, is not blind force nor arbitrary despotism, nor is that Reality a mere uncaring nature-element. We believe that the power behind all existence is not only life, but moral and therefore personal life. We make our supreme venture of faith when we declare, in face of so much that seems to shriek against what we say, that God is love. This is perhaps the only truth about God, in his essential Being, that our human faculties can grasp. We may speak of the omnipotence or the omniscience of God, but what kind of idea can we form of what these words mean? It is only as love that ultimate reality can have any meaning for us. The veiled Creator is still veiled, but there is a light that shines through the veil, and in that light we live.

Yet there is something that awakens awe in us, at the thought of the love of God. For will not infinite love be a consuming fire? Finite beings of time and space may live before an infinite being indifferent to them; but must not infinite love draw all life into itself?

The Grace of our Lord Jesus Christ

By this phrase, St Paul meant that grace is love, acting and initiating, breaking down barriers and overcoming obstacles. If we think of love as the light of the universe, grace is the light that pierces through the mists, until the mountaintops and the valleys are all bathed in sunshine. And grace has no meaning unless there is a real distinction between giver and receiver. If all personal life is a fading illusion, then the Incarnation is an illusion too, and the Divine Love is wasting itself in a world of shadows. Grace is the word that expresses the creative activity of God. Creation is not manufacture, but generation. There is an eternal generation that makes Fatherhood and Sonship a reality within the Being of God; and there is a reflection of that eternal generation in the evolution of a universe with living creatures having the power to will and to act. So the love of God becomes the grace of our Lord Jesus Christ.

The Fellowship of the Holy Spirit
Yet love is something more than grace. Love is not content to give; it asks for a response to its giving. So love is fellowship; but how can there be any fellowship between the Creator and his creation, between finite beings and an infinite God? There is only one answer – the fellowship of human beings with God must be somehow the expression of an inner fellowship of God with himself. So, as the grace of our Lord Jesus Christ means that God is always giving, the fellowship of the Holy Spirit means that the life that God gives, is always returning to him again. At the springs of human thought and will, in the depths of personality, there is a channel through which God comes in. It is only when that channel is choked by human sin that he cannot enter, and then communion with God becomes impossible and the spiritual faculties of our being are paralysed, and – but for the grace of God, we die the eternal death.

Three Persons in One God
Three Persons in One God – let us rather say, three aspects of One Being, three ways in which the one God touches the life of we human beings. It is not the threefold nature of God that was the chief purpose of the doctrine of the Holy Trinity to assert, but rather the essential unity or oneness of God, whether revealed as the Father who sends, or as the Son who comes, or as the Spirit who abides. If the grace, the love, and the fellowship are forms of expression of one great truth, the one God is revealed to us in three modes of being, the permanent aspects of the Infinite Life, to whom we owe our own life and being, our hopes and our aspirations, our devotion and our worship.

Trinity Sunday   *Second Sermon*
Living our Lives

'Those who trust in the Lord renew their strength, they mount up with wings like eagles. They run and do not grow weary, they walk and never tire.' Isaiah 40.1 (ASB EP)

Difficulties

Many people find the idea of the Trinity a difficult concept to grasp, and something not very helpful to their devotional life. Our Muslim brethren accuse us of worshipping three Gods; the Jewish believer regards with great suspicion any attempt which seems to change the One-ness of God. Are we to say that the Trinity idea is a hindrance to the propagation of the Gospel? Or even, as some would say, a deviation from the simplicity of the teaching of Christ himself?

A Late Festival

It is true that the appearance of a Festival devoted specifically to the Holy Trinity is a late event in Christian Church history. St Chrysostom speaks of a festival of the Holy Martyrs, which was held seven days after Whit-Sunday; and the Greek Church still celebrates this, and not a Feast of the Trinity, on the First Sunday after Pentecost. St Thomas à Becket is credited with instituting Trinity Sunday in the English Church to satisfy his devotion to the Trinity, when he was Archbishop of Canterbury; and this may be why our English Church took to numbering the Sundays as 'After Trinity'. The Trinity Festival only became general in the Western Church in the twelfth and thirteenth centuries.

Theological Hair-splitting?

The nature of the Holy Trinity is a subject that lent itself to theological speculation. In the Middle Ages, the medieval schoolmen were fascinated by the subject of order in God's Universe, and they sought to find mystical relationships based upon proportions and numbers in every possible direction. Relics of their efforts remain with us in such things as the listing of Seven Sacraments, the eight sides we usually find to a font – symbolizing completion, the three steps to an altar, and so on.

The Trinity was expounded as part of this view of the great scheme of All Things. Earlier, of course, there were better and even savage quarrels over the exact definition of the Nature of God; and the Great Schism between East and West (still not completely healed) hinged over one line in the Creed – whether the Holy Spirit could be said to proceed from the Father alone, or from the Father and the Son.

A Wider View

Nowadays we tend to leave such problems to gather dust. We are more conscious of the vastness and the extent of this Universe, and the tiny place we have in it, and the mystery of it all, than perhaps our forefathers were. We have abandoned the idea of Heaven being up in the sky, and Hell down below as our ancestors assumed was true from the occasional eruptions of volcanoes spewing up molten red-hot rocks and lava. Our small intellect is, we realize, dwarfed by the great forces and distances and complexities; we may observe and measure with the cleverest of instruments, but the great questions are beyond our ken still.

This view must affect our religious insights also; and I think we tend to see the doctrine of the Trinity (for instance) less as a dry theory and more as our response to the experience of Christian living. We know God our Father, as the loving Creator. We know God as Redeemer, in the person of Jesus Christ. We know God as Upholder, guide and Inspirer, in the Holy Spirit. These are facts which we know from our personal devotional life.

Living our Lives

Do not dismiss the doctrine of the Holy Trinity as mere theological jargon. Of course we can never put into fallible human words the fullness of our living experience; but we should respect, and learn from the attempts that are made, as far as they clarify and help our own ideas, and above all as far as they assist us in the difficult path of our daily life and living. In our daily lives we 'wait for the Lord' and 'renew our strength' in our dependence on God, our Creator, Redeemer, Inspirer; some of us may indeed 'mount up with wings', others 'shall run and not be weary'; and even the least of us can 'walk and not faint'.

PRAYER

May holy Wisdom,
kind to humanity,
steadfast, sure and free,
the breath of the power of God –
may she who makes all things new,
in every age,

enter our souls, and make us friends of God,
through Jesus Christ.

(Patterns for Worship 52.46)

Corpus Christi (*Thanksgiving for the Holy Communion*)   Thursday 29 May   Life

*'Jesus said, Whoever eats my flesh and drinks my blood will live in me,
and I in him.' John 6.50 (Thanksgiving for Holy Communion, ASB;
Postcommunion Sentence)*

Living Bread

With five loaves and two little fishes, five thousand men, we are
told (John 6.10) were fed; and then our Lord gave one of his most
arresting discourses. He began to speak of food for human souls,
more wonderful and precious than had ever been dreamed of. 'I
am the bread of life' – 'I am the living bread which came down
from heaven; if any one eats of this bred, they will live for ever:
and the bread that I will give for the life of the world, is my
flesh.' (John 6.51) When the Jews were astounded at so hard and
extravagant a proclamation, our Lord, far from explaining away
his words, only repeated them with sharper and stronger emphasis
(6.55 and 58).

This teaching of the Lord was a crucial test; after it, many of
the disciples were so dismayed and so puzzled that they went
back, and walked no more with him (John 6.66) Those for whom
Simon Peter spoke were only kept true to their allegiance because
of their boundless confidence in Jesus – 'Lord, to whom shall we
go? You have the words of eternal life – you are the Holy One of
God.' (6.69)

It is easy to picture how the faithful disciples pondered over
these words of the Master, at once so emphatic and so startling,
until at the Last Supper the mystery was explained. Then our Lord
showed how his words were to be understood – he took the bread
into his hands and gave it to them, saying that it was his Body,
and the cup of wine, saying it was his Blood. At last the disciples
understood. St Luke tells us, in his account of the very first days

of the Church, how the Christians persevered in the daily 'Breaking of Bread' (Acts 2.42, 46) and he mentions later on the same rite in the typical Christian Sunday (20.7).

Down the Centuries
The Breaking of the Bread kept always and everywhere its central place; even when the laws were fiercest and persecution the most violent, the cry was 'We cannot get on without the *Dominicum*.' When at last the persecutions were over, and the Church was in peace, great basilicas were built, and the services – now openly performed – became elaborated and even splendid. Always and everywhere, worship culminated at the altar, and there the faithful gathered – men, women and children – to be fed with the bread of life.

It was sad indeed when frequent communion ceased to be usual; in the eighth century the Venerable Bede, the great historian, writing to the Archbishop of York, regretted that the English did not follow the example of the city of Rome, where thousands communicated every Sunday. By the Reformation period, it had become the ordinary practice to receive the Sacrament only once a year. There has been much recovery, but in our own time too many of our own people are still far from what was the universal custom in the springtime of the Early Church.

Heavenly Food
It is probably inevitable that the holy Eucharist should be thought of mainly in association with the Passion, the dreadful night in which he was betrayed. At the altar 'we show the Lord's death, until he come' (1 Cor. 11, 26) and we make before God 'the continual remembrance of the sacrifice of the death of Christ' (BCP Catechism). But the eucharistic banquet may well be conceived of, in another and brighter setting, attached to the scene of the multiplying of bread and fish, a feast of joy and of life; the multitude fed from the hands of Christ. So, through the ages the eternal Saviour offers himself 'as their ceaseless spiritual food to his creatures, possessed as they are by spiritual hunger for himself.' (Hugel)

The spiritual food gives strength and courage, joy and peace; however difficult and hard may be our life, the eucharist lifts us above our sorrows and cares, because it unites us with Jesus Christ. Even in the valley of the shadow of death it will be our provision for the way, and will not fail to bring us safe through the last and most hazardous adventure.

Preparation
The 1980 Book recommends 'careful, devotional, preparation . . . for every communicant' and the older Book suggests that first we should contemplate the greatness of the Gift – 'Our heavenly Father has given his Son our Saviour Jesus Christ, not only to die for us, but also to be our spiritual food and sustenance in that Holy Sacrament' – and we are to come 'holy and clean' to the 'Heavenly Feast' (First Exhortation in the Communion Service). The ancient discipline of the Church expects us to be fasting; and we should always examine our conscience to see what we have done wrong by thought, word or deed, or by omission; and confess to Almighty God. If serious and deliberate sin is on our conscience, we should seek 'the ministry of God's holy Word' and 'receive the benefit of Absolution' (First Exhortation).

> 'Twas God the Word that spake it,
> He took the Bread and brake it;
> And what the Word did make it,
> That I believe, and take it.
> > Queen Elizabeth I

Second Sunday after Pentecost (*Trinity 1*)
1 June   The True Vine
Jesus said, 'I am the true vine, and my Father is the vinedresser. Every branch in me that bears no fruit he cuts away, and every branch that does bear fruit he prunes to make it bear even more.' John 15.1 (ASB Gospel)

Representation
One of the most useful and important cultivated trees in the history of humanity, has been and still is, the vine. From it, of course, come the grapes, and from the grapes come refreshment, sweet juice and of course wine – 'Wine that maketh glad the heart of

126

man' (Psalm 104). The disciples would be familiar with the figure of the vine as representing Israel; Jeremiah speaks of Israel having been planted as a noble vine, but which became degenerate (2.21). Isaiah laments that, although the choicest and best vine was planted in God's vineyard, it yielded only sour wild grapes. The vine became a national emblem, and on the coins of old time, Israel is represented by a vine. Hence it is that when Jesus said, 'I am the true vine', the comparison he was pointing to was that between the present degenerate vine of Israel, and the new ideal of the spiritual Israel brought by the Lord himself as Messiah.

An Emblem

The vine therefore is an emblem chosen by Christ to represent himself, especially as the Source of spiritual life. He is the divinely appointed root and stem upon which the branches depend. The main shaft or stock will survive even if a branch or branches are trimmed off. They will wither and die but not the stock. So it is that we are dependent upon the Lord; but he is not dependent upon us, even though he wishes us to be joined to him. The image of the vine and its branches resembles St Paul's image of the Church and Christ, as the head and the members of the one body, because of the intimate connection, more so than vineyard owner and vines or sheep and shepherd, a close and vital union joining the believers to their Lord.

Unity

'Cut off from me you can do nothing' – and indeed the case is worse than that, for the Lord goes on to say (v. 6) that we, unfruitful, are cast forth and will wither; and the withered branches are gathered up and thrown into the fire.

Withered! Become dry and sapless, like the dry bones in the valley of the desert that the prophet Ezekiel saw. (Ezekiel 37)

There is no doubt that the disunity of the Church is a major reason for its incapacity to proclaim the gospel with power, for its weakness and variety of voices, its lack of true holiness.

'May they all be one, even as we are one . . .' Christ prayed to the Father (John 17, 21); but how far are we still from that ideal.

The Past

At first indeed the Church was virtually all one, and in each place Christians were gathered in one fellowship; thus St Paul could write to 'the church in Corinth', 'the church in Ephesus' and so on. Although there were disagreements over the admission of Gentiles, and some Christians continued to obey strictly the Hebrew law, most of the Church remained one for the first two hundred years; and the great majority remained united for over a thousand years.

Later, through differences of understandings about how Christ's humanity and divinity should be expressed, groups split off, like the Copts in Egypt and the Assyrians, and still survive as small churches in those countries today. The big break came when the Eastern Orthodox and the Western Roman churches divided formally. Then came the Reformation and further serious divisions.

Our Own Country

Here in England the Church was reformed, combining traditional elements with new ideas from the Continent; it was the ancient church of this country, catholic and reformed. However, there were those who desired a more drastic Reformation, and broke away into Baptists, Reformed and Quaker churches; later came Methodism, originally as a protest against the slackness of the Church of England as it was in the 18th century. Not exactly 'withered branches' although certainly 'cut off' from one another; and the Evangelical and Oxford Movements in the late 18th and early 19th centuries did bring revival. And there was the continuing Roman Church, freed from constraints and legal handicaps, and now itself much reformed. Contacts began to grow, and a genuine desire for unity began to make itself felt; especially was this so in the wake of the two great wars, where Christians were finding themselves in close contact, in desperate situations, with other Christians, and knowledge and understanding began to grow.

Today

The churches are much more aware of each other, and of other faiths, of course, not only the ancient Hebrew beliefs but those of Indian, Asian and African communities amongst us today. The interchange of ideas has led to mutual understanding and mutual enrichment, and the introduction of joint projects. There are meetings together of different churches and different faiths, and discussions as well as practical efforts to meet local needs and extend support and witness against prejudice and race hatred.

Let us then pray and work for the unity of Christians and for the fuller understanding of other faiths. In worship and discussion we can enlarge our own spiritual experience and knowledge; we can open ourselves for personal renewal and communities can understand and renew each other. Our aim should be the prayer of Christ our Lord, that 'they may all be one'.

> *To you, Creator of nature and humanity,*
> *of truth and beauty I pray:*
> *Hear my voice when I beg you to instil into the hearts*
> *of all human beings the wisdom of peace,*
> *the strength of justice*
> *and the joy of fellowship.*
> *O God, hear my voice, and grant to the world*
> *your everlasting peace.*
>
> *from the prayer of Pope John Paul II at Hiroshima*

> *O God of many names, lover of all nations:*
> *We pray for peace in our hearts,*
> *in our homes,*
> *in our nations,*
> *in our world;*
> *The peace of your will*
> *The peace of our need*
> *Dear Father of all.*
> *Guide us into your kingdom,*
> *into the paths of peace.*
>
> *Hasan Askari*

Pentecost 2   *Second Sermon*   **The Feast**

'Blessed is he who shall eat bread in the kingdom of God!' Luke 14.15
(ASB EP)

Invitations

In celebration of Her Majesty the Queen's 50th Wedding Anniversary, on 20th of November there will be many parties and events arranged. For important people, there will be invitations which are suitable to be accepted, and those which have to be refused. Drawing-up the lists will be a difficult task, no doubt, but those who are invited will be only too pleased, and anxious to be accepted.

The parable tells the story of some who were invited to a great party, but were reluctant to come on the day and at the time.

In the Old Testament God's relationship with his people is thought of in terms of a marriage; this is the Covenant. Disobedience to the commandments of God is considered to be infidelity and adultery. In the New Testament the Kingdom of heaven is spoken of as a wedding. Jesus is the bridegroom. Opponents ask why Jesus and his disciples fail to fast, as John and his disciples certainly do. The answer Jesus gives is that fasting would be as inappropriate as at a wedding. Jesus is the bridegroom, and there can be no thought of fasting while he is there, among them. As the hymn puts it:

> *'From heaven He came and sought her*
> *To be his holy bride.*
> *With his own blood He bought her,*
> *And for her love He died.'*
>
> *(NEH 484)*

The Feast

The wedding feast speaks of the bliss of the Kingdom. In the parable the invitations are sent to the guests. When everything was ready, it was the custom for a servant to be sent round to remind the guests. But on this occasion he is met with excuses: one guest had bought some land and cannot wait to inspect it, another, a prosperous man, had bought five yoke of oxen and was anxious to try them. A third had just got married, and was not to be separated from his new wife. Not to offer hospitality was rude, but to refuse it when offered was worse.

The master was rightly indignant, and determined that his table was to be supplied with guests. He ordered his servants to go out into the streets, and bring in the poor, the blind, the crippled.

The servants did so, and still there was room to spare.

The master's determination was inflexible; he told his servants to go outside the city walls, and bring in those in the highways and hedges. 'I want my house to be full!'

The Outsiders
Maybe some of the invited guests thought that they could do what they wanted to do, and then come to the feast later. But not so; there would be no room, since there places had been taken by others, by outsiders, the rough and tumble of outcasts and drop-outs, the lowest of the low.

The pious Jews, tied by their religious laws and the complexities of keeping all the complicated rules, rejected their true function, that of bringing people to God. But God's purpose will not be defeated; that refusal was to lead to the preaching to the Gentiles, and their inclusion in the Kingdom of God. Our acceptance of Christ must lead others to the same knowledge and acceptance on their part; otherwise we are being false to the teaching and example of Jesus Christ.

Third Sunday after Pentecost (*Trinity 2*)
8 June   The New Life

'As Christ was raised from the dead, in the splendour of the Father, so also we might set our feet upon the new path of life.' Romans 6.4 (ASB NT Reading)

New Life!
The New Testament epistles ring with the certainty of the newness of life to which believers are called. In some real and actual measure, the Saviour's experience is to be theirs. He lives, never to die again; death has no power over him at all. In his lifetime on earth he had to reckon with sin; but in his sacrificial death he

vanquished sin. His life is now lived utterly in relation to God. St Paul is telling us that we, as believers, are to take the same position regarding sin. When we are tempted to sin, we are to reckon ourselves as to be mere corpses, dead to sin, and upon whom temptation has no effect. Better, to put it another way, we are living in relation to God, and to him alone. We are now 'in union with Christ Jesus' and as he lives to God, so do we.

Change

Cynically, people use the old saying 'Can the leopard change his spots?' when someone says or tries to act 'in a Christian way', after an experience of conversion. It may sound ridiculous, yet something has been affected in the life of that person. The new life of the Christian is the new life of response to God, through Jesus Christ. It has been said, 'Religion begins with the request on the human side, and a response on the Divine.' This may indeed be so, but the New Testament makes it clear that as the desire for God, and the longing for a better and a fuller life is like the implanting of a seed in the human soul, the very desire for God takes its origin in the heavenly initiative. In fact, all living seems to be summed up in the idea of a response to whatever is around us.

Christian Life

For us as Christians, our response, our living, is a response to the Creator, the God who made us, and who gave us – or planned that we should develop – the capacity to respond to him. Gradually, and early on, humanity found the ability to keep the commandments of God, whether given in the form of 'tablets of stone' or as the result of our own observation and learning, as the way of life which produced the greatest happiness for us and around us. Within limits, we have the choice of where we will live and how we will work, so we can select our environment. Not that that means we will, of necessity, be a truly good or helpful person; there are plenty of scoundrels and self-centred humans who show just the opposite.

An Ideal placed before us

Not all of us reach the ideal, as we know only too well. But if we accept the teaching of Christ, we will – with faltering and sometimes falling steps, make the effort to struggle on the way of holiness to our ideal, the City of God. Like St Paul's converts, we are indeed a 'mixed bag' – but our faces are turned towards the light. If we are striving to live the Christian life, our faces are set towards the Heavenly City, and we share in the love of Christ, who said in his last great speech to his friends and disciples, 'As the Father has loved me, so I have loved you. Remain in my love; if you keep my commandments, you will remain in my love, and your joy be complete.'

Pentecost 3   *Second Sermon*   **The Saint of Iona**

'If I dwell in the uttermost parts of the sea, even there your hand shall lead me: and your right hand shall hold me.' Psalm 139, 8.9 (The Cloud of Witnesses)

Columba

St Columba (c. 521–597) or Colim Cille, to give his Irish and original name, was born in Donegal; as a child he lived in a house set on a small hill overlooking three lakes and overshadowed by great mountains, beautiful but the haunt of wolves. A child of a noble family, he was put out to nurse with a woman of the O'Firghil clan, and was brought up in this wild place, where eagles, badgers, pine martens and ravens, as well as wolves, found their homes. From early days, the boy devoted himself to the Faith and to the search for wisdom. He studied under St Finnian at Clonard, as well as at the monastic school of Morville; and beside languages and religion, he learnt to love the songs of Ireland.

As a young and wealthy devotee, he joined the monastic order at Clonard and was ordained priest, and founded many religious houses in his homeland. He became an expert copyist, and spent much time making copies of the Gospels and the Psalter.

Trouble

When Columba was about forty years old, an unfortunate and bitter quarrel arose between the saint and Diarmuid the king, resulting in the deaths of many clan members. Columba was held responsible, banished from his monastery, and after much sorrow and heartsearching left Ireland in the year 563. With a dozen companions, Columba embarked in a coracle and eventually landed on a desolate beach on the island of Iona, bleak and flat and featureless, but sheltered by the mountains of Mull. He could look back and see his beloved Irish mountains away in the far west, rising above the sea.

Missionary Work

Building the monastery took up a couple of years, then he and his companions began an immense work of conversion among the heathen Picts. He journeyed incessantly into the Highlands; penetrated the stronghold of the heathen King Brude at Inverness, and so impressed the man that he was converted, with his people. During what time Columba spent at Iona, he continued the work of copying manuscripts and the 'Book of Durrow' and the 'Book of Kells', two exquisite manuscript books, are thought by experts to have been – if not entirely his work – supervised by him and carried to completion by his pupils.

Visitors and Pilgrims

There was a constant stream of visitors and pilgrims, surprising perhaps, since Columba was not an easy person, and it was said of him 'that of all qualities, gentleness was precisely the one in which Columba failed the most'. He was as hard on others as on himself, but as he became older those who sought him never failed to find sympathy and help.

He prophesied the future fame of the island: 'Unto this place, small and mean though it be, great homage shall yet be paid, not only by the kings and people of the Scots, but by the rulers of barbarous and distant nations, with their people.' He died before the altar of the Abbey in 597.

Today, there are more pilgrims making the journey to Iona probably than ever before. St Columba's Festival is on June 9th.

COLLECT

Most loving Father,
who gave such grace to your servant Columba,
that in his life and works
he reflected the glory of your Son:
Grant that those whom you call to serve you in the gospel
may be radiant with love
and cheerful with adversity,

awaiting the redemption of all things in Christ;
who with you lives and reigns,
in the unity of the Spirit,
one God, for ever and ever.

(The Cloud of Witnesses)

Fourth Sunday after Pentecost (*Trinity 3*)
15 June   The Command of Love

'What I command you is, to love one another.' John 15.17 (ASB Gospel)

Mutual Love

In this chapter, the love of Christ for his followers and the mutual love of those followers for each other, is given great prominence. Our text is clearly related to verses 12 and 13, which begin the Gospel for today. 'This is my commandment: love one another, as I have loved you. A man can have no greater love than to lay down his life for his friends.' We can see clearly here that this mutual love of Christians, reproducing their Lord's love for them, is to be measured in terms of his own precious death. For the disciple's action, the disciple's gift, a willing giving up of the most precious thing we know, a human life – here is compared by Jesus himself, to the tremendous act of his own redeeming love.

'Love one another' – here is the central core of Jesus' teaching to his followers. The old writer Tertullian, heathen that he was, wrote these striking words: 'Behold these Christians – see how they love one another!'

No longer Servants

Up to the time of the last evening together, there was always a certain reserve between Christ and the apostles – broken, perhaps, with the 'Inner Circle' – Peter, John and James – who were on a closer and more personal footing than the rest of the apostles. But here, in the Upper Room, there is a sense of closer communion between the Lord and all his disciples – he speaks as openly now to all the group, as in earlier days he might have been confined to just the small threesome. 'I shall not call you servants any more ... You are my friends.'

But in what sense could it be said that Jesus had 'friends'? In general, friendship was to be defined in terms of mutual advantage. But Jesus had no common interest shared with his disciples; he did not stand to gain anything by their friendship. He was their master, and it would be natural to consider them as pupils or servants.

Friends
But now he is calling them his friends, for the only reason that he had chosen them to be his friends, and had given them his love (13.1) to the full extent possible, and as would be understood soon, they would be receiving the same hate and hostile reaction as he had provoked during his time on earth. All this is implied in Jesus' reiterated commandment: 'Love one another.'

And as Jesus is friends with his disciples, his followers, are we friends with other followers today? Do we see Christ in everyone we meet, do we recognize all others as brothers and sisters in the family of God, the disciples of Christ. Is there any hostility in my heart towards anyone? Is there a smile of recognition for everyone we meet, a gratitude that each is a brother or sister for whom Christ died, as he died for me?

Pentecost 4   *Second Sermon*   **A Guide**

Philip asked, 'Do you understand what you are reading?' And he said, 'How can I, unless some one guides me?' Acts 8.30, 31 (ASB NT Reading)

Not Knowing ...
How many people there are, who cannot understand unless they have 'someone to guide me' as the Ethiopian said to Philip. He had been on a pilgrimage to Jerusalem; no doubt he had been impressed with the sacrifices and the ceremonial, the beautiful buildings, the psalms and the music, and the clever words of the priests and teachers of the Law.

But something was missing. He was returning home unsatisfied; spiritually speaking, he was 'lost'.

Our Task

All Christians must be ready to be, in some sense, missionaries. We are all witnesses to Christ.

True, we may not all go to foreign lands, and win people over to Christ, by our preaching or teaching. But, we can all – besides being witnesses in our own small neighbourhood – through our example and our behaviour, look for the 'lost sheep'. Is there anyone you know who seems bewildered by the problems of life? Anyone who has lost their way, is looking for some guide, baffled by the different answers given to the great questions of the day?

Our Opportunity

Here is our opportunity. We can place ourselves alongside that person, be ready to listen, give them a chance to pour out their problems, difficulties, sorrows, loneliness.

We do not have to be clever talkers, trained theologians, or anything like that; we have simply to listen. In the first place, let the other person know and feel that someone cares. Let them feel they are not alone. Don't try and solve their problems – if need be, take the story to a wise and confidential person, a counsellor, the local clergyman, maybe; get help. Maybe you can introduce the person to the local church community – but move gradually and with care.

The anxious shepherd, trying to reach the sheep caught on the cliff-side, is cautious and careful – lest worse happen and the sheep fall; but he is persistent all the same, and won't leave until some improvement has happened. Likewise the woman in the house – she searches and sweeps and does not give up, until the precious coin is safely found.

Let us open our hearts and minds to the Wonderful Counsellor, and praying, 'Come, thou Holy Spirit, come', be made wise in the things of God, and helpful to others who may be in need of spiritual guidance, sensible advice, and often above all, just encouragement to keep going . . .   G.A.

Fifth Sunday after Pentecost (*Trinity 4*)
22 June   Living in the Light

'Live like people who are at home in daylight, for where light is, there all goodness springs up, all justice and truth. Try to find out what would please the Lord.' Ephesians 5.10 (ASB NT Reading)

The Sacred Law

Although the Jews regarded all the books of the Bible as sacred and holy, they did not give to all of them quite the same place. It was in Exodus, with the Ten Commandments, that the greatness of Scripture reached its full height and grandeur. The Law, they said, was delivered to Moses by God complete and entire, and it was literally and completely the word of God. Jewish boys were taught the Law from the first, and therefore had the Ten Commandments (our first reading today) 'engraved upon their souls', to quote the historic Jewish writer, Josephus.

In our Gospel, Matthew records the incident of a wealthy young man who comes to Jesus, asking how to obtain eternal life – what good deeds should he do? Jesus, if we may make such a comment, seems tired out; he has had crowds of people following him, awkward trick questions, troops of children; and now this smooth youngster, freshly washed and scented, in his expensive robes. He makes an awkward contrast with the Lord and the disciples, dusty from the roads and the traffic, clothes grubby and none too fresh. It must have been annoying; and Jesus gives – not some special advice, but – a very general answer – 'Keep the Commandments!' The young man in his turn is annoyed; he doesn't like being spoken to as if a child. Here he is, talking in public with this rough fellow – striking though he is, he is only a carpenter's son; a nobody, socially speaking!

'*Which* commandments?' he queries sharply. He wants full value for his condescension. Jesus gives a stock reply, as if addressing a schoolboy; he mentions some of the great Ten Commandments, and adds a general one from Leviticus (19.18), which is regarded as a short summary of the Law.

The young man is not to be put down. 'Of course I observe all these; but what else should I do?'

Jesus attaches, apparently, no value to extra 'pious works', i.e. just spending money, which the young man may have in mind.

Instead he replies, bluntly, 'If you really want to go the whole way to perfection, sell off all your possessions and give all the money to the poor – and come and join me!'

The young man goes off, disgruntled and heavy hearted. He doesn't want to give away his wealth, nor break with his social position. No rough road for him!

A Strong Parable
Jesus is still irritated, and gives vent to his irritation with a difficult saying about the impossibility of the rich 'entering the Kingdom', and the historic and bitter proverb about the eye of the needle and the camel. The disciples are upset and astonished – 'Who can be saved?' and Christ – perhaps feeling he had overdone the harshness – reassures them by telling them that 'With God, everything is possible, however impossible it seems to mere human beings.'

> Take away from us, O Lord,
> the love of money,
> forgive our impatience,
> dispel ignorance,
> and perfect our faith,
> for your Name's sake. Amen.

Pentecost 5 *Second Sermon* **Unity in Christ**
'God had granted life-giving repentance to the Gentiles also.' Acts 11.18 (ASB EP)

A Problem – and its Solution
Here is the Early Church confronting a problem which might – if not solved – have meant that Christianity would have survived in the world as a minor off-shoot of Judaism, never as the great and world-embracing religion that it became. The reason? Many – perhaps the majority, certainly at this early stage – of those who embraced the Christian Faith, were Jews; but alongside these, were the non-Jewish converts, the Gentiles, that is to say. These were often from the ranks of the 'Hearers', that is, non-Jews who were attracted to the synagogues by the high ethical standards of the

Hebrew communities, as compared to the confused and mysterious religions of the pagans. Those Hearers who wished to go further than being merely 'Hearers' however, faced the question of circumcision and indeed all the complicated Jewish rules of life and behaviour, to which any convert would have to conform. On the Jewish side, there was naturally a very strong reserve about the admission of Gentile sympathizers, as possibly compromising the faithful with pagan customs and habits; on the other hand, most Jews were prepared to believe that their religion was ultimately destined by God for Gentiles and indeed all peoples of the world.

Unity in Christ

It need not have been a great shock to the apostles to learn that Gentiles also were accepting the Word of God. The problem was that the food laws stood in the way of their full reception. Peter's vision on the housetop (Acts 10.9–16) set him on the path of recognition (vv. 34 to 43) which is confirmed from heaven by the gift of the Holy Spirit, and then by baptism (v. 48). Peter at Jerusalem tells of these experiences to the apostles and others; the conclusion forced upon him, and accepted in due course by the Jerusalem Church (ch. 11, v. 18) is that 'God has granted life-giving repentance to the Gentiles also'.

All believers, whether from Jews or Gentiles, are to be one in Christ. Each believer, with his own particular gift from God, is to serve the Church and the world. St Paul works out this important and unifying fact in his letter to the Ephesians (ch. 2, v. 13), 'You who once were far off have been brought near in the blood of Christ, for he is our peace who has made us both one.'

Diversity

Unity is enhanced rather than impaired by diversity. The believer has to find his or her place and function of service, in fellowship with others and the whole Church. Each member has a contribution to make, to the life of the whole. The root meaning of ministry is service, and the whole Church has a ministry to the world. Doubts and jealousies are to be swept away, and the path made open for all to come to Christ, to carry his word and work to everyone, everywhere, without distinction of colour or of sex. The prejudices and biased traditions of former days – like the prejudices and traditions of the apostles and brethren of Judea –

must be seen as impediments and obstacles to the work of the Spirit. Let the Way of Jesus, in truth and love, bring us together in growing spiritual maturity, thus bringing more and more power to the work of Christ in our world today.

SS Peter & Paul the Apostles (*Pentecost 6, Trinity 5*) Sunday 29 June The Rock-Man

'God who made Peter an apostle to the Jews, also made Paul an apostle to the Gentiles.' Galatians 2.8; or for St Peter, 'Jesus said to his disciples, Who do you say that I am? and Peter answered, You are the Christ of God.' Luke 9.20 (ASB Introductory Sentences)

The Rock-Man
Jesus said, 'You shall be called Peter', which means rock. And Peter was to become a 'rock-man' for his solidity and immovability; the foundation-stone of the band of disciples. Yet his character had to develop before this could be truly realized. Yes, he was loving, devoted, loyal – but wavering at times, mistaken in zeal, impetuous – and was to go to the extent of denying his Master. Yet, he was a rock-like man, and his faith in Christ as Messiah was also to be rock-like. A touching fad or habit of Christ was his liking for giving his friends and companions nick-names; in the case of Peter his choice was excellent. He knew his man – although when under extreme pressure, Peter denied knowing his Lord. 'I would never deny you,' he said, but as we know all too well, when it came to the point, he gave way. Three times he denied Christ; and after the Lord's resurrection, he asked Peter three times the intimate question, 'Do you love me?' Peter's heart, purified from his former fears, was able to make the simple reply, 'Yes, Lord; you know that I love you.' It was Peter who was given the commission to 'Feed my sheep; feed my lambs' and we believe he carried that commission to the centre of the known world, Rome itself, and died there a martyr's death.

The Convert
If Peter was the Apostle to the Jews, Paul was the Apostle to the Gentiles. He was, of course, converted from being the persecutor of the infant Church, to being its greatest missionary. And how

much we owe to his penetrating, wide-ranging trained mind, as revealed to us in his letters.

The story of his life is the story of the spread of the Gospel from Jerusalem, where it was first preached, to Rome, the capital of the Empire – the Empire Paul saw the vast possibilities of, for the evangelizing of the known world, and of which – as a free-born citizen – he was very proud. Paul enabled the Gospel message to break free from its confines among the Hebrew people, and to reach out – with its transforming power – to every country in the world.

He may indeed have differed in opinion in the early days with Peter, especially concerning the mission to the Gentiles. More than once, Paul speaks of rebuking Peter to his face for what Paul saw as an out-dated Jewish exclusiveness. And Peter cannot refrain from giving a somewhat double-edged compliment to Paul on his letters, written 'according to the wisdom given him' but with 'some things in them hard to understand'. (2 Peter 3, 15–16) But the joy is that their common commitment to Christ, and the proclamation of the Gospel, were stronger than any minor differences.

Martyrs

And both eventually carried that cause to Rome, and both in the end bore witness to their faith and their cause, by martyrdom.

Upon these two 'foundation pillars' may the Church of God ever stand, and in firmness of faith proclaim the Gospel of her Lord and Master, Jesus Christ the King of Martyrs.

A PRAYER FROM THE EASTERN CHURCHES

Lord, you have founded your Church
upon the firmness of Peter's faith
and upon Paul's wisdom and understanding,
and the inspired teaching and writing of both,
to combat error and to defeat ungodliness;
taught by both your Apostles
in the knowledge of God our Father,
we praise you, Lord Jesus, our Lord and Saviour,
for both these Pillars of power and truth,
and grant that we may come to share with them
in your kingdom of eternal life. Amen.

SS Peter & Paul the Apostles   *Second Sermon*
The Two Pillars

(ASB EP Lessons: Ezekiel 3.22–end; John 21.15–22)
'Lo, the glory of the Lord stood there ... and I fell on my face; but the
Spirit entered into me, and set me upon my feet. 'You shall say to them,
'Thus says the Lord God.' Ezekiel 3.23

Conversion

The Bible scholars who choose our Lessons, picked for tonight an
Old Testament event which foreshadows the story of the Conversion of St Paul; it is the story of the Conversion of Ezekiel, we
might say. The message that the great Old Testament Prophet
brings to the people of Jerusalem of his own time, was God's
promise of the coming of a Messiah, with a new Covenant replac-
ing the old, and new life revitalizing the nation. The prophet's
messages include the Messiah being 'a shoot from the root of
Jesse' (17.2–24), and the prophecy of the miraculous new life being
brought to the 'valley of dry bones' (37.1–14), and finally a vision
of the land at peace, with a New Temple from which pure water
will continually flow, and which will have around it (as in Revelation) great trees, whose leaves have the property of miraculous
healing.

Yes, Ezekiel certainly looked forward to the rule of the Messiah,
and the regeneration and new freedom of the People of God, that
would be brought about by the Messiah; so Ezekiel is regarded
as a prophet of Christ and the Church, and in particular the
missionary work of St Paul and the Early Christians, under the
guidance of the Holy Spirit.

Peter

For St Peter, we have the almost private conversation between
Jesus and himself, on that strange morning when the unknown
figure on the beach turned out to be – wonder of wonders! – the
living Lord. After breakfast, the two, apart from the others, entered
into a private conversation. 'Simon, son of John' (note Jesus does
not use the nickname 'Peter' – Rock, which he gave him at the
start of their relationship – for the moment, it is back to formality
as between two strangers), 'Do you love me, more than these?'
(the other members of the band). Peter can only reply very simply,

'Yes, Lord; you know that I love you.' A second and a third time the Lord repeats his question. At the third time, Peter breaks down; and Jesus accepts him once again.

The Lord tells Peter that there will come a time when he will be bound and dragged off to death; 'Follow me,' he says – maybe he sees all too clearly the martyrdom that Peter eventually faces in Rome, and is preparing him for that day.

'Follow me' is the same command that Jesus gives us today, in our own age and our own place. Let us make up our minds that we too, will follow our Lord, and do all we can to carry out the rest of the command – 'Tend my sheep, feed my sheep, feed my lambs.'

> Almighty God,
> who inspired your apostle Saint Peter
> to confess Jesus as Christ and Son of the living God:
> build up your Church upon this rock,
> that in unity and peace
> it may proclaim one truth and follow one Lord,
> your Son our Saviour Jesus Christ.

Collect for the Confession of St Peter (January 18) (PHG)

Seventh Sunday after Pentecost (*Trinity 5*)
6 July   Forgiveness

Peter went up to Jesus and said, 'Lord, how often must I forgive my brother if he wrongs me? As often as seven times?' Jesus answered, 'Not seven, I tell you, but seventy-seven times.' Matthew 18.21 (ASB Gospel)

Is Seven the Perfect Number?

It seems that Peter was not taking account of how God views forgiveness, but looking at the human and personal aspect. After all, he was offering not a bad attitude; quite a long distance from the strict Hebrew view – 'An eye for an eye, and a tooth for a tooth.' And seven was a reasonable number of forgivings; it was a sacred number, surely – the seventh heaven, the seven virtues and the seven deadly sins, to take just a few examples of the sacred

ORDER FORM

CHURCH PULPIT YEAR BOOK 1998

to be published October 1997

by Chansitor Publications Limited
(a wholly owned subsidiary of Hymns Ancient and Modern Limited,
a registered charity)

ORDER NOW
TO ENSURE YOU RECEIVE YOUR COPY

The Church Pulpit Year Book 1998
will commence from Advent Sunday
30 November 1997

*Please supply .... copy(ies) at the special pre-publication price
of £13.99 incl. U.K. postage. (Thereafter published price: £14.99 incl. U.K.
postage.
Overseas postage extra – a quotation will be supplied on receipt of order.*

Name Revd/Mr/Mrs/Miss/Ms ....
(Please PRINT details clearly)

Delivery Address

....

....

....

.... *Postcode* ....

Tel. No ....

To order this form must be returned, with your payment, to:

CHANSITOR PUBLICATIONS LIMITED
16 BLYBURGATE
BECCLES
SUFFOLK NR34 9TB
Tel: 01502-711231

(see overleaf for Church Times details)

***Mary had not realised how interesting
Church Times was***

seven. However, Jesus has been giving fairly stern rulings on a number of matters, including a condemnation of any follower who causes another to sin, perhaps especially aimed at those false leaders who lead the simpler brethren astray. In any case, it must have been something of a surprise to be told that forgiveness must be like God's, limitless – 'seventy-seven times, not seven'.

Forgive Us As We Forgive Others
We have been taught to pray:

> *'Forgive us our trespasses (sins)*
> *as we forgive those who trespass against us'*

After all, it is only the forgiving spirit that can be forgiven. That is the meaning and application of the parable in the Gospel for today. There can be no arithmetic in forgiveness.

Yet in some aspects of life, there is a limit which is expected to be kept. For instance in the matter of ordinary honesty, we recognize that we must pay what we owe, pay a decent price for what we buy, in other words obey the Eighth Commandment – 'Thou shalt not steal', in spirit and in actual dealings. Then we shall have done what is expected of us.

But as to forgiving and forgiveness, here is a spiritual obligation laid upon us, with no limits. How is this, we may query? The answer is, that forgiveness is God-like, and is part of the heavenly ethics.

> *'Forgiveness is above law, as the king who pardons*
> *in clemency, is above the judge who in justice*
> *is compelled to condemn.'*

God's Forgiveness
Forgiveness from God depends on two things. First of all, upon repentance. We are bound to ensure that penitence must be a real sorrow for sin. It is not sorrow for being 'found out', but sorrow for the actual sin itself. Then there must be confession and a real attempt at restitution.

Then, secondly, there must be a sincere and steadfast purpose to achieve an amendment of life. Forgiveness is neither easy to grant – nor to receive. Yet, it is the gracious gift of God to those who truly are seeking it, and the Church has the authority and the power to grant it. We are wise if we avail ourselves of it, for if we neglect so to do, it is to us a grievous loss. After all, it is the religion of the Cross which – knowingly or unknowingly – our human hearts are seeking; the religion which speaks of pardon and peace, of sin forgiven and of grace bestowed.

Pentecost 7 *Second Sermon* A Short Course on Discipline **(1) Discipline of the Body.**

'Glorify God in your body' 1 Cor. 6,20 (Suggested second lesson: Romans 12,1–13)

Giving Things Up?

Mention the subject of discipline of the body, and many people will think we mean 'giving things up' – like in Lent, we give up sugar, alcohol, tobacco, sweets and so on. Or rather, maybe we think of other people giving things up! Or on the other hand, we may think in terms of physical exercise, running round the block morning and evening, taking a bicycle instead of the car, using one of those home exercise machines that promise an almost immediate loss of weight and a new, slim look. We prefer to take a machine, maybe, because it's a short cut to our new look, and also we can do it 'in the privacy of our own home'.

In the literary history of this country, one of the great giants was Dr Samuel Johnson, he who invented the dictionary, and wrote much else. He was a physical giant as well as a literary one, or at least he had a much huger body than would be thought healthy today. His tongue was sharp, his mind acute, yet he was a very religious man and his prayers are very beautiful. It was Dr Johnson who remarked:

> Wickedness is always easier than virtue, for it takes the short cut to everything.

Do we slip up on our discipline, do we take short cuts in what we do – not least in our spiritual life? Do we find time for penitence, which means taking some time to look back at what we have been doing, and seeking forgiveness of our sinfulness, especially sins of laziness, indulgence or carelessness? Fasting is a form of discipline, and expresses our intention well; it places a check upon ourselves where we can really feel it – or even see it – as we get our weight down to something like what it should be.

Right Values
Our Christian faith (unlike some other religions) values the body; but at a realistic price. St Paul illustrates this: 'Do you not know that your body is a temple of the Holy Spirit, which you have from God. You are not your own; you were brought with a price – so glorify God in your body.' (1 Cor. 6.19f) The implications of this are profound, for the spiritual finds much of its expression in the physical frame we inhabit. God himself chose to become incarnate, to take a human body, and so he shows us how it should be holy. One of the greatest images of the Christian community is that of the living Body of Christ.

Taking care of our bodies is part of our duty as Christians. We should take an assessment of how well – or badly – we are treating our physical needs. Maybe we should get more sleep, rather than taking on more and more extra work or activities. Do we check from time to time with our doctor and our optician? Do we exercise – just straightforward walking whenever possible, helps to keep us fitter. To each our own assessment, remembering that abuse of the body, in whatever way, is a denial of God's gift of our creation.

'Natural'?
A common expression today is 'If it's natural, it must be good.' This is a dangerous idea, not least because it is wrong; for the Christian vision has always seen human beings as fallen creation, incomplete on our own until we refer ourselves and all we do, to our Creator God. St Paul sees the need to keep his body in check, under daily discipline; he uses the image of the athlete running in the Marathon, or the boxer in the ring –

'I do not run aimlessly, I do not box as one beating the air; but I pommel my body and subdue it, lest after preaching to others I myself should be disqualified.' (1 Cor. 9.26f)

Just as the individual body needs care and right management, so also does the community, the communal body. Nationally, and as a parish, we need to have a discipline on how we act. Parts of our life as a community can all too easily become distorted, and the result can be that our purpose, or rather, God's purpose, can be frustrated. St Paul spoke of the need for a careful discipline of the body, that all its members might work in harmony together. Such a discipline demands a realistic acceptance of ourselves – as we are, not pretending to be someone or something different.

Return
Ultimately, of course, our bodies will return to the dust from which they came; for they are but temporal items. We cannot cling to them, yet they are the framework given us by God for our time on earth. And during that time, they should reflect something at least of his glory. Part of that reflection begins at the altar, as we receive the sacrament of the body of Christ, the gift through which we can grow to the fullness of life

> *'I appeal to you, by the mercies of God, to present*
> *your bodies as a living sacrifice, holy and acceptable*
> *to God, which is your spiritual worship.'*
> *St Paul: Romans 12.1*

Eighth Sunday after Pentecost (*Trinity 7*)
13 July   The Command of Love
'What I command you is, to love one another.' John 15.17 (ASB Gospel)

The Key-note
In our Gospel reading this morning, the love of our Lord Jesus Christ for his followers, and the mutual love of those followers for each other, is given the strongest prominence as a vital key to the true Christian life. Our text is clearly related to verses 12 and 13:

> 'This is my commandment, that you love one another as I have loved you. Greater love has no one than this, that a man lay down his life for his friends.'

We may well comment on this saying of the Lord, that the mutual love of Christians (reproducing their Lord's love for them) is now – it is made perfectly clear – to be measured by his death upon the Cross. What such love involved, had been illustrated already by the Lord's servant-role in the washing of his friends' feet. The lowly task of the lowest was taken by the Lord and Master. The love it signified is about to be seen in its full and dreadful extent of cruelty and pain, in the bitter and agonizing execution of Jesus on the cross.

Friendship

Jesus calls his disciples 'friends' for the first time; the question may be raised as in what sense could it be said that Jesus had 'friends'? To be blunt, it could be asserted that Jesus had no 'common interest' with his disciples; he did not stand to gain anything through their friendship. However close they were in their travels along the dusty roads of Palestine, however much they depended on one another, the fact was that Jesus was their Master, their Leader, their Teacher; and it would be natural and right to consider them as 'pupils' or 'his servants'. In the carpenter's shop they would have ranked as 'Learners', no doubt! But now he calls them his friends, because he has chosen them and loved them to 'the fullness of his love' (v. 1). All this is implied by the reiterated use, by the Lord, of his 'New Commandment' – 'Love one another!'

Three Notes

We may well say that faith in Christ, love for him and for one another, and a loving effort to bring in the world's salvation – these are three of the 'notes' of true Christian discipleship. If we have a true faith in the Lord, and a confident trust in him through all events and troubles, we do not only offer him our adoration and love, but also give – joyfully and willingly, our total obedience. Christ's command of love is not a sort of general philanthropy, but rather a deep and sincere affection, care and trust, towards our brothers and sisters. There may indeed be difference between Christians in many ways in our human life 'here below' – differences of tastes, habits, outlook and so on – yet these do not, cannot, interfere with those ties of loyalty and love which are so strong that no force can separate them.

Motive
This mutual love has its source, its inspiration, and its strength in the love of Christ for his people. 'As I have loved you' is the phrase by which our Lord refers all duty and all virtue to himself and his example. For the believer, Christ is the Master in all our life and all our conduct. Jesus loves the whole world – this little spinning planet in the vastness of the universe, with its crew of living creatures – with a love in which he identifies his People with himself. We are to show our devotion to him, by loving humanity as he loves us. Christ alone is our perfect example; he loves his people with a love that is constant, patient and forbearing.

Proof
The love we show to our brothers and sisters in Christ and to others, is the test which our Lord has chosen. It is the proof to the unbeliever: 'We know that we have passed over from death to life; we know this, because we love our brothers and sisters' (1 John 3.14) Here then is proof, proof to be recognized by our people: Love is a means of recognition. It is the language that tells us we have met a fellow national; it is also an argument calculated to convince the world.

> *O God, our Creator and Father,*
> *your Son has founded the Church*
> *to be a divinely ordered community,*
> *to be holy and loving,*
> *caring and serving,*
> *for all peoples and all truth;*
> *a pattern for the world's life,*
> *a servant community to humanity*
> *a force for goodness and love.*
> *Give us your grace and strength*
> *to bring freedom and fullness of life.*
> *G.E.*

Pentecost 8   *Second Sermon*   A Short Course on Discipline   **(2) Discipline of the Tongue**
'Out of the abundance of the heart the mouth speaks.' *Matthew 12,34*
(Suggested second lesson: Matthew 12,22–32)

Neglected Subject?

Discipline of the tongue is something not often spoken about in our time. But the importance of words, either spoken or written, is something that most of us will recognize all too well. Lawyers, writers, and others all know the need for careful discipline in the use of words. Upon the choice of perhaps one word jobs, fortunes, even life itself may depend. We allow – our society allows – freedom of speech, but slander is illegal; where exactly the line is drawn is a tricky problem and can give rise to furious debate. There is perhaps too much speech around today; the media gives ever-increasing opportunities for more people to give more comment on more issues – too often, we may think, at the expense of truth, for many issues are trivialized by the quick comment which necessarily skates over the complexities that may be involved.

> 'To everything there is a season, and a time to every purpose under heaven' said the writer of Ecclesiastes, and added,
> 'A time to keep silence, and a time to speak.' (Eccl. 3.1,7)

Silence, and Emphasis

A priest tells us: 'I well remember watching at a scene of great distress, where the priest went straight to the person concerned, sat beside them and held their hand. Nothing was said. Yet, more was communicated in that simple action than words could ever say. A time indeed to keep silence. If this is true of our communication with one another, how much more is it true of prayer, our communication with God.'

A proper economy of words is part of the discipline of the tongue. In the Sermon on the Mount, Jesus spoke against the use of great oaths and embellishments, whose intended purpose seemed to be to support or emphasize our meanings. He said: 'Do not swear at all, neither by heaven ... nor by earth ... Let what you say be simply "Yes" or "No".' (Matthew 5.34–37)

All of us can recognize the danger and temptation of over-emphasis; we try to give credence to what we are saying by adding this or that. How easy it is from there, to enter into the treacherous realms of half-truth and then falsehood. 'Speak the truth openly and simply,' said Jesus. Let the argument stand or fall on its merits alone.

Influence of the Tongue

Again, Jesus said: 'Not what goes into the mouth defiles anyone, but what comes out of the mouth, that defiles.' (Matt. 15.18) The tongue gives expression to the inner person; in the Book of Proverbs we read 'The tongue of the righteous is choice silver', or 'A gentle tongue is a tree of life.' But also we read: 'Death and life are in the power of the tongue.' There are times when a word has brought hope to despair; but also a word may cut us to the quick, dashing our hopes, bringing pain and disappointment. The bitter aspect is that the speaker is often quite unaware of the effect the words may be having. How many times it has been necessary to mend fences broken down by sheer misunderstandings – words carelessly thrown out or misheard.

The danger of gossip is always present – the chance to run down someone, or to be seen as the one who knows more than others. How subtly easy to do this under the guise of concern or fellowship; and how easy to cause damage by a word 'casually' dropped. The mere hint – nothing direct said – but suspicion aroused; and rumour – a word whispered 'in confidence' or 'just a joke' but which takes on a life of its own. The discipline of the tongue must involve absolute discretion, however tempting that little jibe may be.

St James

Always the practical man, St James writes about the tongue: 'A little member, yet boasts of great things'; like a rudder on a ship – small but influencing the whole direction. He goes on:

'How great a forest is set ablaze by a small fire; and the tongue is a fire. The tongue is an unrighteous world among our members, staining the whole body . . . No human being can tame the tongue; a restless evil, full of deadly poison. With it we bless the Lord and Father, yet with it we curse men, who are made in the likeness of God; from the same mouth come blessing and cursing.' (James 3.6f)

Tradition

Again, we should be disciplined in our use of our tongues, since we stand in a tradition that has afforded great respect to the spoken word. In Hebrew thought the word, once spoken, took on a life of its own: 'God spoke and it was done' – 'Let there be light' – the word gave birth to the action. And it is in Jesus Christ that we see God's Word spoken once more. That same Word which called creation into existence also calls us into the promise of new life. The Word of God incarnate is the Good News of the Gospel, that we have to speak out as a community under the discipline of our corporate tongue. For what we say as a community is under discipline, just as much as what we say as individuals.

> 'May the words of our mouths, and the thoughts of all our hearts,
> Be now and always acceptable in thy sight,
> O Lord, our strength and our Redeemer.'
>
> Ps 19.14

Ninth Sunday after Pentecost (*Trinity 8*)
20 July   True Strength

'Be strong in the Lord and in the strength of his might. Put on the whole armour of God, that you may be able to stand against the wiles of the devil.' Ephesians 6.10,11 (ASB Gospel)

Tight Corner!

When someone has courage, determination, and strength of character; when we feel that he (or she) would be useful to support us in a tight corner, we would say, 'He (or she) is a right toughie!' It need not necessarily be some kind of rough approach in a narrow street, say; it might just as well be some hard-line argument in an office, unlikely to descend into physical action but rough all the same.

There are really two ideas of what constitute real strength in current use. One is found among people who only look for things like strength of body, physical courage, and an unbending will. This is not, really, a very high definition of toughness. Why, a gangster or a political assassin is 'a real man' as much as say, an SIS soldier defending his post or some hostage. The growth of the use of force and physical violence may in some small respect be due to the lower view of 'real strength'.

True Strength

Look again at the higher ideal of strength which we started with: to strength of body and strength of purpose, there must be added strength of character as well. To bodily strength there must be added moral strength; to physical courage must be added moral courage too. We must be loyal to our friends, we must be true to our word once given, we must be able to control the lower side of our human nature, and we must be gentle in spirit when gentleness is needed. It is not easy to describe someone in this better sense, briefly and simply. Perhaps poets have attempted it more successfully than prose writers. For instance, Rudyard Kipling deliberately set out to so in his famous little poem 'If', which begins,

> *'If you can keep your head when all about you*
> *Are losing theirs and blaming it on you'*

and contains lines like:

> *'If you can wait and not be tired by waiting,*
> *Or being lied about, don't deal in lies,*
> *Or being hated don't give way to hating,*
> *And yet don't look too good, nor talk too wise . . .'*

Bible Example

The poetry of the Bible contains an attempt to picture a man worthy of the name of Psalm 15, which tells us that someone fit to dwell with God is,

> *He that leads an uncorrupt life*
> *and does the thing which is right:*
> *who speaks the truth from his heart*
> *and has not slandered with his tongue.*
> *He that has done no evil to his fellow:*
> *nor vented abuse against his neighbour;*
> *in whose eyes the worthless have no honour:*
> *but he makes much of those that fear the Lord.*

154

In God's Image
A definition of what manhood should be is found in the story of Creation in the Book of Genesis, which says 'God created man in his own image' – Bear in mind that here 'man' means the human race, and does not refer exclusively to males. God meant us to be like himself; the more like God we are, that is to say, the better lives we lead, the closer we come to attaining what God intended true manhood and womanhood to be.

The Perfect Man
To say that we have been created in the image of God, and should live up to that honour, is to give advice in abstract terms – but God sent his Son to become human himself, and show us clearly what perfect humanity really can be. Jesus Christ, in the life he lived on earth, sets us the example to follow. In that way we can approach, as far as is humanly possible, what is ideal in being manhood and womanhood. As we heard in the Gospel for today, the Lord prays that we may be true to his holy Name, consecrated as we are at our Baptism into that Name. Protection we will be given, but we are not to avoid the conflict, instead we can rely upon the strength given through the Son of God.

Pentecost 9 *Second Sermon* A Short Course on Discipline (3) Discipline of the Mind
'To set the mind on the Spirit is life and peace.' Romans 8,6 (Suggested Second Lesson: Mark 12.28–34)

Engaging the Mind
The discipline of the mind is something we need to be specially careful about; for the life of faith engages the mind, and if it fails to do this properly, then either faith will flourish with our emotions, soaring to great heights one minute but plunging to unknown depths the next. The cause of these variations has little to do with the reality or otherwise of our faith; they are dependent upon external influences that may occur at any time, often trivial in themselves. Or perhaps our faith is one that was learnt in child-hood, but has not developed much since; it has not matured along

with the rest of our understanding. So, we find a belief in God and his world that is held quite separately from our adult perception of life. At some stage, sooner or later, a problem arises when we find our immature grasp of faith cannot carry the weight of interpretating our experience of life – and so we lose what little faith we had.

Heart and Soul – and Mind

Jesus clearly states that love of God must be not only with heart and soul, but also with the mind. Does this mean, then, that one needs to be greatly intelligent to be a follower of the Lord? No. There have been and – thank God – are now, many simple folk whose holiness has shamed those of greater intellectual capacity. I firmly believe that the life of faith is open to all; but must be lived by each to the fullness of his or her capability. After all, love of God is not dissimilar from love of another human being – and people of widely differing abilities are blessed in loving human relationships. But also in a human relationship, that love must engage the minds of the people involved and not just their hearts.

The human mind is a highly complex mechanism. We appreciate something of its complexity when we see it going wrong. With mind as with body – only in illness do most of us begin to realize the extraordinary wonder of our own creation; normally we take it for granted, so long as all is going well.

Education – and the Church

Our minds are essential servants of our being, and deserve proper attention and a right discipline. Education is the way in which young minds are trained. This has always been recognized by the Church, which has played and still does play, an important part in the history of education in this land. The Church is rightly concerned to be involved and active in the debate on the future of our nation's schooling. The mind is dependent upon what it is fed; we therefore need to be disciplined in its diet. St Paul wrote: 'To set the mind on the flesh is death, but to set the mind on the Spirit is life and peace.' (Romans 8.6)

It must be a matter of real concern to the Christian that our society feeds itself upon presuppositions which underlie much of what we see on television, read in our papers, and are subject to in our legislation. After all, is life really just concerned with acquisition: the getting of more and more, owning goods, wealth and even people? Must everything be valued solely in money and economic terms? And what, we should ask, is the proper level of individual responsibility in our society today?

The Church is called to give a stronger moral lead. This we should clearly heed, so long as we remember that such morality cannot be selective – 'The sins of the boardroom should be just as much a matter for concern as the sins of the bedroom' (Bp of Oxford). We should start with things as they are, rather than as they appear. The Church, then, must begin unashamedly with God; that is where our moral vision originates. In our failure to appreciate fully the demands and the gifts of God's world, we are in bondage and rendered powerless in the face of so many problems.

God Revealed

Our minds are to be disciplined to listen and learn from others – using Bible notes and commentaries, and also the wealth of literature, classical and modern, about all areas of our faith. We should nourish our vision continually; to despise scholarship is to deny the gifts of understanding that God has given to us throughout the ages and in our own time.

Our Lord spoke of the need for a childlike quality in our faith; but childlike is different from childish. It properly retains an openness of enquiry, and a sense of wonder and excitement – the readiness to be surprised. This is very different from what some devout people call 'their simple faith' – which can be no more than a faith whose head is buried in the sand for fear of what it might see or where it might lead.

Set Your Mind on God

Christians are called to set their minds on God, to think in God's terms. St Peter was first commended by Jesus when he answered, 'You are the Christ!' (Mt 16.13–28) No human thinking had led him to that realization – it was a gift of God's grace. But, a moment later Christ was to rebuke Peter – 'Get behind me, Satan!' Why? Because the way he was thinking was not God's way, but man's. We must never cease from exercising a discipline in our minds, to keep them thinking along the Way of Truth – God's way, not man's way. We should, as St Paul said, 'Let this mind be in you, which was also in Christ Jesus' so that we, who make up the Body of Christ, may also have the Mind of Christ.

There is a right restlessness of enquiry in the human mind; if it is allowed to wander aimlessly, it will only tire itself, and the whole person. But open it to the gift of faith, and it finds much to stimulate and guide it, until we discover the truth that:

'The peace of God, which passes all understanding, will keep our hearts and minds in Christ Jesus.'

(Philippians 4.7)

Tenth Sunday after Pentecost   27 July
The Mind of Christ

'Let your bearing towards one another arise out of your life in Christ Jesus. For the divine nature was his from the first; yet he did not think to snatch at equality with God, but made himself nothing, assuming the nature of a slave.' Philippians 2,5–7 (ASB NT Reading)

Preparing for Martyrdom

'Life in Christ' is the expression used by St Paul in our reading for today, from his letter to the Philippians. The Philippians were in great difficulties through persecution; their leaders had been arrested, and they appeal to Paul for help. His letter in reply is virtually a tract on martyrdom – written *by* a martyr to a church *of* martyrs.

Whatever minor difficulties had arisen in the past, the Apostle and the Christian community were now drawn closely together. A contrast here with the Corinthians, who had known no suffering for the Gospel, but who almost broke Paul's heart with their contentiousness and their sins.

An Appeal for Unity

In today's passage from his letter, Paul is appealing for unity in the desperate position they find themselves.

Unity in the Church will show itself in likemindedness, 'the same turn of mind' as he puts it; a unity expressed in humility towards, and concern for, other human beings. The human unity must be an expression of the divine unity. Paul says, 'If our common life in Christ yields anything to stir the heart, any sharing of the Spirit' and 'to the glory of God the Father' – Father, Son and Holy Spirit are the supreme example of true unity.

If these Christians can show the common care for unity, the same turn of mind, Paul's joy will be completed, his 'cup of happiness' will be filled up, fulfilled in fact.

Unity
Through Christ, by means of Christ, in Christ's power – all this, yes; and not only through Christ but in a deep, intimate sense we are to be united with Christ. Christ is the atmosphere we breathe, the very air in which we live. The old life is dead and driven out; the new life is born and fills us; we live *in Christ* and Christ lives *in us*. Here follows a description of Christ's humility; 'he made himself nothing, assuming the nature of a slave' and Christ's exaltation – 'God raised him to the heights'. His is the example we are to follow, as the Lord himself makes clear in the Gospel reading 'I have set you an example; you are to do as I have done for you.'

A Hymn?
The scholars tell us that these seven verses – 5 to 11 – are a question by St Paul, from what is probably the earliest hymn to Christ. He quotes the hymn in much the same way as I might quote,

> *'The head that once was crowned with thorns*
> *Is crowned with glory now . . .'*

Here, it seems almost certain, is a precious example of the thinking and the devotion of the Early Church, meditating on the mystery of the 'emptying' of Christ in his glory – 'making himself nothing, assuming the nature of a slave'. Not that he abandoned his divine nature, but he laid aside that glory to which his Divine Nature entitled him, the glory which had been his before the Incarnation and which was revealed at the Transfiguration on the Holy Mount, the feast we keep on August 6th.

Then, for a moment, the Lord is seen by the astonished disciples as he is, in glory beyond time and beyond peace.

Exaltation
That glory which Christ laid aside, God restored to him, 'raising his Servant to the heights'; therefore as you have always obeyed, work out your own salvation (v. 12) or as we would say, pursue

your Christian calling to its victorious conclusion 'blameless and innocent'.

As surely as God gave glory to his Son, so he will give grace for the working out of his will. 'In Christ' will be not only the redemption of individuals, not only of humanity, but in the end the redemption of the whole universe, the cosmos; and the Kingdom of Creation will become the Kingdom of God and of his Christ.

RENEWAL

> *God our Shepherd, give the Church a new vision*
> *and a new charity, new wisdom and fresh understanding,*
> *the revival of her brightness*
> *and the renewal of her unity;*
> *that the eternal message of your Son*
> *may be hailed as the good news of the new age;*
> *through him who makes all things new,*
> *Jesus Christ our Lord.*
>
> *Percy Dearmer*

Pentecost 10   *Second Sermon*   A Short Course on Discipline   (4) Discipline of the Spirit

'If the salt has lost its taste, how shall its saltness be restored?' Matthew 5.13
(Suggested Second Lesson: Matthew 5.13–20)

Salt that has lost its taste

A striking image – salt that has lost its taste – and many of us may well be forced to admit that our spiritual lives have indeed lost something of the flavour and the savour with which they began. Through tiredness, indifference, lack of growth, we may be feeling somewhat jaded spiritually.

If we were to feel this same sense of weariness or lack-lustre in our physical being, we should look for a remedy – a course of vitamins perhaps, a fresh and interesting diet. So too in our spiritual lives, it is appropriate and right that we should consider afresh our discipline in matters spiritual. Such concern is of no less importance than our physical well-being, and indeed is more important in the long run. St Paul recognized this when writing to Timothy:

'Train yourself in godliness, for while bodily training is of some value, godliness is of value in every way, as it holds promise for the present life and also for the life to come.'

(1 Tim. 4.8)

A right discipline of the spirit, therefore, is vital not only in the here and now, but also in the hereafter. It is so easy for us to become preoccupied with our everyday things, the daily routine that makes up our life, to the exclusion of a wider understanding of ourselves as a part of God's creation, made in his image and brought into fellowship with him, through Jesus Christ.

The Spiritual Life

The spiritual life brings another dimension into all that we see and do. It is like the picture printed on a sheet of paper, which suddenly becomes alive when it appears on our TV screen in full colour and three-dimensional. Or, it resembles the hologram we find on so many things, from greeting cards to credit cards, giving depth and perspective to an image. So, the spiritual provides that depth of meaning and that perspective of understanding for life, as we live it day by day. What then are the ingredients that make up a proper discipline of the spirit? High on the list will be worship; the coming apart from all else to spend time focusing our thoughts and hearts in giving praise and worth-ship to God. So we come to church; but we need to make this a regular part of our life. For growth of any sort builds up slowly and on a regular diet. Ask yourself: Is your own pattern of churchgoing adequate? Is it perhaps *just* sufficient exercise for your spiritual health – rather like walking a set mile every day to keep you moderately fit. But why not think in terms of the athlete; try to grow stronger in faith. The athlete needs training – he goes to the gym regularly. Maybe we should find room for more than just one Sunday service; we might find it beneficial to get to a weekday service, in the Parish Church or in somewhere near your place of work.

Growth

All growth needs assessment, and occasional pruning or redirection. The Christian life is no exception. We grow spiritually for instance in our reading. There is no shortage of literature on the spiritual life. You can choose from classics of old or the shared experiences of our contemporaries. Books on prayer can feed our own prayer life; we can find much to inspire ourselves in the biographies of men and women of faith. It is good to have at least one book on the go, in your pattern of reading. Then there are things like retreats – times set aside to reflect and take stock at a greater depth than usual. We have the practice of confession, helpful to many as a time to assess ourselves before God. Or there is spiritual direction: regular appointments with a priest (perhaps one of your clergy, or someone outside the parish) with whom you chart your pattern of growth in the spirit. Do any of these form part of your own spiritual discipline – or might we ask 'Should they?'

The Spiritual Life

Time is elusive in today's world. A discipline of the spirit raises the issue of our use of time. Any worthwhile endeavour demands its proper share of our time. The musician, for example, must allow sufficient time for practice; a business man or woman must take time to prepare for meetings. So with the spiritual life. As Rabbi Mendel of Kotzk said:

'He who is about to pray should learn from a common labourer, who sometimes takes a whole day to prepare for a job. A woodcutter who spends most of the day sharpening his saw, and only the last hour cutting the wood, has earned his day's wage.'

The spiritual life involves spending time in the presence of God. The temptation is to fill that time, so we prattle away at God and call it prayer. But there is far more to prayer than just our words – for how then should we be aware of what God is saying to us if we do all the talking? 'Be still, and know that I am God.' Regularly throughout the Gospels Jesus is portrayed as withdrawing to be apart from others, and quietly with God. So, part of our discipline of the spirit involves time for reflection in God's presence. At the start of the day we need time to consider the events ahead; at the end of the day time again to reflect on what has happened. In each case, we bring before God our actions, our hopes and fears. We lay them before him, as it were, and let the light of his Spirit shine upon them to illuminate them and put them into perspective for us – the perspective of eternity.

There is a further skill to be developed. This is the way in which we hold things for a moment longer than usual – anything that we see or are involved in – hold them for a while longer, let them linger before God to seek upon them his blessing or his judgement. Thus, we can begin to learn the secret of hallowing every moment of every day. St Paul wrote 'Pray continually' – he did not mean a stream of uninterrupted words, but rather the cultivation of a life lived permanently in the presence of and awareness of God. The discipline of the spirit is, to cultivate just such a pattern in our everyday living.

P.B.

Eleventh Sunday after Pentecost (*Trinity 10*)
3 August   Pots of Earthenware

'We are no better than pots of earthenware to contain this treasure, and this proves that such transcendent power does not come from us, but is God's alone.' 2 Corinthians 4.7 (*ASB NT Reading*)

Appraisement

Today we are constantly being appraised. In business, assessments are used to check performance, and to decide if workers are to keep their jobs. If we ask for a loan, the bank weighs up our assets and liabilities, to see if we're creditworthy. Assessment begins before birth, as babies are checked with ultra-sound scans. Appraisal continues after death, when estates are valued: 'How much was he worth?' people ask.

The Church has had assessment from its very beginnings; in today's letter to the Corinthians, St Paul is trying to establish the value of his credentials against those of wandering preachers, who were trying to mislead these volatile new Christians. So the Corinthians are appraising Paul and his message. But at the same time Paul is assessing them; in his earlier letter, he had rebuked them for quarrelling, disorderly worship and immortality. If he'd been writing a company report, it would have been so bad that this particular office would have been shut down. But when the letter we heard today was written, things had improved greatly; so we can see a mutual process of assessment at work

History
At this time, when the Church was new, it wasn't valued very highly. Most people thought Christians were crazy. In his Governor's report back to Rome, Pliny the Younger wrote of Christians' 'insanity' and 'obstinacity'. He ordered 'two maid-servants called deaconesses' to be tortured; 'but,' he concluded, 'I uncovered nothing but a perverse and extravagant superstition.' A poor assessment indeed. Paul was not using abstract figures of speech when he wrote, 'Hunted, we are never abandoned to our fate; struck down, we are not left to die.' There are many miracles recorded in the first centuries of the Church, but surely one of the greatest is the survival of Christianity itself.

Today
That's history; and today many people do not rate the Church very highly. We are constantly told that we live in 'a post-Christian society'; and we know that right now, and every Sunday morning, there are more people down on their knees washing the hubcaps of their cars, than on their knees worshipping God. Prominent commentators go out of their way to attack Christianity; but it is not these Hampstead village atheists who are a danger; instead, they often provoke believers into a thoughtful defence. The worst threat comes from widespread and insidious indifference, the silent moth and rust that corrupt.

Expectations
This indifference may be partly at least caused by expectations which are misplaced, and therefore bound to be disappointing. When today's reading from Isaiah (42, 1–7) was written, the Jewish people were expecting a warrior king who would protect them from the Persian Empire. Instead, the writer prophesied a Messiah as a suffering servant, quiet and gentle.

Christianity does not always give the world what it expects – instant solutions to complex questions, absolute answers to difficult moral dilemmas. This disappointment is one reason why people often give the Church a poor assessment. We are bound to agree with some of these. The Church is far from perfect. Most parishes can think of better ways of spending £200,000 than on the elaborate trial staged by the Diocese of Lincoln to determine – amongst other things – whether it is indecent to blow down a lady verger's neck.

Hopeless?
Do the failings of the Church mean that Christianity itself is hopelessly flawed? No. The gospel of Christ is indeed a treasure, but one that requires flawed human beings, earthenware vessels, to transmit it.

We are the Church. When we appraise ourselves as Christians, we have to admit that we are indeed earthenware vessels. We all know our failings. If I'm in a beautiful church holding a candle, surrounded by clouds of music and incense, I all too easily indulge in fantasies of loving my neighbour. However, if I'm gripping my steering wheel in the middle of a traffic jam, and some idiot cuts in, I don't think of him as even human – much less made in God's image, and my neighbour whom I'm commanded to love. Then if we are honest, our own assessment of ourselves is not very flattering.

God's Assessment
So, if our many failings are obvious to others, and we are all too well aware of them ourselves, what must God think of us? His opinion is the one that really matters. How will he assess us?

In today's gospel the answer is clear and simple. 'By this love you have for one another, everyone will know that you are my disciples.' There are links between God's love for us, and our love for others, and other people's recognition of us as disciples of Jesus.

God's love is the treasure in our earthenware vessels. If we allow this treasure to overflow from our ordinary, flawed selves, then the people around us will know God's love. Revealing the love of God to others is not always easy or obvious. Yet, in small unexpected and surprising ways, the treasure of God's love shines forth, because of what we *do*, and in spite of what we *are*. With God's help, we can challenge the cynics, rouse the indifferent, and show love to the lost.

R.B.

Pentecost 11   *Second Sermon*
(*Transfiguration*)   **Light and Glory**

'If there was glory in that which lasted for a while, how much more glory is there in that which lasts forever?' 2 Corinthians 3.11 *(ASB)*

A Strange Story

On Wednesday, August 6th, this week, the Church commemorates a striking and mysterious event in the life of our Lord Jesus Christ. We know it as 'The Transfiguration' and we hear about it in the gospel according to St Luke, in chapter 9, verses 28 to 36; or St Mark 9, 2–13, or St Matthew 17, 1–13.

The festival we keep brings to us a strange story to our modern ears. The evangelists were writing to the people of their own time, and in the old Roman and Greek worlds, visions and voices, and the appearance of the gods to human beings, were in a sense everyday occurrences.

In the Hebrew literature also, images and colourful descriptions were in frequent use. If the writers wanted to say 'God spoke with anger' they would write – 'A sharp sword proceeded out of his mouth'. To make clear God's strength and protection, they would write – 'God is our high rock, our fortress.' We might say? 'God's presence could be felt' – they would say: 'A shining cloud over-shadowed us.' We might say: 'God's will became known' – they might say, 'The voice of God was heard, speaking his commands.'

The Transfiguration

So, bearing in mind these differences between them then, and us now, what is the message of the Transfiguration for us?

Take the circumstances. Only a little while before, St Peter made his great declaration of faith. 'You are the Christ', he said, 'the Son of the Living God.' This man Jesus, who went about teaching and preaching, was not just a holy man, not even just a prophet. He was the long-awaited Messiah, the Leader of Israel. What a leap of faith this was, and what a commitment Peter made.

Jesus re-names him 'Rock-Man' – for on this rock of faith, the Church, the society of his followers, would be built. Eagerly, Peter awaits the Leader's orders – only to be told that this Messiah is not the 'Warrior King' he and the others expected, to lead them against the heathen occupiers of their sacred soil. Instead, he is a

'Suffering Servant', and his followers will share his fate – trials, tortures, sufferings and death.

Refusal
A shattering re-appraisal is forced upon Peter; at first he refuses to accept the new version of the Messiah and his role. 'Heaven forbid, Lord, this shall never happen to you!' Jesus' reply is stern – 'Get behind me, Satan!' Crushed, rejected, Peter is in a state of turmoil, spiritual and mental. And if Peter himself is in turmoil, may we not also with the all reverence, suggest that Jesus himself is at a moment of crisis? Humanly speaking, Jesus needed reassurance that the path he has chosen, the path of failure, pain and torment, and death itself, is indeed the right choice.

There is an intense spiritual struggle in the minds of the disciples, and also in the mind of Christ himself.

A Flood of Light
Suddenly, the crisis is resolved: flooding down, like a great white light, comes the reassurance that this choice *is* the right one, that the Father's will *is* being done, that ancient prophecies *are* being fulfilled. 'This is my Chosen One, listen to him!'

So the little band is strengthened to go forward on the road that has been chosen, the road to Jerusalem, the road to suffering, torture and death – but the road which will lead to renewed life and to triumph in the end.

Twelfth Sunday after Pentecost (*Trinity 11*)
10 August   No Choice
'The love of Christ leaves us no choice, when once we have reached the conclusion that one man died for all.' 2 *Corinthians 5.1 (ASB NT Reading)*

A Changed Way of Life
There is a new world, for men and women who accept the love of Christ, whose lives have been changed by Jesus Christ. Most of us take a long time to move from the proposition 'God exists' to the practical consideration, 'Then that has practical consequences for me.' Paul saw that there was no choice.

He had been a bitter opponent of Christianity, an enemy of Christ, and when he set off on his journey to Damascus for the special purpose of persecuting the Christians there, only to meet with that astonishing vision and challenge that converted him, he found himself living in a new kind of world. 'When anyone is united to Christ, there is a new world; the old order has gone, and a new order has already begun.' (2 Cor. 5.17)

Two Kinds of Change
Paul was thinking mainly of the inner and spiritual change in himself, that made him feel new and different. But in his case, and in the case of many people, the spiritual change was accompanied by a second change, a change in his way of living and in his circle of friends. By becoming a Christian, he cut himself off from the world of the Jewish upper class and the well-to-do Rabbis and religious leaders of his home town of Tarsus, to say nothing of such respected figures as the great Rabbi Gamaliel of Jerusalem, where Paul had studied at one stage of his life. Now he mingled mainly with the followers of Christ, who were in the main poorer and rougher than his former friends, and after a time included many non-Jews.

Instead of living a life of security, he and his friends were sometimes in danger – even considerable danger – for their faith. Their surroundings were as likely to be rough-and-tumble as before they would have been elegant and even fashionable. The practical considerations of the change of faith were by no means easy to take to!

The Whole of Life
Christianity, if it is sincerely accepted and practised, has consequences for the whole of life. It gives a standard for the measurement of all experience. Its heart is a personal relationship with god; a personal love, a personal loyalty. The personal, living God makes demands; the living Christ addresses us and calls us to personal service.

Our calling is to do what we believe Christ asks of us.

Sometimes it may be difficult; the demands can be severe. And the further one goes, the more severe, the greater, the demands may become. We do know, however, that if we can but pluck up courage and start – and even more important, perhaps – persevere, then strength will be given.

Witness

Probably the most important aspect of our service – and this surely applies to all of us, whatever our 'station in life', whatever our 'gifts and talents', whatever our intellectual or artistic – or non-artistic but practical – outlook and capabilities – is that of witness.

'We are entrusted with the message of reconciliation' says St Paul; and our Lord's great prayer includes his petition for those who, through the words of the disciples, will believe in him.

Here to hand, then, is a task for each one of us, laid upon us by the Master himself.

Not to 'preach' in any patronizing or condescending way; not to try and ram our beliefs down the throats – willy-nilly – of those we meet and those we know, our friends, those who share our interests and life. But to show in ourselves the effects of our belief; then, to lead others along the same path, or at least to point them in the same direction, as we ourselves have walked. It is personal conviction and personal example that will really make an impression; a love that leads to reconciliation.

In the words of the collect for today: 'Help us so to proclaim the good news of your love, that all who hear it may be reconciled to you.' My friends, we have no choice.

Pentecost 12 *Second Sermon* **Jonah**

'The waters closed in over me, the deep was round about me, weeds were wrapped about my head.' Jonah 2.5 (EP ASB)

A Great Story

The story of Jonah and the Whale is one of the great old folk-tales that everyone knows, like Noah and the Ark, Adam and Eve in the Garden, the Tower of Babel, and so on. They lend themselves to dramatic illustration and every artist worthy of his salt loves to seize the opportunities they offer. Walt Disney's people would make a wonderful cartoon film to add to their successes; certainly the mediaeval artists carved the story of Jonah on the capitals of their columns, painted it in their frescoes, drew it in their stained-glass windows, in churches and cathedrals all over Christendom.

Marvels

The mediaeval mind loved marvels and delighted in stories of the miraculous. But in fact the astonishing adventure with the whale is really almost incidental to the real story, and the true purpose, of the Book of Jonah. The author uses the adventure as angler might use his bait – as a means of catching his audience's attention, then putting over his message. What is his message?

Pride and Exclusiveness

The Book of Jonah belongs to the period of Hebrew history after the return from the Exile. The new settlers in the Old Country were obsessed with two aspects of their religion – their pride in their possession of the exclusive worship of the One True God, and their pride in the purity of their race. True, these two spiritual forces had provided the driving power that eventually brought about the Return of the Nation, the rebuilding of Jerusalem, and the reforming of the people and the land of Israel.

A Wider Hope

But they also meant that there was a turning-inwards of Jewish thought, a rejection of that aspect of their Faith that had always maintained the wideness of God's mercy, and a rejection of the belief in the Jews as an instrument in God's hand, for bringing in the rest of the world's peoples to an acceptance of the Lord as God.

In contrast, the author of Jonah is recalling his people to that wider view, and making a plea for a renewal of missionary activity amongst the nations.

A Parable

'Jonah' is a parable, and its message is that in the providence of God, even a non-Israelitish nation may turn to the Lord in repentance of their sins, and in recognition of him as their Creator and their God. Their repentance of their sins and their worship of the Lord will be acceptable, and their faith is to be commended.

Jonah himself is shown – with more than a touch of humour, incidentally – to be much in the wrong, and in him is caricatured the over-zealous and anti-foreigner attitude of the Pharisees and other strict Jewish devotees. Like them, Jonah is wrong – both in his refusal to preach the message of salvation to the 'foreigners' of Nineveh, and in his anger following God's acceptance of their repentance and the giving of his forgiveness.

Two Mistaken Ideas

Jonah believed that the Lord is a 'local' God; if one can get physically far enough away, the Lord's power cannot reach one. So, Jonah flees to Tarshish away in the west, to be out of God's territory; but he learns that God's power is not by any means to be confined to any one area, but is indeed universal. Jonah believed also that God is an exclusively 'Jewish' God, a 'tribal' God if you like; to him, only his Chosen People are of any real concern. Jonah learns instead that God's mercy, like his power, extends over all peoples everywhere.

The Message

At the end of the book, the Lord in effect is saying, 'You are terribly upset about this plant, which cost you no pains at all, which you did not cultivate, which grew up overnight whilst you slept, and is now fading away – but what of me? I created the people of Nineveh, watched over them whilst they grew up, as it were, cared for them, sorrowed at their sorrows, rejoiced at their joys. So, should I not be sorely distressed over this teeming great city and its fate?' God loves and cherishes all that he has made, even the ignorant multitude of busy self-centred folk – and even their cattle – in that depraved great city!

The Moral

We Christians should learn the lesson; never be complacent, believing we are sure in God's love and affection, if we are not playing our part in proclaiming his love throughout the world that he has made. The riches he has given to us are not for us alone, but are to be shared with others less well off. We cannot keep God for ourselves; he is for all the world!

Thirteenth Sunday after Pentecost (*Trinity 12*)
17 August   Following the Example of Christ

'As they were stoning Stephen, he prayed, "Lord Jesus, receive my spirit." Then he fell on his knees, and cried aloud, "Lord, do no hold this sin against them," and with that he died.' Acts 7,59 (ASB NT Reading)

Persecution

Jesus made it quite clear to his disciples, as we hear in the Gospel reading today, that they must be prepared to face persecution and even death. Jesus was hounded along the rough and brutal road, spat at, bedaubed with filth, on the way to death on the cross. This is the kind of world he lived in, and we live in also. In his Sermon on the Mount, Jesus spoke of the happiness of those who bear hatred and persecution for his sake. 'How blessed are those who have suffered persecution for the cause of right; the kingdom of Heaven is theirs.' (Matt. 5.10) Those of his followers who bear a faithful witness to Christ, and are loyal to him, are drawn very close to him, and experience the joy that follows from this.

The world has always, and will continue, to savagely attack those who confess their faith in Christ, and live by that faith and trust. But faithfulness brings great joy, and the reward is certain: 'Be thou faithful unto death, and I will give thee the crown of life.' (Rev. 2.10)

Loss for Christ's Sake

To follow Christ, and to do what we believe is right, may lead to suffering and loss. Bishop George Bell, the distinguished Bishop of Chichester, disapproved of the saturation bombing, as carried out by our side in the Second World War, and expressed in many speeches and on many occasions his constant disapproval. Those who know have said that they believe Bishop Bell would have been Archbishop of Canterbury, if he had not so publicly expressed his strong belief that such bombing was wrong.

Dietrich Bonhoeffer felt that Hitler was so evil, that it was right for him to engage in a plot to assassinate the Fuehrer. Bonhoeffer's courage resulted in his imprisonment in a concentration camp, and his execution by hanging.

Faithful unto Death
We must at times ask ourselves whether if we were faced by persecution, we would have the strength to remain faithful to Christ. We know the appalling nature of modern methods of interrogation – cruel torture, physical and mental, and the use of drugs to compel confession. Let us pray that if such a time should ever come, we should be able to confess to Christ boldly. We are, after all, pledged to be Christ's faithful soldiers and servants. We can take comfort too, from considering the eventual release of prisoners and the open revival of faith, in what was Soviet Russia with its intense and expensive anti-religion campaign over many years. Now a new Cathedral is being built in the centre of the Kremlin – symbol of a victory for Christ over Marx.

> Lord God, the refuge and strength of your people in every hour of need, sustain all who suffer for their allegiance to the faith of Christ. Give them courage and patience to endure to the end, that by their example and witness, they may win others to the service of him who suffered for all humanity, our Saviour Jesus Christ.
>
> Prayers for Use at the Alternative Services

Pentecost 13 *Second Sermon*
'Farewell, my Friends'

'Now, behold, I know that all of you among whom I have gone about preaching the Kingdom, will see my face no more.' Acts 20,25 (ASB EP)

Paul's Farewell and Good-bye

The first part of the chapter from Acts, from which our reading is taken, tells of Paul's travels. He goes to Macedonia, then to Greece, where he spent three months (did he write the 'Letter to the Romans' here? See Romans 15,23–33). Then there was a plot against him, which he avoids, and goes on to Troas, where he joins in the Sunday eucharist and gives a long sermon (20,7) with the famous result of the young man falling asleep and falling out of the window (9–12). He goes on, in a hurry to get to Jerusalem for Pentecost, and on the way he calls the elders of the church at Ephesus to come and meet him.

We learn (chapter 21.4) how the Christians at Tyre prophesied that Paul should not go on to Jerusalem; and then at Caesaria the prophet Agabus tells him he will be bound and delivered into the hands of the Gentiles (i.e. Romans). But Paul seems inwardly forced to make the journey; he strongly believes it is the will of God for him to return to Jerusalem. Does he perhaps feel that the city where his Master was arrested, beaten and tortured, and executed, has a similar fate in store for himself? The prophecy of Agabus is very like the forecast of Christ's passion. Does he also see – perhaps dimly – that his own great desire to go to Rome and preach the Gospel there, is to be fulfilled?

Good-bye, my Friends

Paul knows all too well that the fledgling church he is leaving behind, is going to be leaderless and vulnerable, strange teachers will come in with heretical doctrines ('fierce wolves') against whom he does his best to warn the flock. Some had made difficulties; one his hinted at in Paul's self-defence – 'I have not wanted anyone's silver or gold or clothing'. Why should Paul be accused of such a thing? Did anyone suggest that his handling of the money collected for the Jerusalem church, was just a little suspicious?

Altogether, a sad letter, full of foreboding, yet with a sense of fixed purpose and inexorable strength in fulfilling the Lord's commands.

After his address, he knelt down and prayed with them all; and all wept and kissed Paul, sorrowful that they would see his face no more. 'And they brought him to the ship.'

Afterwards

We do not know exactly how things went; but events fell out in much the way expected. Paul was arrested, taken before various authorities, including the High Priest – who struck him in the mouth, as his Master had been struck; and eventually he was sent to Rome.

'You have appealed to Caesar; to Caesar you shall go.' In Rome, we are told, he lived 'two whole years, preaching the kingdom of God and teaching about the Lord Jesus Christ, openly and unhindered.' (Acts 28, 30–31)

Fourteenth Sunday after Pentecost (*Trinity 13*)
24 August   The Heavenly Ladder

'Truly, truly, I say to you, you will see heaven opened, and the angels of God ascending and descending upon the Son of man.' John 1.51

The Calling

The scene is Bethany beyond the river Jordan, where John has been baptizing. Amongst those who have come to him is Jesus himself, and John bears witness to him as the 'Son of God' (John 1.34) and relates the descent of the Spirit as a dove from heaven at that baptism. The next day, standing with two of his disciples, as Jesus walks by, John says 'Behold the Lamb of God!' The two disciples forthwith follow after Jesus and are invited to stay with him; one of them is Andrew, Simon Peter's brother. He goes off to Simon, tells him they have found the Messiah, the Christ, and brings him to Jesus. Jesus looks him over, is obviously pleased, and presents him with a new name – or nickname, a custom Jesus is fond of – as 'Cephas', meaning Peter, i.e. 'Rock'. To Philip Jesus says, 'Follow me' – that is, he is now accepted as one of Christ's disciples.

Philip goes off to Nathaniel and gives the significant testimony: 'We have found the man spoken of by Moses and the prophets.' That is, he to whom so many passages of the Old Testament pointed, the Messiah, the Christ.

Doubts

What Nathaniel finds hard to accept is that the Messiah would come from a small, remote place, without even a mention in the Old Testament to give a clue to its future importance. 'Can anything good come out of Nazareth?' Nevertheless, his initial doubt soon yields to recognition, and he gives the most important testimony so far: 'Rabbi, you are the Son of God! You are the King of Israel!' Jesus had said, 'Here is an Israelite worthy of the name; in him is nothing false.' Jesus was drawing a comparison with his Jewish opponents in Jerusalem; unlike them, Nathaniel is a true Israelite, one who recognized and acclaimed Jesus for what he was.

'Under the fig tree, I saw you'

How did Jesus know Nathaniel was trustworthy? In Jewish law, one had to give the exact place and time of any event witnessed (as in Daniel and Susanna, 'What kind of tree did it happen under?'). Jesus passed the test; he then goes on to make his astonishing prophecy – 'The heavens will open, you will see God's angels ascending and descending upon the Son of Man.' The scene is taken from the story of Jacob in Genesis 28,12 – 'Jacob dreamt there was a ladder set up reaching to heaven; and angels of God were going up and down upon it.' The last word could in Hebrew equally well mean 'upon him', and the scholars came to take the meaning that Israel on earth had some kind of spiritual counterpart in heaven; when Nathaniel saw Jesus it was as if the true Israelite saw the true Israel in heaven, and his counterpart on earth. The picture is one which emphasizes one aspect of the title 'Son of Man' – a figure whose destiny was to be played out both on earth and in heaven.

An Apostle

Although Nathaniel is not named in the lists of apostles, the Church includes readings which refer to Bartholomew, with whom Nathaniel is identified by tradition. He is said to have visited India; and a Hebrew copy of the Gospel according to Matthew is said to have been found there by a Greek visitor, c. AD 150, left behind by 'Bartholomew, one of the Apostles'.

Pentecost 14   *Second Sermon*   Human Cruelty

'Brother will deliver up brother to death, and the father his child, and children will rise against parents and have them put to death.' Matthew 10.21 (ASB EP)

Horror

What appalling sufferings, cruelty and deaths, have been happening in our world recently. We look back with horror at the fearful murders of thousands of people in central Africa; one race, the Tutsis, committing genocide on their neighbour black race the Totsis. Terrible pictures of churches scarred by battle, their inner walls splashed with blood and torn by bullets and rockets; and the streams of dispossessed families trying to reach safety, any safety ... No sooner has some sort of settlement been reached here, than we see and hear how Liberia's civil war has reached a desperate state. Troops sent in from neighbouring countries are unable to cope; helpless civilians have swarmed onto ships, hoping to reach some shore where peace – any kind of peace – is possible; only to find that they are stuck out at sea, with no chance of reaching a port where they can get back to dry land. Sickness, lack of food, lack of water and of the barest decencies reduces their wretched numbers day by day ...

Bosnia
The facts are emerging of the terrible reign of terror in north-west Bosnia in 1992. The indictment issued by the International War Crimes Tribunal describes the Serbian Dusan Tadic as a sadistic killer who supervised a reign of terror, torturing, killing and raping his Muslim neighbours.

Also in Bosnia are coming to light dreadful crimes committed under General Ratko Mladic, including the murder of Muslim prisoners and their burial in fields, using a mechanical digger to gouge out mass graves. Laughing soldiers made up the execution squads, shooting at night-time by car headlights. Those who gave evidence escaped miraculously, though terribly scarred by the experiences they went through, both in body and mind, and burnt into their memories were fearful pictures of stacks of bleeding corpses, piles of mangled flesh, men dying, moaning and crying out in the darkness. Perhaps almost worse was the eventual fate of the town of Srebrenica, where hope of UN air strikes, which would stop the Serb advance, gave confidence to the inhabitants. Some strikes were launched, but too late; the town was firmly in the hands of the Serbs. Thousands of its inhabitants, who believed they were under the protection of the UN, were murdered in cold blood in a matter of days. (Based on article in the *Sunday Express*, 12 May 1996, headed 'The Damned').

Fifteenth Sunday after Pentecost (*Trinity 14*)
31 August   Paying the Taxes
'Tell us your opinion then; is it permissible to pay taxes to Caesar, or not?' Matthew 22.17 (ASB Gospel)

Paying Up

The Jews of our Lord's time felt doubly annoyed about their taxes. Apart from disliking having to pay taxes at all (well, we all would share that dislike, would we not!) they did not consider that the Romans had any right to tax them. Therefore Jesus had two matters to deal with, when some stooges (as we might call them) – put up the question, being tools of the Pharisees and the Herodians, both sets against Jesus but for different reasons. The Pharisees thought he was destroying the sacred Law; the Herodians were pro-Roman and presumably hoped Jesus could be marked down as a political rebel. Whatever reply he made, they hoped it would get Jesus into trouble with the Romans.

Paying For What We Get

Jesus ignored the second and dangerous issue – the question of who were the rightful rulers of Judaea and Galilee, the Romans or the Jews. That was where his enemies, posing as genuine questioners, hoped to catch him out.

Instead, he indicated that on the question of taxation in general, a government has a right to tax its subjects. 'You use Caesar's money,' he said, holding up the coin he had asked for. 'Very well, for this you must pay; pay Caesar what is due to Caesar.' The evangelist does not record whether he went into details about the benefits the Roman government provided; the existence of such benefits as implied by what he said about the coin which he held. Nor did he touch on the question of how much taxation is fair, nor when it becomes excessive.

A Different Claim

To this answer Jesus added a short sentence, which moved the discussion from the subject chosen by his questioners, to another point, one Jesus considered far more important. Having said, 'Pay Caesar what is due to Caesar,' he went on, 'and pay God what is due to God.'

Like earthly governments, God makes claims upon us. He seeks not only our obedience to his laws, but a due proportion of our time, our money, and our services. Some of these things are given through what we may do for his Church, but the interpretation of what gifts and actions may be counted as 'given to God' is very wide. Many things we do for the benefit of our fellow human beings may fairly be said to be given to God too.

Unforced

Of course, in one important respect, the claims of God upon us are entirely unlike those of the State. The Government of a country enforces payment of its taxes by laws and penalties. As far as God is concerned, we can give to him and work for him, or we can hold back, as we wish and choose. This freedom to decide for ourselves is one of the blessings which God allows us. The fact that God gives us freedom to say 'Yes!' or 'No!' in the matter, as well as all his other acts of trust, should make us all the more ready to obey his will and help in his service.

Shortfall

All of us, says St Paul (Romans 3.23) fall short of God's glory. Glory shines, when God's will is done, as perfectly as possible, under the circumstances. 'Let your light so shine before men that they may see your good works and give glory to your Father who is in heaven.' (Matthew 5.16)

We fall short of God's standard of goodness, we fall short of his will for us, which is our sanctification, let us remember. We fall short of the God-given conscience within us, which passes judgement on past deeds and on our future plans. Let us pray that we can become, by the enabling of God's grace, what he wants us to be, and do the things he wants us to do by his inspiration and strengthening.

> *Sanctify me, dear Father,*
> *that others may see*
> *a little of your glory*
> * shining through.*
>   G.A.

Pentecost 15 *Second Sermon*
A Faithful Saying

'The saying is faithful and worthy of full acceptance, that Christ Jesus came into the world to save sinners.' 1 Timothy 1.15 (ASB EP)

Devoted Companion
Timothy was a native of Lystra in Asia Minor, the son of a Greek
father and a Jewish mother who was a Christian. In the Acts of
the Apostles we read that 'He was well spoken of by the brethren
at Lystra and Iconium. Paul wanted Timothy to go with him; and
he took him and circumcised him because of the Jews who were
in those places, for they all knew his father was a Greek.' (16,1–
3) In addition to being a devoted companion of Paul, Timothy
was entrusted with missions to the Thessalonians, to encourage
them under persecution, and to the Corinthians, to strengthen the
converts in the faith. Timothy became Paul's representative at
Ephesus, and according to Eusebius the historian, the first bishop
of that city. Paul wrote this letter, probably from Macedonia, while
Timothy was in Ephesus.

Keep the Faith
It seems that Paul felt his end was near, and he must have felt it
his duty to warn his young helper against the speculations and
new ideas which were going around; and if taken seriously could
make a shipwreck of the Faith. As a help, Paul presents Timothy
with the text at v. 15 – Here is a saying you can rely upon, and
nobody should doubt:
  'Christ Jesus came into the world to save sinners.'
  These words were obviously not Paul's; he seems to be quoting
a saying that had currency in the Church. It appears, the historians
tell us, that there were a number of short sentences, maxims,
phrases of hymns, pieces of catechetical teaching, and dogmatic
sayings in frequent use in the Church. It is possible that they
had originated in some of the inspired utterances of the Church's
prophets. Probably the Apostle was appealing to one of these
sayings, and giving his own approval of it.
  Whilst we do not know who first uttered the phrase, we are
glad to have it. Like many of the lovely things in the world, it is
the outpoured faith of an unknown soul.

A Divine Saying
The phrase about a saying being 'faithful and worthy of acceptance' occurs five times in the Pastoral Epistles. In the case of this
particular saying, it would appear to be derived from our Lord's
own words about himself. It puts Christ's own words into a more

condensed form, perhaps; and it casts a bright light on God's own character.

The temptation to cherish hard thoughts about God is a very old one; and indeed in some people, rather a modern one also. 'I was afraid of you, because you are a severe man' (Luke 19.21) is the evil thinking that too many human hearts have held in secret – and with God a loving Creator! When God saw the evil that was spoiling his creation of humanity, he found a remedy; he gave his only Son to save the world. What a tenderness of redeeming grace; what love was revealed.

A Vital Saying

Vital because it states the greatness of Christ's work. He came to this world to save sinners. Salvation is a very different thing from 'more civilized' or 'lofty enlightenment' or 'improved conditions', all of which may exist side by side with spiritual disaster. Salvation is gained by an act of surrender of the entire person, including the will; our Lord gives freedom from the bonds of sin, a new and true direction, and spiritual strength to enable us to obey God. This saying tells us we have a Saviour, Christ Jesus who came into the world to save sinners. Here is the offer of God's grace, and we would be advised well to take it.

> *Almighty God,*
> *you sent your Son to redeem the world,*
> *and will send him again to be our judge.*
> *May we so imitate him*
> *in the humility and purity of his first coming*
> *that when he comes again,*
> *we may be ready to greet him*
> *with joyful love and firm faith*
> *through the same Jesus Christ our Lord.*
> *(PHG 4)*

Sixteenth Sunday after Pentecost (*Trinity 15*)
7 September   The Good Samaritan

'Overcome evil with good.' Romans 12.21 (ASB NT Reading)

Questions

At a meeting or conference, the number of questions asked of
individual speakers is a good indication of the interest their contribution has aroused. So here, on this occasion, amongst the questioners is this lawyer. By the way, the title he is given does not
mean he was an expert in the law of the land, entitled to wear a
wig and gown in court, and address the bench and the jury, but
rather a learned man in the Law of Moses, an expert in the Torah,
the five books of Moses or Pentateuch, and in all the details of the
decisions made by the scribes and theologians over difficult or
disputed points, in the law.

On this occasion, a lawyer followed up his first question with
a second. He had asked Jesus how to achieve eternal life, and
Jesus gave the stock and perfectly correct answer, on which they
were both in complete agreement – at least as far as general principles were involved. But on the practical application of those
principles – 'And who is my neighbour?' Jesus had something
quite new to say.

Difficulties

Too often our own attitude to our Lord's teaching is not unlike that
of the lawyer: we raise difficulties, we say we don't understand, we
make exceptions, and we plead that our case is a special one. The
lawyer implies by his second question, that he was not at all
sure exactly *who* was 'his neighbour'. For our part, when we see
someone in trouble, how often do we say to ourselves 'Don't want
to seem interfering' or 'Time's too short – I must be at' – wherever
it is – 'by six o'clock, and it's now five forty-five . . .' Then in these
days, what can one single man or woman do in the face of a dozen
roughs, or a group of schoolboys (or girls) in a tough area or late
at night . . . Get away, find a phone, ring the police, call for help,
bang on a door . . .

Jesus' Answer

We all know the story Jesus told in answer to the lawyer. It answers both his questions but is more concerned with the second one. The first two travellers who come along the road give no help; they cross over and pretend not to see the injured man, robbed and half-naked. Their failure was the more disappointing since one was a priest and the other a Levite; nevertheless the audience would have more sympathy with the priest and Levite than we have, for they would know the two were in the grip of conflicting obligations. And by their Jewish upbringing they would regard the concept of 'neighbour' very narrowly; they would feel no obligation to come to the aid of any traditional enemy of the Jewish race, as would be a Roman, a Samaritan, or indeed most Gentiles.

A Shock

Jesus' answer, therefore, of the Samaritan who was prepared to regard his worst traditional enemy as 'his neighbour' was intended to shock that attitude right out. 'Go and do as he did' meant – and means – treat anyone, of any race or colour or background, as your neighbour, with all in the way of help or care or provision that the word implies.

This parable – probably the best-known of all the stories that Jesus told – is taking as its target the exclusive nationalism of the Jewish people of the time; but there has never been a society, or indeed a civilization, to which it would be irrelevant.

Pentecost 16   *Second Sermon*   **Mary the Mother**

'Mary said, Behold the handmaid of the Lord; let it be done to me according to your word.' Luke 1.38 (ASB Introductory Sentence)

Mary, Mother of Our Lord

Tomorrow, September 8th, is our Church's special festival day in honour of Mary, Mother of Our Lord Jesus Christ. In the older Prayer Book, it was given as the commemoration of the Nativity of St Mary the Virgin; now in the New Book it is given the more general title, remembering not only Our Lady's Birthday but also giving thanks for her whole life and example.

Son of God

It is a sign and a measure of the greatness of spirit of this modest Jewish maiden, that God Almighty should choose her as the vessel for the coming of our tiny spinning globe, this Planet Earth, of his beloved Son our Saviour Jesus Christ in human form and shape. Joy mingled with sorrow was from the beginning the mark of the life that lay ahead; the shadow of the Cross fell over the stable in Bethlehem and the house in Nazareth, and the words of ancient Simeon rang in Mary's ears: 'This child is destined for the fall and for the rising of many in Israel, destined to be a sign that is rejected – and a sword shall pierce your own soul also.'

Son of Mary

As Jesus grew 'in wisdom and in stature' as St Luke writes, love for her son was the mainspring of her life and all that she did; every manifestation of her son's future – his words, his way of life, his stories – all were treasured up; 'Mary kept all these things in her heart.' Then came the time of separation, when the call of his Heavenly Father took Jesus away to preach and teach. She no longer saw so much of him; she worried, as any mother would, and as St Mark records (3.31–35); and she must have been saddened by the unbelief the neighbours showed when he came and preached at Nazareth (Matthew 13.53–58). But there was good news also, and the great day when he rode into Jerusalem was wonderful: how pleased Mary must have been at this note of triumph. All too soon, however, the news was bad – her Son was arrested, tortured, taken out to the 'Place of the Skull', to be executed like a common criminal – indeed, side by side with two thieves. She was there; along with his close friends John and Mary Magdalen, and some other women who travelled with Jesus on his long preaching tours. His last words were to John concerning his mother, and to Mary concerning John: 'Be to him a mother!' and to John, 'Be to her a son!'

Last Days

It was with the news of the Ascension that Mary is mentioned as attending meetings for prayer in the 'Upper Room' with the apostles and 'his brethren' (Acts 1.14) but after this we hear no more. Mary may well have preferred to slip quietly away from public notice and crowded places; one tradition is that having made her home with St John, as Jesus wished in his last moments, when he left Jerusalem she went with him to Patmos and eventually ended her life there.

> *Almighty God,*
> *who by your grace called the Blessed Virgin Mary*
> *and opened for all the door*
> *of infinite mercy and eternal light:*
> *Fill us with your grace,*
> *that, through our obedience and faith,*
> *the world may rejoice in your mercy,*
> *and walk in your light;*
> *for the sake of Jesus Christ our Lord.*
> *(The Promise of his Glory: 91)*

Seventeenth Sunday after Pentecost (*Trinity 16*)
14 September   The Seed
'Quietly accept the message planted in your hearts, which can bring you salvation.' James 1.21 (ASB NT Reading)

Action, not Talk
St James is a very direct apostle. He goes straight to the point, for that is his practical approach to the Faith. The keynote of his letter is that the religion of Christ is less something to talk about, than something to act upon. Our holy Faith is nothing, if it is not a power acting upon us – love-controlling, life-moulding.

His words remind us of our Lord's parable, where the seed sown is the Word of God or as we might put it, the teaching in the Gospel.

Parable
Christ points out a real correspondence between one aspect of God's world, and another, and St James does the same. The Master takes his metaphor from the farmer's life, and his disciple follows on. We have to be receptive, we are to be good soil, and as the field receives the seed and allows it to germinate and grow, so we are to take in the Gospel message, accept it, allow it to grow within us, accepting God's message as from him. To us, it can be the

means of regeneration; we receive into our hearts the Word of God, and it will prove to be the power of God bringing salvation.

As the seed grows, our lives should change; Christ says that as we know a tree by its fruit, so his followers should be distinguished by their lives and their behaviour, that is by their increasing ability to help, to encourage, to strengthen, to support their fellow human beings. The lives of Christians should show the 'fruits' that St Paul mentions: 'love, joy, peace, patience, kindness, self-control: he also repeats Christ's condensed version of the entire Jewish Law – 'You shall love your neighbour as yourself' (Galatians 4.14) and as he says earlier, 'Through love be servants of one another' (v. 13).

Reception
When Christ preached to the Jews, the ordinary, common people 'heard him gladly'. Those who later became his worst enemies did not receive his words gladly, nor with meekness. We remember the people of Nazareth who resented him (Luke 4.28–9) and how his enemies tried to throw him over a cliff-edge to his death. And we might remember how the Jews of Antioch resisted St Paul's preaching. Far too often people were impatient, unready to allow the words to reach them even, wrathful at what they thought were invasions of their religious doctrine. St James bluntly condemns this: 'You must be quick to listen, slow to speak, and slow to be angry.'

To Listen is Not Enough
Yes, certainly listen – but there again, merely to listen is not much use. You are just like the person who glances into a mirror, then immediately goes away and forgets what he looks like. You must not be like that when you hear the word of God – listening for a moment, then going away and forgetting what the message is.

And what is our religion? One thing is clear, however pious you may think you are, unless you can control your tongue, you are not going to get very far. 'What's in a word?' someone may ask; but a word is in itself a kind of act. The more we become accustomed to violent words, the more prone we become to violent acts. And below both word and act, our minds grow accustomed to violent habits of thought.

This is the cause of much un-Christian talk and behaviour today. We must learn to cultivate the steady, quiet, unhesitating strength that comes straight from the immutable kindness of God. After all, that is our proper nature; and whatever is contrary to it, however frequent, is in the true sense, unnatural.

Religious?

It is all too easy for us to imagine that we are 'religious', but punctilious observance of outward forms and ceremonies is not religion. True religion is characterized by acts of charity and helpfulness to those in need, and keeping ourselves pure from worldly selfishness.

Pentecost 17   *Second Sermon*   **Salt**

'Salt is good; but if salt has lost its taste, how shall its saltness be restored?' Luke 16.34 (ASB EP)

Taste – and Preservation

Preservation is no problem in our time and our world; we keep any kind of food that will rapidly 'go off' in our fridge; and anything that is to be kept for some time, perhaps for a party a week or more ahead – well, that goes in the same fridge, but in the deep freeze. Salt, for us, is only a flavour which we can add, or not, to the dish placed in front of us. But think for a moment of earlier days; our ancestors prepared for winter by salting away the foods they would need – the meat from cattle, deer, and sheep, and the fish, carefully cleaned, then all packed away in salt to keep eatable during the long hard months of the year. How useful; and how important, to make sure the family had enough, preserved to carry them through the winter. And all the year, salt was precious just from the pleasure of its taste, it gives savour to otherwise rather dull-tasting food. Useful also for its preserving power; salt was and is a purifier, keeping good and useful foods from decay and corruption.

Parable of the Salt

God is the salt – God incarnate placed in this corrupt and evil world. 'Behold, I bring you good tidings' proclaimed the Angel to the Shepherds, men of this our corrupt world; 'for unto you is born this day a Saviour' – that is, One who, by his purifying power, can cleanse and preserve from corruption and decay this human race of ours. The Holy Spirit, the Salt of Heaven, is sent to cleanse and preserve from evil; the Church, as Jesus says, 'you are the salt of the earth', is God's agent. Why is the influence not as strong as it was, not so powerful now, in our days? Because the salt has lost its flavour. 'It the salt has lost its flavour, it is henceforth good for nothing, but to be cast out and trodden underfoot of men.' What a tragedy – to be 'good for nothing'!

Recovery
There is only one power, one influence, that can purify, preserve and save from extinction and good-for-nothingness; and that is the power of God operating upon the world, through the Church. No other power will ever bring to an end family, parish, political, industrial, national or international quarrels. That is the salt that the world needs; God is the salt of the world. Let the doors be opened of the individuals, of the families, of the nations, of the world, to receive the Spirit of God; if this was only to be done, the corruptions, the sorrows, the problems, the evils of this world would be at any rate arrested – and in time healed. Are we ourselves lacking salt? Are we, professing Christian folk, dull and savourless? Are the services and the Church and all its doings also dull, savourless and unattractive? without the Holy Spirit of God permeating and giving power and flavour to the whole? Let us look to our provision and our life, that we can indeed become the salt that defeats decay and evil, keeps for nourishment, growth and true life, the energies of humanity and the world.

St Matthew the Evangelist
Eighteenth Sunday after Pentecost (*Trinity 17*)
21 September   The Call
'Jesus saw Matthew at his seat in the custom-house; and he said to him, Follow me.' Matthew 9.9

Choosing an Apostle
Although St Matthew is not one of those apostles who are names and nothing more, we know only three things about him. First, we know that he was a customs official, and it was while he was

doing his work, sitting in his office, that Jesus came to him and said very simply – but very decisively without doubt – 'Follow me.' And Matthew got up, left his accounts and figures on the desk, and there and then walked out and joined Jesus. If, as seems most likely, the incident is the same one as is reported by Mark (Mark 2.14) as happening at Capernaum, there is no reason to doubt but that Matthew had heard the message of Jesus, and had had time to ponder over it, before he responded to Jesus' summons.

His Friends
Matthew's house, conveniently near the office, was a presumably fairly sumptuous place, large enough to accommodate a good number of his associates round the table; he was therefore probably a senior civil servant customs officer in the service of Herod Antipas. He did not hurry off without any thought of his fellow-workers and friends, but invited them home to meet with, and eat with, Jesus, which is the second fact we know. The third fact is that one of the four gospels – the one printed first in our Bibles – is called by his name, though the experts do not think that he wrote it all. Matthew and Luke have a number of passages in common which do not appear in Mark, but very little of Mark does not appear in Matthew or Luke, or both.

The Party
The Pharisees criticized Matthew's choice of guests, saying to the Lord's disciples that they were not suitable company for a religious leader. The tax men were disliked intensely by most of the population, since they worked for the Romans, the foreign tyrants, and also because the taxation system gave great opportunities for enriching those who worked it, at the expense of the ordinary people. No ordinary decent Jew would have anything to do with such shysters. Perhaps Jesus was intending to reassure Matthew, disturbed and embarrassed, when the Lord answered half-jokingly, 'It's not the healthy folk that need a doctor, but the sick', and added, 'I did not come to invite virtuous people, but sinners.'

The Pharisees
There is a subtle criticism of the Pharisees in the Lord's answer. Do we not sometimes come across people who are obviously far from well, yet if family or friends suggest seeing a doctor, they

reply obstinately, 'Nonsense! I'm not ill!' The Pharisees behaved in just this way; their disease was sin, their pride and self-satisfaction, and they could not begin to admit they were sinners; but they were quick enough to point out the sins of others.

Easy to criticize; suppose we ask ourselves, 'How far does our Lord's implied reproof apply not only to them, but to people like me?' We may not be narrow and self-righteous, as they were; but sin takes many forms – are we blind to the presence of some sin in our own lives?

And Today?
This story of faults and sins raises two other matters of some importance to the Church today. What should be our attitude to people who are openly living sinful lives, and have no intention, it seems, of making any change? And, what place have gatherings for pleasure, and social events, in the life of the Church? Waste of time, and distraction from more serious aims and objects? Or are they of value in promoting Christian fellowship, and in bringing in outsiders who may be put off by far too much solemnity?

If we take a strict view, both about the kind of company we keep and the place of pleasure in Christian life, we easily make our faith look gloomy and severe, we misrepresent its teaching, and we alienate other people; and there is the danger of self-righteousness, like the Pharisees. A more liberal view on both pleasure and people has its own pitfalls, even if we avoid the troubles of the Sheffield Nine-o'clock Service.

Our Lord's View
Jesus mixed freely with all sorts of people, attended wedding celebrations and parties, and illustrated his teaching by stories about such occasions. He was no killjoy. His rebukes of those who acted otherwise, were because they condemned and found fault, with those whose lives were unlike their own. 'I came that they may have life, and have it abundantly.' John 10.10

Pentecost 18 *Second Sermon* Contentment

'There is great gain in godliness with contentment; for we brought noth-ing into the world, and we cannot take anything out of the world; but if we have food and clothing, with these we should be content. But those

who are rich fall into temptation, into a snare, into many senseless and hurtful desires that plunge them into ruin and destruction.' 1 Timothy 6,6–9 (ASB EP)

Our Responsibilities

At times, we should sit back and take stock of the matter of living, both for ourselves and for others. What is it that we mean when we speak of ourselves as 'I'? What is this inner being which thinks, feels and acts? Yes, and perhaps more important, what is that inner being which feels it is responsible for thinking, feeling, and acting? It is because of this endowment which is ours that we know our lives are of importance, and that we are aware of the seriousness of the present moment. Each human being, as a moral being, is a worker, each working on himself or herself; working for the future, but is that future limited to what we know as 'time'? In our hearts we yearn for fulfilment, and we instinctively know that the fullness of completion is not to be attained during the span of time. Our hearts long for eternity; as St Augustine put it long ago,

> *Almighty God,*
> *you have made us for yourself,*
> *and our hearts are restless*
> *until they find their rest in you . . .*

> *(Collect for Pentecost 18 ASB)*

Yearnings

All of us are aware – more at some times than others, no doubt – aware of the brevity and uncertainty of our human life. As we look back on history, we see how times change; regimes that seemed for all time have vanished, others take their place but already begin to show signs of alteration, of change, of decay. Fashions change; in thought and philosophy no less than in clothes and decor, in styles of politics, no less than the shape and colour of the latest car. We do see and feel uncertainty everywhere; changes are thrust upon us, even with violence at times. There is increasing movement and change everywhere.

> 'All flesh is grass,
> and all its beauty as the flower of the field:
> the grass withers, the flower fades . . .'
> (Isaiah 40.6)

Passing

Withering grass and fading flowers are a true picture of our physical life. But though human physical life has these characteristics, immortality is the destiny of the human soul. We were made for fellowship with God. We need reminding that 'the world passes away, and the lust of it; but whoever does the will of God abides for ever' (1 John 2.17) Earthly things do not, and cannot, satisfy. God has set eternity in our hearts – 'He made everything beautiful in its time, also he has put eternity into human minds, yet so that we cannot find out what God has done from the beginning to the end.' (Eccles. 3.11) In a changing world, the one thing enduring is God's purpose: and in Christ it is being fulfilled, now and in the times to come.

Nineteenth Sunday after Pentecost (*Trinity 18*)
28 September   Why be Anxious?

'Consider the lilies of the field, how they grow; they toil not, neither do they spin: and yet I say unto you, That even Solomon in all his glory was not arrayed like one of these.' Matthew 6.28,29 (ASB Gospel)

The Providence of God

We believe in God's loving providence because Jesus makes that belief possible. We believe, because of him, quite literally in God's loving care. Jesus, in some of the loveliest passages in his teaching, reminds us of the concern God the Creator shows for the birds and the flowers, and gives us an assurance of God's care for us. 'Solomon in all his glory was not arrayed like the flowers of the field. But if that is how God clothes the grass in the fields, which is there today, and tomorrow is thrown on the stove, will he not all the more clothe you?' God knows our needs, and if we trust him, he will provide for them. Here is the reasoning that tells us that worry and anxiety are foolish. If we really have faith in God, we should be content to feel that we are in his hands – and they are loving hands, we know – and thus in the end all will be well.

This does not mean that we are not to bother to take such obvious steps to care for others and for ourselves, as to use what natural gifts we may have, and the wages or salaries we earn, together with the money we may have from such things as investments or legacies, to the best advantage for ourselves and for others.

And of course we look with wonder at the world of nature, and with amazement and awe at the astonishing universe of which we are only a tiny part. God's creative power and God's amazing mind – if we may use that term – astonish us as we see more and more into the depths of outer space and into the depths of inner space – the workings of the Cosmos on the one hand and the workings of the microscopic world of molecular science on the other.

Yet we can still believe that as we are made in God's image, so by a kind of reverse logic, God in his infinite power, wisdom and love is in a sense a reverse image of humanity – an immeasurably greater and more wonderful power and mind than we can begin to grasp, and yet, somehow, something is shared between God and us. This is one message of the Gospel reading for today.

Money

The other message is about our attitude to money. We are to try to do what is right, what we believe is God's will; and then our belief is that he will not fail us, and somehow our needs will be met. The prayer Jesus taught us to say, is not 'Give *me* my daily bread' but 'Give *us* . . .' There is nothing selfish about that prayer. God's bounty is sufficient for all, and is to be shared by all. Yet the world is divided between the rich who have too much, and the poor who are hungry, without enough food, shelter, clothing – and without the opportunity or opening to begin to improve their state.

Yes, we do what we can; contribute to Christian Aid and Oxfam – but the great solutions will not be solved until governments take a realistic attitude to the solutions of the problems – solutions they already have in their piles of reports and recommendations and UN documents of every size and colour. More self-sacrifice among the well-off nations, and more readiness to contribute to relieve distress, feed the hungry, care for the sick.

At the heart of the Gospel stands the Cross, the challenge to self-sacrifice. Whenever we pray 'Give us our daily bread', that is a challenge to help to feed the hungry of the world.

> *The burgeoning greed*
> *that never heeds the need of others*
> *involved in a merciless system*
> *looking only at profit and dividend*
> *the lust of possessions*
> *that cannot accompany us*
> *   at our last migration:*
> *Take away these sins,*
> *   O Lamb of God.*

from *The Word is the Seed (S.P.C.K.)*

Pentecost 19 *Second Sermon*
The Hosts of Heaven

'You shall see heaven wide open, and God's angels ascending and descending upon the Son of Man.' John 1,51 (ASB EP for St Michael & All Angels)

'Angels and Archangels'

'Therefore with Angels and archangels, and with all the company of heaven,' we join together in saying at the Holy Communion, praising God's holy Name, and echoing the wonderful hymn that is continually sung by all creation before the Creator, God almighty. It is difficult perhaps for us, in our day and age, to accept in the same way as our ancestors accepted, the idea of a 'heaven' up there 'above the bright blue skies', and perhaps just as difficult to accept the idea of messengers from God. Yet these parts of our faith are just as much proclaimed to us in the Bible as many other things; the Bible begins and ends with angels, cherubim guard the gates of Paradise, the angel of the Apocalypse gave God's commission to St John, and instructed him to seal it up.

Jesus himself told the people that the 'guardian angels' of children always behold the face of God the Father in heaven.

Messengers
The scholars tell us that our word 'angel' is a translation from Hebrew and Greek words meaning 'messenger'; and the phrase 'the angel of the Lord' can denote an appearance of God himself in human form. In the older times, the clear-cut distinction we make between 'natural' and 'supernatural' did not exist; human beings are bodies animated by the breath (Gen. 2.7) or spirit (Eccles. 12.7). In Hebrew thought, there was a belief in supernatural beings attending upon God (ascending and descending the heavenly ladder, as in our lesson tonight) and as messengers and intermediaries, bring God's help or revelation. Then in addition there are evil spirits, including Satan, the prime rebel against God, and lesser evil spirits who cause illnesses or disease.

In Art and Life
Angels are often depicted in art, in paintings, stained glass windows, and carvings. Sometimes these depictions can be magnificent and idealistic – like the St Michael by Epstein at the entrance to Coventry Cathedral – but they can also be unfortunately rather effeminate and leading us to dismiss 'angels' as either mythical or a kind of adult fairy tale. This would be a great pity, and a stronger attitude needs to be taught and displayed. In our Christian life, we should be clear that God does use and send his messengers – visible and invisible – and we should be alert to look for 'angels' in our daily living. Voices on radio, pictures on TV, the words we read in a book or paper or hear as we go about our lives, all can be messengers of God's love, truth, and enlightenment. They can also be warnings, and the role of a warner is another that is traditionally given to the angels.

Twentieth Sunday after Pentecost (*Trinity 19*)
5 October   Keeping Up Morale
'These three men, Shadrach, Meshach, and Abed-nego, fell bound into the burning fiery furnace.' Daniel 3.23 (ASB OT Reading)

Daniel in the Den of Lions

One of the first Bible stories to be told to small children is the extraordinary story of Daniel in the lions' den; indeed, it is for adults as well, one of the best-known Bible stories. We know how Daniel was thrown into the lions' den by the wicked King of Babylon, because he would not be false to his Jewish faith; and we know how the lions did not eat up Daniel, and all came right in the end. We would understand it better, though, and value it more, if we knew not only the story but its background.

Other Stories of Daniel

The Book of Daniel contains other stories, not as famous as the lions' den story, but quite well-known. One that is not unlike that story is what we have heard today, the story of the three friends who remained true to their faith and were thrown into a great fierce furnace – and escaped miraculously alive and unburnt. Of a different kind is the story of Belshazzer, the proud and powerful king who feasted in his imagined security, little dreaming that his enemies were in the very act of breaking into the city, and his death was at hand (Chapter 5). This story has been a favourite subject both for great artists and for great musicians. Two other stories, incidentally, are pointed out as being really the very first detective stories ever written: they are 'Susanna and the Elders' which is how false evidence was shown up by clever Daniel, and a beautiful lady saved from execution; and 'Bel and the Dragon' which is about (I'm sorry to say) cheating clergymen who took the offerings made in their temple, all for themselves, until clever Daniel put dust over the floor, and next morning showed the king the very footprints of the greedy priests.

Why were these Stories Written?

All these stories are supposed to take place when the Hebrew people were all taken to Babylon as slaves, far from their native land. The Bible scholars took it for granted that that was also the time and place the stories were written; but eventually they realized first, that the Book of Daniel was not written until hundreds of years after the Captivity, as it is called, and second, that the clue to the meaning of the stories is to be found in what was happening when the Book was written.

In fact, of course, the Hebrew people had long since been freed from slavery and had come back to Jerusalem and their country;

but now new enemies had appeared and once again, their religion and Israel itself were in great peril. This was the life-and-death struggle between the Jews, and the Syrians who wanted to impose the Greek religion and culture upon them; a struggle which went on for over forty years of bitter fighting and terrible cruelties. The books known as 1 and 2 Macabees tell us in sometimes very savage details how the struggle went on. It is all too reminiscent of the terrible slaughters and cruelties performed in Serbia and parts of Africa, in our own days, and the brutalities in Northern Ireland.

Value of the Stories Now

It is a bad sign of the times we live in, that little we see on the box or in our films today is calculated to encourage goodness, generosity or mercy, courage and unselfishness. General standards are low and there is little to admire; the stories are of violence and cruelty, betrayal and hatred. Rarely do we see anything of goodness or generosity, pity or mercy. The spirit shown by the heroes of the Book of Daniel is needed throughout our nation as never before.

And it is needed as much among Christians. The Faith is ignored by many, despised by some, sneered at by others; we need to hold fast with the courage and faith and good sense shown by Daniel's characters, and we all need Daniel's trust in God.

> Lord, pour upon us the fullness of your mercy,
> and by the power of your Spirit remove our divisions.
> Bring your Church to become a sign for all nations,
> that the world may be filled with the light of your Spirit,
> and believe in Jesus Christ whom you sent
> to proclaim your Way and to purge the nations
> from errors, corruptions, greed and brutality.
> Let humility triumph over pride, generosity over greed,
> humanity over cruelty and revenge,
> and your peace fill our hearts and minds.

Pentecost 20   *Second Sermon*   Our Voyage

'When the ship was caught and could not face the wind, we gave way to it and were driven.' Acts 27.13 (ASB EP)

The Last Journey

Paul had escaped an attempt to assassinate him (Acts 23.12–24) and as a Roman citizen, had been sent on as a prisoner to the Governor, Felix. After a preliminary hearing, as we might call it (24,1–24), and another before Festus the tribune (25,1–12), and yet another before King Agrippa (25.14–26), in the end it was decided that Paul should be sent to Rome and stand trial there at the highest level. Tribune and king summed up the result of their investigations as 'This man is doing nothing to deserve death or imprisonment.' And Agrippa said to Festus, 'This man could have been set free if he had not appealed to Caesar.'

The Roman legal system was very protective of the rights of a citizen, although those outside that classification had little but rough justice served upon them. The citizen, however, could, in the last resort, appeal to Caesar, as Paul had done in asserting his rights.

Why did Paul want to go to Rome?

Basically, the decision was made at Ephesus (Acts 19.21) where Paul resolves to go to Jerusalem and adds, 'After I have been there, I must also see Rome.' He also makes something of a dire prediction, speaking to the elders of Ephesus at Miletus in a farewell discourse: 'And now, behold I am going to Jerusalem, bound in the Spirit, not knowing what shall befall me thereafter . . .' (20.22)

Interestingly, the writing from the first verse of chapter 27, resumes the diary form, written by Luke himself, if we may take the use of 'we' as meaning just that. The use of 'we' began at v. 10 of chapter 16, where the writer describes the vision Paul had seen of a man of Macedonia asking for help, and continues 'When he had seen the vision, immediately *we* sought to go on into Macedonia . . .' and goes on to v. 16, but does not appear again until v. 1 of chapter 27 – the writer then continues with vivid descriptive passages about the voyage and the perils of shipwreck on an island, which turns out to be Malta. The last mention of 'we' appears in chapter 28, when after three months in Malta, at last they set sail and eventually reach Rome – 'And so we came to Rome.'

What an adventure! and a friendly meeting with the Roman brethren at 'The Forum of Appius and Three Taverns' which was quite a triumphal entry, the Forum being forty miles out from Rome and 'Tres Tabernae' thirty. In Rome, Paul was allowed to stay by himself, and teach with a soldier as guard. So ends Luke's great literary feat; we believe that Paul was not put to death in Rome, and there are allusions in letters by him or ascribed by him, of at least one period of imprisonment, and of his own uncertainty as to the outcome of his trial. It is hard for us to forgive Luke for not telling us all about it; but he makes the climax the arrival of Paul at the capital of the Empire technically a prisoner, but able to teach and preach 'openly and unhindered'. That is a great finale.

Twenty-first Sunday after Pentecost (*Trinity* 20)
12 October   Pray Continually

'Now will not God see justice done to his chosen who cry to him day and night, even when he delays to help them? I promise you, he will see justice done to them, and done speedily.' Luke 18.8 (ASB Gospel)

On our Knees all Day?

Our Lord tells a parable in the gospel for today, to the effect that we should pray always. Now clearly, Jesus does not mean that we should spend all day on our knees, nor that we should be praying amid every activity of the day! Nor can he mean that we should be thinking of God all day long. That is not possible! James Thurber told of a man who was always afraid he would stop breathing. He even set his alarm clock to go off at regular intervals during the night, to wake him up to see if he were still breathing! Obviously, we really cannot be like that in regard to God.

Always?

How then *are* we to pray always?

When two people love one another, they are constantly in each other's thoughts. Even if their minds are on other things, they have each other, as the saying goes, 'at the back of their minds'. So it should be with us and God. We should constantly think of God, and pray to him, and in this way we create a supernatural atmosphere in our lives, so that, even when we are not thinking of God, he is still at the back of our mind. Our normal, formal, daily prayers help to sanctify our day. They make of our daily work, a prayer.

Rooted
Our activities become rooted in prayer, so that they in themselves *are* prayer. In this way, there is a real meaning in saying that our whole day is prayer, and that therefore we are praying always. Today's parable stresses the necessity of perseverance in prayer. So much prayer is, or can be, merely casual, without very much depth to it. Where there is real love, there will be depth of understanding. We must so create our relationship with God that, although he remains a mystery to us, yet at the same time we can feel we know him. His presence becomes a reality in our lives. It becomes a constant presence, even though we do not, or cannot, with our busy conscious mind, be aware percipiently of it all the time.

> *Lord Jesus Christ,*
> *help me to follow and find you*
> *in our world today:*
> *in the places where I work,*
> *meet people, spend money,*
> *and make plans.*
> *Take me as a disciple of your kingdom*
> *to see through your eyes*
> *to welcome all with your trust and truth*
> *by the power of your Cross*
> *and the freedom of your Spirit.*
>
> G.A.

Pentecost 21   *Second Sermon*
A Good King   St Edward the Confessor

'In his time shall righteousness flourish, and abundance of peace.' Ps.
72,7

England at Peace

The mid-eleventh century was a period of peace in England. Alfred
the Great and his immediate successors, Edward the Elder and
Ethelstan, had succeeded in defeating the Danes and in effect
uniting England under one ruler. Edgar was the first to be crowned
(by St Dunstan, Archbishop of Canterbury) as 'King of all England'. Much of this, however, was lost by Ethelred the Unready,
though King Canute brought peace and overall unity. After
Canute's son's death in 1042, the mighty Earl Godwin made
Edward, son of Ethelred II and Emma of Normandy, King of
England. He was forty years of age when he was crowned;
although in his veins ran the blood of Alfred the Great, he had
lived most of his life in France, and the language of that country
was what he spoke. He brought over many Normans with him to
hold positions of power in both Church and State, so that with
his coming the 'Norman Invasion' of England could be said to
have really begun.

Peaceful

However, the mid-eleventh century was a period of peace, a fitting
era for one whose holy life was marked by gentleness and piety.
His coronation in Winchester Cathedral by Archbishop Eadsige,
with most of the English bishops assisting at the ceremony, must
have been a truly magnificent spectacle.

In appearance Edward was very tall and blond, almost an albino,
but of regal bearing. Even during his lifetime his people regarded
him as a saint, crediting him with powers of healing, and with
the gift of seeing into the hidden mysteries of the future.

A contemporary poet wrote of him as being 'noble, chaste and
mild, guarding his people' until death came and the angels bore
his soul into the Light of Heaven. Despite his piety and austerity,
he was an ardent sportsman; he would spend hours in prayer,
and then go off happily to the chase.

Marriage

Earl Godwin of Essex arranged Edward's marriage to his daughter, Edith, thinking the union would strengthen his (Godwin's) influence against the influx of Normans, already remarked upon with some jealousy and fear as forming a kind of centralized administration of the country. It is said that Edward himself had but little inclination for matrimony; he was however a staunch supporter of the monastic system, and built a great abbey at Westminster near his palace. This was the result of a vow which he had made during his life in exile at Rouen. He had sworn to make a pilgrimage to Rome, but this obligation was impossible to fulfil when he was made king; so he sent a party, including two bishops, to beg the Pope for absolution from his vow, if he built a mighty abbey to the glory of God and the Apostles, in London. His request was granted, and the Abbey built.

Revered

The Confessor-King died in his Palace at Westminster in that fateful year 1066, and his body placed in a shrine behind the High Altar of the great church, where countless generations have paid homage to the king and saint. He was quickly revered by the ordinary people, and during the bitter times after the Norman Conquest they looked back to his reign as something of a golden age. (It was said that 'a woman could travel from one side of England to the other, with her bosom full of gold, in complete safety.' Sadly, one would not care to give such an assurance today ...) 'Many of those who sleep in King Edward's Abbey were devoted servants of their time, who left the world better for their passing. But this is certain, that true satisfaction came to them, and success crowned them, only so far as their ambitions were for a cause, not for a party; for others, not for themselves. Man's happiness lies in devoting himself; his success in the offering he can make. And our Confessor was a successful man, yes, even in this world, because in his simple piety, in the unaffected generosity of his nature, he set himself to serve those about him by easing their burdens, by relieving their necessities, by confirming their allegiance to the Faith.' (From a sermon by Ronald Knox, in *The Cloud of Witnesses*)

Last Sunday after Pentecost (*Trinity 21*)
19 October   The Promise of Life

'I strain ahead for what is still to come; I am racing for the finish.'
Philippians 3.13

Fascination
Part of the fascination of the words of Christ, is that they promise life and have the power to give it. His words are like no other words, in that they are loaded with grace and, if accepted, have a transforming quality. They make life worth living because they impart a wholeness, a fullness, an abundance to it. They promise a life beyond a life.

'I have come that they may have life and have it more abundantly,' Jesus said. He tells us that 'he will give eternal life to all that the Father has entrusted to him'. Without Christ, human life tends to sink to the animal level. He is the key to human existence, and indeed the reason why it exists at all. 'I am the Resurrection and the Life,' he said; what is dead, meaningless, unproductive, becomes alive, fruitful and significant – in him.

Eternal Life
It is not simply that his words give a promise of the future, but they give eternal life *now*. A superhuman power is imparted by them; a power which can indeed impel a human being across the grave to a new and finer existence; but which – at the same time – gives to our present life a glory and a splendour beyond human comprehension – because it is a sharing in the life of God. We can now say with St Paul, 'I no longer live, but Christ Jesus lives in me.' The power of Christ envelops us – not that we lose our identity, but that we are caught up in the life of Christ, in such a way that we become one, not in identity, but in unity of purpose and love.

Power
In the Tower of London, awaiting execution, St Thomas More wrote,

> 'The sayings of our Saviour Jesus Christ were not a poet's fable, nor a harper's song, but the very holy Word of Almighty God himself.'

This is what gives these sayings such power; all the might of God is contained in them. Our part is, to respond to them; and this we do when we try our best to live in accordance with their teaching and exhortation.

Last Sunday after Pentecost   *Second Sermon*
Citizens of Heaven

'Sir, sir,' they cried, 'open the door for us!' But he answered, 'I declare, I do not know you.' Keep awake then, for you never know the day nor the hour.' Matthew 25.13 (ASB EP Reading)

Visions of the Redeemed

From visions of happiness and peace, after the trials and terrors of earthly life, that Isaiah puts before us, the gospel reading brings us back to earth with a resounding crash. Christ warns us not to relax; we must continue to be prepared for the coming of the Lord. Our vigilance must be continual, and we must be ready for the moment when it comes. If we are not ready, then we may all-too-easily share the fate of the unfortunate girls, who found themselves shut out from the festivities at the last moment.

Where exactly did they fail?

Well, it was not in dozing off, for all the girls fell asleep. The fault must lie in that they had forgotten to bring with them the needful oil for their lamps. The bridegroom went in to the wedding feast, with the girls who had lighted him on his way; but he was certainly not going to admit a group of girls whom he had never seen until the moment they came to his doorway.

Repentance

What is being impressed upon Christ's listeners (and ourselves) is this – The new life offered to all who believe – and how often does not Christ describe this new life under the guise of a banquet, or a feast, or a wedding breakfast – is freely offered; but on condition that those who wish to accept prepare themselves. The wedding garment provided must be worn (Matt. 22.1–14); those who are invited but do not bother to come on time, because they are so busy (Luke 14.12–24) these must expect to find themselves turned away and the doors shut, and others preferred before them.

Preparation
Let us on this last Sunday of the Church's Year, so prepare ourselves that we may – not only join the worship and the fellowship of the New Church Year, but also – be able to enter in to the final Wedding Feast with our lamps burning. If the appointed hour should suddenly strike, and the noise and singing of the Bridegroom's journey be heard, and our opportunity present itself – would our lamps be ready and burning, or empty and cold and useless . . . ?

> Withhold not from me, O my God, the best,
>   the Spirit of thy dear Son:
> that in that Day when judgement is set
> I may be presented before thee
>   not blameless but forgiven,
>   not effectual but faithful,
>   not holy but persevering,
>   without desert but accepted
> because he hath pleaded the causes of my soul,
>   and redeemed my life.
>
> *(Eric Milner-White)*

Ninth Sunday before Christmas (*Trinity* 22)
26 October   God at the Centre
(The ASB Readings now change to Year 2)
'Thou art worthy, O Lord our God, to receive glory and honour and power, because thou didst create all things; by thy will they were created, and have their being!' Revelation 4.11 (ASB NT Reading)

What Sort of a World?
How do you see the world? What sort of a world is it? Do you see God in it? What role do you see him having in it?

We have a choice of view; it is not forced upon us. We are

dealing with questions of the invisible and spiritual, and we cannot see all the realities with our eyes. What we perceive as the landscape of the world is what is in our mind: it is how we choose to see it.

What about the great questions of purpose – Why am I here? Why is the world here? What is the purpose of it all? These questions cannot be answered just by looking around at the buildings and the cars and the buses. These do not give us the meaning of it all. Bishop Lesslie Newbigin says that if you see a building going up, there are only two ways to find out its purpose: Either you wait until it is finished and see how it is furnished and equipped and used; or you ask the architect or builder. It's like that, the bishop says, with the world; but we haven't time to wait until the development of the world is complete, in order to find out its purpose! We need to know now, in our lifetime. The only way we have, therefore, is to let the builder tell us.

God at the Centre
The first book of the Bible, Genesis – which means the Beginning – although it was actually written later than the other parts of the Bible, is placed right at the start in order to answer some of our questions. What sort of a world is this? What sort of a God is there? What is the purpose of human existence? Our readings, in the most emphatic ways, call us to see the world with God right at the centre – whether as a celestial gardener, planting food and providing animals for human sustenance, and ensuring the continuation of the newly-created human race, male and female. Or as an almost unapproachable Deity, enthroned in glory, and about whom swells and rises the vast chorus of praise from the whole universe; and finally, in the words of Jesus to Nicodemus, giving the mysterious aspect of spiritual power, available to those born again.

'Why am I here? What is our purpose?'
The answer we take from the Bible is that we are here to develop and manage God's world: this is what human work and effort is all about. Because we are in the image of God, our partnership should mean that our work, like God's, is both creative and satisfying. Sadly, this is not often so; people have to do jobs in routine and boring ways, and initiative and imagination are not used. Why? This is usually so that the owners retain control, get-

ting maximum output for the minimum of time and money; but this reaps a terrible harvest as it tends to dehumanize people, treating them less than God intended, and they become poorer – and poorer workers.

'Together'
This points to the concept of service. We do things for one another. We make our skills and energy available for the common good. And it must be the common good; this work enterprise that God has given is good – that means good for everyone. Sadly, all work is not all creativity and satisfaction. A great deal of it is a sheer struggle to stay alive. This is what we call The Fall, and it is related to human disobedience of God. Our aim must always be to return, as much as possible, to creative management, because this is God's original purpose and aim for us. So we return finally to the centrality of God. It remains our human choice whether or not we will see things this way. But if our vision of the world has God as designer, first great Cause, and chief actor, it yields a fruitful understanding of our purpose in the world. We are made by God to share in his work of managing the world, together, for the good of everyone and all of his creation.

Ninth before Christmas   *Second Sermon*
'The Word'

'In the beginning was the Word, and the Word was with God, and the Word was God.' John 1,1 (ASB EP)

A Mystic Title
One title of our Lord Jesus Christ does present some people with some difficulties – it is 'The Word of God', associated particularly with St John's Gospel, where it appears right at the beginning, 'In the beginning was the Word, and the Word was God . . .' and then a little later – 'The Word became flesh and dwelt among us' (v. 14) In the first place, there is some easily-made confusion between the 'Word of God' meaning the Scriptures, and the 'Word' who was *with* God and also *was* God. This needs a certain clarification; the Scriptures contain truths about God, written down by inspired

writers – that is, the evangelists and apostles in the New Testament, and the prophets and poets of the Old Testament.

Mediated to us in different styles and varied ways, by the scriptural writers, *this* 'Word' is the message of salvation, the message of the Bible for us all, and it follows and points out the road we should take in life, with the history of the Hebrew people and their – at first – crude and primitive ideas of God and his worship, then the long and gradual process of refining and clarifying the words and the worship, the rules and customs, the rights and the wrongs; then on to the New Testament, in particular the Four Gospels which contain the words and teaching of Christ as well as his earthly life, the Acts – the first struggles and growth of the infant Church – together with the Epistles of Paul, John, Peter, James and then the final strange, if beautiful and mystic, book – Revelation. As the author of the Letter to the Hebrews puts it,

'In many and various ways God spoke of old to our fathers by the prophets, but in these last days he has spoken to us by a Son, whom he appointed the heir of all things, through whom he created the world' (1,1–2).

'Logos'
Again, the 'creative force' of the universe was widely recognized by ancient philosophers, Greek and Roman, and they gave the Greek name 'Logos' ('word') to it; to some this word denoted the divine reason immanent or indwelling, and pervading permanently the universe and in the minds of humanity; to others it signified a creative power or agony which mediated between a God, thought of as wholly transcendent – that is, outside the world of matter, and the world itself.

The Early Church adopted this idea in its efforts to make clear the faith it was committed to teach; it used the word 'Logos' to mean the direct and personal incarnation of Jesus Christ.

Problems
Problems arose before long between the philosophers and theologians, as to the exact meaning of the concept, and varied points of view soon developed into heresies, such as the Arian, which took Christ as being essentially *less* than God; or the view ascribed to Apollinaris, which was that Christ was not fully human like us, but at best a human body with a divine principle within it. The answer to these propositions was eventually reached, by

declaring that if Christ was not fully human, he could not have been the Saviour of the human race: 'What he did not assume, he did not heal.'

Paradox

Many divines have expended immense time and thought upon the problem of the nature of the Incarnation, down the ages from the Early Fathers through the Council of Chalcedon (which produced the 'Nicene' Creed we use Sunday by Sunday) through the Reformation period (when both Luther and Calvin took up differing positions) to the present day.

Perhaps the best, or present at any rate, view might be summarized thus:

There is a paradox in the Incarnation, as there is in Creation: all things created out of nothing ('Big Bang' or not). There is a paradox in grace: the Christian conviction that everything good we do is the work of God within us, and not our own. So, this paradox expresses best the mystery of the Incarnation itself in its fragmentary form in our own Christian lives, it is a reflection of that perfect union of God and Humanity *in* the Incarnation, on which our whole Christian life depends.

Deep Places

No doubt the theologians will continue to explore the deep places of our religion, and produce ever more subtle explanations; but for us ordinary people it is surely best to take refuge in the thought that the Christ, who is now exalted and living enthroned in heaven, is still the same Christ who tramped the dusty roads of Palestine, talked and laughed, sweated in the sun and shivered in the frost, ate and drank with beggars and prostitutes, showed his faith and his love, cheered his friends and told off his opponents, lived and died and was raised by God to new life.

Through him we present our prayers and petitions; to him we look for our example of life and love, and from him we hope to receive our reward in the world to come.

Almighty and everlasting God,
grant that we who have seen your glory revealed in our human
    nature,
and your love made perfect in our weakness,
may daily be renewed in your image,

and conformed to the pattern of your Son.
Jesus Christ our Lord. Amen.

Eighth Sunday before Christmas (*Trinity 23*)
2 November **Redemption**

'God sent the Son into the world, not to condemn the world, but that the world might be saved through him.' John 3.17 (ASB Gospel)

Obedience and Disobedience

We Christians are men and women, human beings; we are not angels. We all have our weaknesses and our faults. We may not like apples, but there is bound to be something in our lives that fascinates us, draws us away from the right path, and we wander away from our true calling and vocation, the love and the service of God. St Ignatius Loyola, founder of the Jesuits, at the beginning of his remarkable and widely read and used book, *Spiritual Exercises*, wrote this: 'Humanity was created to praise, reverence and serve God.' This is by no means always an easy precept to follow. The joys of *Vanity Fair* may lure the Christian away from it. The desire of making money may become the be-all and end-all of our work and life. Our real direction of ourselves and all that we do, to be an offering of service to God, may be forgotten. But if we are fundamentally persons of good will, trying in spite of problems and difficulties, to do God's work in the world, our Christian beliefs should in the end, win us back to a truer and better view of living.

God's Attitude

Sometimes we may be like the first son, who says 'No!' in Jesus' parable of the father who asks his two boys to work for him in his vineyard; but like that son, afterwards he repents and went. You see, God understands failures and is always ready to transform them into success, provided we do our part. As the poet wrote,

> 'But what if I fail of my purpose here?
> It is but to keep the nerves at strain,
> To dry one's eyes and laugh at a fall,
> And baffled, get up to begin again . . .'
>
> (Robert Browning)

210

God allows us to get up again and again, after having failed him. What he wants is our repentance. He hates us to shirk our responsibilities. This is what poor old Adam and Eve did in our Old Testament story – they promised God not to eat the famous fruit, the apple of discord; but didn't keep their promise. Unreliable, not conscientious – there go our first parents! People like that in our world today can be a menace in business (did I hear someone say 'Barings'?) and even more dangerous in personal relationships.

Moral for Today
The lesson for us all is that we must be honest and sincere in our lives, as a matter of human trust and human contracts, and for our relationship with God. We may fail at times, but at least we should try our best, after our failures, to start again – come to the light, as St John puts it today in our Gospel reading – and work for God with renewed energy, hope and love.

8th before Christmas *Second Sermon*
True Religion

Jesus said, 'You leave the commandments of God, and hold fast the traditions of men.' Mark 7,8 (ASB EP)

The Commandments
Many problems faced Moses in the wilderness; perhaps the greatest was the making of wise laws to maintain proper discipline and regard for one another, among what was a very mixed collection of people, coming from differing tribes and with different – often antagonistic – customs, rules, beliefs.

He did his work well – somehow on this mixed and confused mass of refugees from the brutality and domination of Egypt, he imposed a set of rules or laws which, by and large, kept the peace; and enabled them to successfully get through the inhospitable desert regions, and moulded them into a disciplined nation. Did Moses write, as the old scholars maintained, all the first five books of the Bible, including his own obituary (Deuteronomy 34)? The present form of these books, and probably the original writings from which they were edited, date from much later than the great leader's time.

Fame
But Moses was undoubtedly the author of many of the laws embedded in the books as we have them today, and to be the author of the Ten Commandments of God is fame indeed. What an achievement, and what a power and a personality was – with God's help – able to perform the marvellous task of union and conversion of very varied tribes into the beginnings of a nation.

Later, when we reach the time of the Lord Jesus, we can see what had happened to the code of laws when we read in St Mark's gospel the lesson appointed tonight. (Mark 7.1–23) Over the years, clever lawyers and scribes (theologians, we would call them) had so enclosed the original simplicity of the Laws as to make it possible to do many things which the Laws themselves were intended to prevent. As Jesus says, 'You have a fine way of rejecting the commandment of God, in order to keep (or allow) your traditions! . . . You make void the word of God through your "tradition" which you hand on.' Jesus went through the form of words, to arrive once again at the essential truths of the ancient Law; a spiritual thing, not arrived at or achieved by physical acts, but by spiritual means only. Nothing outward can defile; uncleanness comes from within.

The Early Church
Eventually, of course, this teaching was taken up by the early Church (though the disciples did not grasp Jesus' point – vv. 17, 18, 19 – and Peter had to have a separate revelation (Acts 10, 9–48) which opened wide the way of salvation to Gentiles. Though there was still difficulty, as we read in Galatians 2.11ff. Paul rather bitterly reproaches Peter – 'If you, though a Jew, live like a Gentile and not like a Jew, how can you compel the Gentiles to live like Jews?' Paul in fact was tolerant of the Jewish Christians' reluctance to abandon the ritual prescriptions of the Law, but was equally insistent that they should not be forced upon Gentile Christians. (Romans 14.1–15.13)

*Dear God, You burst our narrow bonds. We cannot
confine You, monopolize You, control You. Out,
beyond Israel, beyond Christianity, beyond the religions,
to the ends of the world, to the end of time,
embracing every creature – O God, my God, God of all.*

G.A.

*   *   *

First Sunday of the Kingdom – *See 'The Promise of His Glory', p. 383 for full details*
(7 before Christmas ASB)
COLLECT: *O God,
       by whose command the order of time runs its course;
       forgive our impatience, perfect our faith,
       and, while we wait for the fulfilment of your promises,
       grant us to have a good hope because of your word;
       through Jesus Christ our Lord.*

Second Sunday of the Kingdom
(6 before Christmas ASB)
COLLECT: *Be to us, Lord, a crown of glory
       on the day when you come
       to judge the world by fire;
       that in your grace and mercy
       you may clothe us now in this life
       with the robe of righteousness,
       and in the life hereafter
       with the perfection of a glorious liberty;
       for with the Father and the Holy Spirit
       you are one God, now and for ever.*

Third Sunday of the Kingdom: Feast of the Kingship of Christ
(5 before Christmas ASB)
COLLECT: *Eternal Father,
       whose Son Jesus Christ ascended to the throne of heaven
       that he might rule over all things as Lord:
       keep the Church in the unity of the Spirit
       and in the bond of his peace,
       and bring the whole created order to worship at his feet;*

who is alive and reigns with you and the Holy Spirit,
one God, now and for ever.

*   *   *

Seventh Sunday before Christmas (*Trinity 24, 3 before Advent*)   Remembrance Sunday
(see p. 262)   (*First Sunday of the Kingdom (PHG)*)
9 November   The Ancestor of Faith

'By your descendants shall all the nations of the earth bless themselves, because you have obeyed my voice'. Genesis 22.18

Abraham your Father

If Jews and Muslims and Christians are to recognise each other as children of Abraham, we must all be ready to be like him, and imitate him in faith and obedience. He is called the 'Friend of God' in both Old Testament (2 Chronicles 20.7) and in the New Testament (James 2.23) because of his faith in God, and the way he takes all his problems to God. He was troubled about the destruction of Sodom and Gomorrah; he worried that the good people there should die with the wicked. His pleading with God resulted in the sparing of the inhabitants for the sake of the righteous folk who may be there ... 'Shall not the judge of all the earth do right?' Before this, of course, he had left his native land and moved with all his family and tribe to the South, where he could be free to worship his God and bring up his people who would, God told him, be a blessing to all nations.

Jesus, in argument with his critics, said of Abraham that 'He rejoiced to see my day' suggesting that Abraham was still living, and taking a deep interest in the purpose of God for all nations, which he himself had glimpsed.

We may be puzzled at our Lord's words 'Before Abraham was, I am' – this could refer to the Name of God, revealed to Moses at the Burning Bush (Exodus 3.4, 13–14) as 'I AM WHO I AM' – the divine title, mysterious and solemn.

Isaac

Abraham's willingness to sacrifice his son Isaac, through whom – humanly speaking – the divine purpose was to be fulfilled, shows us that he put faith in God and obedience to him as his highest priority, even though his belief that God wanted human sacrifice was mistaken. (Or did Abraham, disgusted by the human sacrifices (usually children) which the people offered in those remote and primitive times, go through a kind of acted parable, and return from the mountain with his victim unharmed, and the account of God's voice from heaven telling him to stop, and not offer up his son, but take a ram instead and offer that ...)

'Where?'

Sometimes we may obey an inner urge to set out on some course or journey, the end of which we cannot see. 'Where will all this lead to?' we may well ask ourselves. But if we obey the driving force, we are sharing the faith of Abraham. We set out trusting in God, as Abraham did.

Seventh Sunday before Christmas
Second Sermon   Truth

Jesus said, 'If I tell the truth, why do you not believe me?' John 8,46 (ASB EP)

Hostile Hearers

The crowds who came to listen to Jesus, came for different reasons and had differing responses to what they heard. There were those who were much impressed, and who at least for a time, tried to follow what they had gathered – maybe later they came to form the Jewish Christian Church, centred at Jerusalem, with James 'the brother of Jesus' and Peter as leaders. Then there would be those who were not moved, or if they were, they went home and soon forgot all about it. And from a certain number of his hearers Jesus met with active opposition and hostile criticism.

Opposition

The criticisms were varied. Some hearers accused him of disrespect for the laws laid down by the Scribes and Pharisees – for instance the observance of the Sabbath in its very extreme form. They declared him to be devil-possessed, and of course that his healing powers came from not God, but Satan. The priests and leaders must have been particularly hurtful to Jesus – for of all the Jewish people they should have understood what he was saying best of all.

Violence

One of the saddest outbreaks of violence occurred against Jesus in the very early days, at Nazareth, the very place where he was brought up. The locals resented – or some of them – this jumped up fellow, the son of Joseph the carpenter, who was known by everyone as a decent craftsman, but hardly an expert in the Bible or the Laws of Moses, telling them what to think and what to do. They even went so far as to try and throw Jesus over a cliff (Luke 4,28–30). This must have distressed Jesus particularly, since he and his assailants were personally known to each other; taken up by strong emotion however, his countenance must have been so stern that the crowd parted, and he walked through the midst of them untouched.

Insults

Bitter insults were hurled at Jesus in the scene described by John today, and particularly over the references to Abraham. In reply Jesus comes close to replying in kind, telling his attackers that they are children – not of God, nor of Abraham, but – of the Devil. Further insults provoked him, it seems, and he made a clear claim to divinity, 'Truly, truly, I say to you, before Abraham was, I AM.' Here is an indication of Christ's eternal existence as God, for by the use of the ancient and sacred name – first appearing when Moses was called by God from the burning bush – he claims to be nothing less than Incarnate God, here on earth. Not surprisingly, the crowd took up stones, but Jesus hid himself . . . (v. 59) It is for us to give the welcome to Jesus, that he should have had that day back in the Temple, when the crowd of God's Chosen People instead of recognizing who he was, wanted to put him to death.

Sixth Sunday before Christmas (*Trinity 25*)
(*Second Sunday of the Kingdom (PHG)*)
Deliverance and Freedom
'I will reclaim you with arm outstretched and with mighty acts of judgement.' Exodus 6.6 (ASB OT Reading)

Moses
What a great figure Moses was; he inspired, bullied and threatened the raggle-taggle mixture of Bedouin tribes into a cohesive body with a sense of purpose, which became – against all odds – the nation of Israel. Moses must have had many of the characteristics of another great desert leader, Lawrence of Arabia. He found how vast the desert is – there men could begin to grasp something of the vastness and the unity of God.

And how like the tribes Lawrence loved, and strove to master, must the early Hebrews have been. Brave but quarrelsome, brutal at times, but loyal to tribe and family. Only gradually could they be pulled and driven into some wider unity, and become a nation.

Unity
This wider unity Moses was able to bring his followers to accept through a striking combination of religious instruction, with promises of a country for them all to share – plus the treasures of the peoples they would dispossess. He led them through the bitter desert and hostile territory until they at last arrived at the Promised Land. There, without setting foot over the frontier, Moses was able to see the country his followers were to take over; and having made them into a nation, given them a language and a code of conduct, and a powerful religion, he died in peace, leaving the final battles to his successors.

Religion
Moses was brought up at the court of Pharaoh, as the Bible tells us in the first two chapters of Exodus. It is possible that he came under the influence of those who followed the faith of the famous Pharaoh Ikhnaton, a ruler who taught belief in One God – perhaps for the first time in recorded history. What is certain, however, is that to the ancient figure of the Patriarch Moses are attached two great ideals.

The first is the worship of One God alone. What had been previously revealed to others under various aspects, was now fused into the Creator God, the Living God, Jehovah, 'I AM THAT I AM.' The second is the ideal of Freedom. Moses led the Hebrew people – as they became – from slavery in Egypt, to freedom in their own land.

A Type of Christ

For us Christians we see in Moses a 'type' of Christ, that is, a foreshadowing or symbol of the freedom of all God's people that the Resurrection victory won. In our Lord's suffering, obedience and sacrifice, all human suffering is taken up and transformed by his victory, made fruitful and creative.

Sixth Sunday before Christmas *Second Sermon*
'The Bread of Life'

'I am the bread of life. He who comes to me will never be hungry; he who believes in me will never thirst.' John 6.35

Victory

What an amazing event the Resurrection of our Lord was! The disciples were astonished, amazed, swept away in a wave of surprise and relief, unable to understand – yet they knew their Lord was there. Mary Magdalene saw him through eyes filled with tears, as 'the gardener', until she heard his voice. Then she knew who it was. Thomas would not believe, until he touched the wounds. Then he said, 'My Lord and my God!' The two disciples – were they husband and wife? – on the road to Emmaus, knew him not – until he broke the bread.

Recognition

We hear the words of Jesus. We know he is with us. We touch the bread, taste the wine. We know his Presence with us. 'I am the bread of life', he says. We receive the bread, broken; drink the wine, poured out.

The Seaside
The people who followed Jesus and his disciples after the miraculous feeding of the five thousand, may well have been thinking about the wonderful supply of food; yet there was also the urge to know more about the wonder-working Prophet and to hear more of what he had to say. 'Would he not give them another sign, perform another work? If he is really a prophet, do something like the greater leader Moses did – bring food down from heaven?'

Bread from Heaven
'I am giving you the Bread of Life; I am bringing you spiritual food and drink; if you believe in me you will never die eternally, for I will raise you up at the last day (v. 40). It was not Moses who gave your ancestors the bread from heaven, but my Father.'

The Will of the Father
Jesus comes to do the will of the Father: 'All that the Father gives me will come to me; and he who comes to me I will never turn away.' God's will is, that all should come to him. 'It is his will that I should not lose even one of all that he has given me.' The message of Christ crucified and risen, is that he will not lose anyone who comes to him; we are not to be so preoccupied with living, earning a living, making our way in the world, that we neglect the spiritual. Nor should we be content to rely upon our attendance at our church, our devotion at our Eucharists, our reception of the Body and Blood at our Communion-time.

Witness to Power
We should test the power of our faith by bearing witness of it to others, outside and beyond the limited – though lovely! – area of church and worship. It has been rightly said, 'No feeling is worth anything, if it is not the child of truth and the parent of action.' Our faith must be such that we can justify it and explain it to those who would ask us for the reason behind the hope that it is in us. And, even more important, that hope must translate itself into deeds, service, help for the helpless, direction to the vigorous.

Fifth Sunday before Christmas (*Sunday next before Advent*) (*Third Sunday of the Kingdom (PHG)*) 23 November End of the Journey

'But you be on your guard; I have forewarned you.' Mark 13.23 (ASB Gospel)

Forewarning

The day before Martin Luther King was assassinated he gave a speech at Memphis in which he said, 'I've been to the mountain top, and I've looked over, and I've seen the Promised Land. I may not get there with you, but I want you to know that we as a people will get to our Promised Land.'

This longing for a dawn out of darkness has become the basis of many a nation's legends and aspirations. We are all of us on a pilgrimage, and within us in one way and another we have this longing for better things at our journey's end. We know there will be trials and tribulations, on the way, but one day they will make way for a happy ending.

The Ending

In today's Gospel, Christ points out that one day the whole of the human pilgrimage will come to an end. The picture presented in the Gospel is a dark and sombre one; it is a picture of chaos, with an earth shaken to its foundations. But just as at the beginning of the world, there was darkness and confusion, from which God brought light and harmony, so will it be at the end, when Christ comes in majesty.

The world will be dark then only for those who have turned their backs on Christ. The Gospel does not mean, then, that the world will end in a terrible catastrophe; what it is telling us is, that the world as we know it, will no longer exist but that a completely new order of existence will come into being. Christ tells us in the gospel that no one knows when all this will happen, but we are to be constantly on watch. 'Be on your guard, I have forewarned you.' Our faith and love must never fail, nor our hope; and so let us prepare ourselves for the unknown Day.

Fifth Sunday before Christmas   *Second Sermon*
Broken Off

'They were lopped off because of their lack of faith.' Romans 11.20 (ASB EP)

Cut Off by the Tide
A not uncommon happening, down by the seaside, is for a small group of people to be cut off by the tide. They went too far over the rocks, perhaps to a small island, or perhaps they did not know some of the local peculiarities; anyhow, they were rather ignorant of the tricky ways that the sea can get up to. Hopefully, these people escape with something of a scare, maybe a wetting also; sometimes, however, there may be a tragedy.

Cut Off in Other Ways
Some other people may be cut off from their fellow humans, perhaps for longer periods and different circumstances. We all worry very much when some students or travellers are cut off by people of primitive tribes in remote parts of our world, and are held captive for money or for some political end.

Then there are those of us who are more or less 'cut off' from the rest of us and the people around about them, by deafness or blindness, or other handicaps. We give thanks for all those agencies and helpers who give assistance in various ways for such people, and make their lives less difficult and less isolated. And there are people who cut themselves off. They give way to feelings of suspicion or distrust or dislike of those neighbours or other people round about, and withdraw into what can be a sad and lonely life.

Cut off from God
And apart from these men and women who isolate themselves, or are isolated from the world round about them, there are all too many who are cut off from God, a much greater tragedy.

How is this?

Perhaps it is through lack of opportunity. There are still large parts of the world where Christianity has made no impact, or very little; and other countries where the State or the religion of the country is against Christianity. On the other hand, the great anti-religious area of Russia has opened its borders to Christians from other countries, and the wonderful Othodox Churches are able to come out into the open.

Selfishness and Sin
Selfishness and sin are what separate us from God; it is sad to see someone who once was closely and deeply involved with a Church and seemed to hold the Faith with joy and delight, but who has – through sin, perhaps, or lack of teaching, or some personal cause – gone away from God.

Although we may cut ourselves off from God, in various ways, God does not cut himself off from us. Look at the Parable of the Lost Sheep, for instance; here the Good Shepherd follows the lost sheep, and eventually brings it home rejoicing.

Our Part
We have a part to play here. How important it is, not to allow our knowledge of another person's decisions to stop us from friendship, from including that person in any activities or interests, and using the opportunities that may be presented – not to 'missionize', press too hard, but to bring the facts of our religion to their notice. Those who have – for whatever reason – shut God out of their lives, but have come to realize what they have done and their need of Him, can look with confidence for their Rescuer. God does not fail those who seek him.

*   *   *

Sermons for Saints' Days and Special Occasions 1996

Friday 29 November   *Eve of St Andrew*
Day of Intercession for the Missionary Work of the Church
'Go into all the world and preach the gospel.' Mark 16,15

On this day we are asked to pray for the missionary work of the Church, that is, the spreading of the Gospel throughout the world. Many well-known societies are devoted to the mission of the

Church; our first duty is to interest ourselves in their work, pray for them, and support them financially. Our giving should be regular and our prayer constant, and our getting to know the societies and their needs a definite aim as a priority in our religious life. Christian missions are in a very difficult position in many countries – in some, Christian teaching is expressly forbidden, often under harsh penalties, and Christians are badly treated. Discriminated against, persecuted, brutally martyred – these things are happening today, in our own time, not in some long-ago persecution. Find out how you can help through your local representatives.

PRAYER

> Almighty God,
> who called your Church to witness
> that you were in Christ reconciling people to yourself,
> help us to proclaim the good news of your love,
> that all who hear it may be reconciled to you;
> through him who died for us and rose again,
> and reigns with you and the Holy Spirit,
> one God, now and for ever.
> *(ASB: For the Missionary Work of the Church)*

Saturday 30 November   *St Andrew the Apostle*
The Brothers

'Come, follow me, and I will make you fishers of men.' Matt. 4.19

The Call of Christ

On the day that Christ came to the shores of the Sea of Galilee, an entirely new life began for the fishermen casting their nets. This was not only because of the completely new conditions under which their lives would be led, but also because both their past and their future would have an entirely new significance. It wasn't that Andrew and his brother Peter would lay aside their fishing tackle and undertake very different work, no longer piloting their boats and catching fish, but treading the dusty roads of Palestine – it was also that all their work, whether past or future, would shine with a new light. The Light of the World would shine within them, adding lustre to all they did. They would become new men, with new life and new powers.

Andrew and Peter

What happened to these two men, Andrew and Peter, brothers, has happened to a greater or lesser degree to countless men and women down the ages. They have heard the voice of Christ calling them – not indeed as a physical sound, but as a compelling force urging them to become his followers in a special way. It means leaving their careers and giving themselves wholeheartedly to his service, to whatever aspect of the Lord's service they find themselves directed. Teachers, evangelists, missionaries, doctors and nurses, priests and nuns and ministers. While Andrew became a bold preacher of the gospel, his brother Peter became the recognized leader of the Apostles. Without Andrew, Peter might never have become a follower of Christ, let alone the chief of the band of apostles. Andrew brought people to Jesus; the gospels tell us of the Greek visitors, of the boy with the loaves and fishes, but the most important instance of his bringing a person to Jesus must certainly be that of Peter.

Our Task

Let us follow his example. Can we not bring other members of our family to Christ? Can we not influence those who work beside us, or live close to us, to come to Jesus? We need not be preachers, but we do need to be helpful, friendly, ready to listen to troubles and problems. Are we the sort of person others turn to in times of trouble?

Above all, before we can exercise any influence at all in advancing the faith of Christ, we ourselves, like Andrew, must have committed ourselves to Christ and learnt to love and follow him.

OUR PRAYER

God of hope,
by your Spirit you make known your truth.
Remember the many who, though created in your image,
have known neither you nor the dying of your Son,

their Saviour Jesus Christ;
and grant that by the prayers and labours of your Church
they may be delivered from ignorance and unbelief
and brought to worship you;
through him who is the resurrection and the life of all,
Jesus Christ our Lord.

(PHG 83)

Monday 9 December *The Conception of the Blessed Virgin Mary* (tr. from Dec. 8)
Hail Mary

'We know that in everything God works for good with those who love him, who are called according to his purpose; for those whom he foreknew he also predestined.' Romans 8.28,29 (PHG)

History

The doctrine that the Blessed Virgin Mary was preserved from any stain of original sin was widely accepted from early days, in both East and West. It does not mean that Mary was conceived without the sexual union of her parents; rather, it is perhaps most simply stated as the belief that Mary received it, at the moment when her soul was infused into her body, the graces that Christians normally receive in Baptism. Since 1854 (the date of the definition by the Roman Church of the Immaculate Conception) Orthodox theologians have generally rejected the doctrine; before then many of them accepted it in some form. The Anglican Bishop Ken (1637–1711) taught it in his stanza:

> The Holy Ghost his temple in her built,
> Cleansed from congenial, kept from mortal guilt;
> And from the moment that her blood was fired
> Into her heart celestial love inspired.

St Thomas Aquinas, writing c. 1272, says that although the Church of Rome does not keep it, some other churches do, and therefore its celebration is not to be entirely reprobated!

Present Usage

The feast appears without the adjective in the BCP Calendar, but is omitted from the ASB, which gives prominence to the Birthday (September 8th) as the principal feast of Mary. However, *The Promise of His Glory* gives proper readings and the following collect, and notes that the festival 'is appropriate to the Season of Advent'. (p. 401)

> *Almighty and eternal God,*
> *who prepared the blessed Virgin Mary to be the mother of your Son:*
> *Grant that, as with her we look for his First Coming as our Saviour,*
> *so we may be ready to greet him when he comes again as our Judge;*
> *for he is alive and reigns with you and the Holy Spirit,*
> *one God, now and for ever.*

Readings:
Gen. 3.9–15, 20; Ps. 98 1–5; Eph. 1.3–6, 11–12; Luke 1.26–38.
Additional Psalms and Readings indicated in PHG, p. 401.

Thursday 26 December   *St Stephen the First Martyr*   Steadfast

'He full of the Holy Spirit, gazed into heaven and saw the glory of God, and Jesus standing at the right hand of God!' Acts 7.55 (BCP & ASB Gospel)

'Full of faith and of the Holy Spirit'

St Stephen is mentioned first in the list of seven (Acts 6.5) chosen by the body of Christian believers to help the Apostles in their ministry as stewards of the Church and ministers to the poor and distressed. Although not named as such at the time, these seven are taken to be the first of what became known as the Order of Deacons. The scope of their work expanded; in particular Stephen gave vigorous and convincing witness to the Lord. He was probably a Hellenist, a Greek who had embraced the Hebrew faith, and been led to the confession of Christ as Lord. He proved to have other qualities valuable to the Church besides being a practical organizer; he had gifts of healing (Acts 6.8), he was an eloquent preacher and teacher of the Faith, and had the ability to convince his hearers.

Martyrdom

All this stirred up bitter opposition; he was accused before the Council, and made a courageous speech in defence of the Faith and himself, which infuriated the assembly and resulted in his being dragged out of the city, and stoned to death. At the climax of his trial Stephen was totally swept up to heaven, as it were, and was thinking so devotedly of Christ, that he saw the Lord in the glory of God in the heavenly places: 'Behold, I see the heavens opened and the Son of man standing at the right hand of God' (ch. 7.56) As he died he had Christ's words on his lips and Christ's example in like circumstances before him.

Paul

Luke makes the point that at this dreadful affair was the young man, who later we meet and revere as St Paul; and this young man was not only consenting to the brutal death meted out to Stephen, but was actually taking part, in the sense of looking after the garments thrown aside by those eager to get hold of large stones to smash down upon the heretic. Was this event perhaps the beginning of a turning-point in the life of Paul? Later on we know that he also had a vision of Christ in heaven (Acts 22.6–11) which brought about his conversion; and as a result, of course, he became the great apostle of Christ and co-founder of the Church of God, with St Peter.

Shake off Prejudice

The contrast between St Stephen's approach to the new Faith, and the attitude to it taken by the priests and scribes, should warn us against being prejudiced, and against clinging to things of religion just because they are familiar. We need freshness of outlook in a changing Church and a changing world; we need to be able to see and judge what is good in the new, and give it our whole-hearted support. Yet we must also keep in mind that St Stephen joined the new Church, not because it was new, but because he believed in Christ and in what Christ taught. There is as much danger in following what is new, merely because it *is* new, as there is in clinging to old things merely through obstinacy and prejudice.

Friday 27 December *St John the Evangelist* **The Apostle of Love**

'We love the children of God, when we love God and obey his commandments.' 1 John 5.2

Love and Life

John the Apostle is often referred to as 'The Apostle of Love'. This is a fitting title, since John stresses the necessity of love in the life of the Christian. He points out to us that while love of God is primary and utterly essential, yet love for our fellow human beings flows out from this love. His long life shows a distinct spiritual development, as we see from the contrast between early days and his life later on. We see how a man of quick spirit and active disposition ('James the son of Zebedee and John the brother of James, whom Jesus surnamed 'Boanerges' that is, 'Sons of Thunder') became the disciple whom Jesus loved, and later, the Apostle of Love. His writings show how deeply the spirit of his Master had entered his soul; his keywords are Life, Light, and Love.

Firebrands

James and John were obviously young fire-brands; once they wanted to call down fire from heaven to burn up certain Samaritans who refused hospitality to the Master, and they were pushful in asking to be given the chief places in the Kingdom of Christ. This sort of youthful hot-headedness, however, gave way to a spirit of love and tenderness as the brothers developed under the loving and tender influence of the Lord.

It was John who was privileged to enter a closer intimacy with Christ than was granted to any other disciple. Though he is named 'the disciple whom Jesus loved', there was no favouritism in the relationship. John was in the 'inner circle' and saw Jesus in his Transfiguration Glory. He was beside him at the institution of the Holy Communion; he was near to him in the Agony in the Garden. At the cross he stood beside the Mother and Mary Magdalene; and it was to him that Jesus confided his Mother, and John who took her to his own home.

Maturity
John's first Epistle is often compared to a sermon on the Fourth Gospel; his love for Jesus enabled him to grasp spiritual truths so plainly that, of all the Evangelists, he most strenuously asserts the Lord's Godhead. It is upon the basis of the Divinity of Jesus, who was sent to redeem the world because of the Father's love for his creation, that John bases his stress on love as the priority in the true Christian character. There is tenderness as well as insight in his appeal, which means as much to us in our time, as it must have done to its first recipients: – 'Little children, love must not be a matter of words or talk; it must be genuine, and show itself in action.' (1 John 3.18)

Saturday 28 December *The Holy Innocents*
Bitter Weeping
'Rachel weeping for her children, refusing to be comforted, because they are no more.' Matthew 2.18 (ASB & BCP Gospel)

A Cruel Death
The human heart yearns over the cruel death of those little ones of Bethlehem, and enters with grief into the sufferings of their parents. Helpless babes who were offered as unwilling sacrifices, in which the Saviour of the world himself was saved, for Joseph's dream meant that the family left Herod's territory in time. Egypt was the natural place of refuge – it was not far away and many Jews had settled there, so the refugees would be sure of a reception and reasonable care. But alas for the children and the families in Bethlehem; the brutal carrying-out of Herod's order would cause great pain and distress; one of the last cruel acts of a most cruel ruler. Throughout his life, because of his suspicions and blind rages, he was capable of sacrificing the innocent without a pang and without any regret, if they seemed in any way to cast the slightest shadow on himself as ruler. His own family members could be executed at a moment's notice to achieve any political end or safeguard his political position.

In Our Own Time
In our own time, what terrible massacres we have known: in our own land with the killing of little children – and their teacher – at Dunblane. Then the killing of children in Central Africa as part of brutal murderous attempts at extinction by one tribe against another. The murders of children in Bulgaria as part of the attempted killing-off of Muslims. The killing of the 'street children' in Brazil; the constant slaughter on the roads. The killing off of Innocents has become part of our lives.

Worse, in a way, even than these horrible acts, are the brutal men who indoctrinate the minds of children with their bitter political views – so we get infant soldiers in Iran, child terrorists in Palestine, boy revolutionaries in Liberia.

Christmas and Suffering
When we consider the birth of Christ at Christmas, we do so in an atmosphere of rejoicing at his coming – so it is easy to forget the kind of world into which he chose to be born, a world as full of sin and suffering as is ours today. And it is easy to let ourselves be persuaded that the people among whom Christ came to live, were all good, kind, and gentle; whereas in fact they were the same mix of well-meaning but soft, foolish sinners, evil characters and good characters as we have today. The Innocents' Day reminds us of the depth of God's love in coming to our human world, and of our call 'not to stand indifferently by, but to defend the weak from the tyranny of the strong'.

1997
Wednesday 1 January *The Naming of Jesus* (Circumcision) **The Holy Name**
'At the end of eight days, when he was circumcised, he was called Jesus, the name given by the angel before he was conceived in the womb.' Luke 2.21

The Law of Moses
The Jewish Law requires that every male child shall be circumcised on the eighth day from his birth (Leviticus 12.3). This day is made a festival, when family and friends come together to witness the

naming of the child, rejoice in the new life, and pray for the child and parents.

How did this custom of circumcision originate? Ancient history is wrapt in mystery; the most likely possibility is that in dark and primitive days, there was revulsion away from the dreadful ceremony of the sacrifice of the first-born, as demanded in primitive tribal worship of Jehovah; so the experts tell us. Instead of the first-born being actually killed, a humane substitution was made; some of the child's flesh – the part closely associated with the power of generation, yet also most easily dispensed with – was, by the hands of the priest, cut away in a substitute ceremony, as ordered by the Law of Moses.

Obedient

Old writers take this first shedding of the sacred blood of Christ as a first intimation of his saving Passion; or as a sign that Christ was 'obedient unto the Law'. St Paul takes the ceremony as a sign that we should suffer circumcision voluntarily not outwardly in the flesh, but 'inwardly, in the heart, according to the Spirit' (Romans 2,29). In principle this experience has already befallen us in baptism, which the Apostle calls the 'circumcision of Christ' (Col. 2,11)

Suffering

The year begins with the record of the suffering of the Lord, as his blood was shed in circumcision. In the year which lies ahead of us, there must of necessity be some suffering, some pain, some grief. Let us make an act of offering now to God, uniting any pains of our own with the sufferings of our Lord. The thought of the Passion thus enters into the joy of Christmas, as Mary's joy was tempered with the pain of the birth. Pray for courage to face what suffering in our lives, there may be.

The Holy Name

The New Year begins for Christians with the holy name of 'Jesus'. This name is the same, the experts tell us, as 'Joshua' – and this signifies 'The Deliverer' or 'The Saviour'. In the Name of Jesus, Peter performed the first miracle after Pentecost; in the Name of Jesus millions of people today go about their work and their lives, continually sending up small 'arrow-prayers' – 'Lord Jesus, help me! – 'Jesus mercy' – 'Jesus my Saviour'. In the Name of Jesus, we too can 'in all things obey his blessed will'.

Saturday 18 January *The Confession of St Peter The Rock*

'Jesus asked his disciples, "Who do you say that I am?" Simon Peter replied, "You are the Christ, the Son of the Living God!"' Matthew 16.15,16

Speaking for All

We may be sure that when St Peter declared that Jesus was the Christ, he was speaking for all of the little band of disciples, as well as for himself. The disciples had recognized a definite correspondence between the Jesus they knew, as they walked the dusty roads of Palestine, and the Messiah, long-promised in the prophecies of Holy Scripture. What, however, formed a point of contradiction and held them back from the whole-hearted decision of Peter, was the strange (to them) prediction of suffering and even death.

Contradiction

We look back and can clearly see, in the utterances of the prophets, that a proud earthly monarch could not occupy the spiritual position of the Christ. In fact, his death would be the profoundest testimony that could be given to the righteousness of God. So, to the deep student of prophecy and life, Messiahship had to imply suffering – and not accidental, but as a necessary way of accomplishing his mission. When Peter, in all conscience, sought to persuade Christ to turn away from the path of suffering, he was doing the Devil's work and rightly was strongly put down by Jesus.

Spiritual Experience

Peter did not realize sufficiently all that had been revealed to him. He had divined the true dignity of the Master, but not realized all that it meant. The disciples all needed a deeper spiritual experience and a fuller understanding of the mission of Christ; even their leader, Peter. A man of impulse and affection, rather than calm spiritual intuition, or careful reflection upon the words of the prophets and the psalmists. It was due to his forward and impulsive temperament that he became the spokesman for the rest, and was so confident concerning himself, Jesus, and the future. Christianity and the Church indeed owe much to such spirits, but more sober thinkers may keep them in check, and the lessons of God's providence may provide a discipline that is needed.

Errors

Peter – and the rest – had more worldly hopes and ideas of the coming Kingdom of God, as we can see from their expressions of hopes for 'thrones' and questions about 'What shall we have in the new world?' Had he – and they – cherished purer and definitely spiritual hopes, the mischief might have been minimized, and Peter's impulsive nature perhaps kept in check. 'The world has many Peters, who wish to be wiser than Christ, and to tell him what it is needful to do,' says an old aphorism. But let us not be too hard on Peter; his strength of character, 'The Rock' as Jesus named him, formed a strong basis and foundation with his vital faith, which made him the leader of the disciples and the figure to whom they turned when in despair or trouble. Above all it was his deep and strong love for the Lord that made his position so clear and important. After the Resurrection, at breakfast on the lake shore, he confessed his love three times, and Jesus accepted it. The Lord's command was 'Follow me.' He says the same to all of us.

The Promise of His Glory gives proper readings and the following Collect, and notes that this festival is observed as a celebration parallel to that of the Conversion of St Paul. The two Apostles thus begin and close the Week of Prayer for Christian Unity. (p. 402)

COLLECT

Almighty God,
who inspired your apostle Saint Peter
to confess Jesus as Christ and Son of the living God:
build up your Church upon this rock,
that in unity and peace
it may proclaim one truth and follow one Lord,

your Son our Saviour Jesus Christ,
who is alive and reigns with you and the Holy Spirit,
one God, now and for ever.

(PHG p. 363)

(Readings: Ezek.3,4–11 or Acts 4,8–13; Ps.23; 1 Peter 5.1–4; Matt.16.
13–19. Additional Psalms and Readings are indicated in PHG p. 402;
also for 18–25 Jan., Week of Prayer for Christian Unity, and Sunday
in the Week, also instruction for the Unity Candle; pp. 246–258.)

Saturday 25 January   *The Conversion of St Paul*
Turned Around

'Get up; go into the city, and you will be told what to do.' Acts 9.6
(ASB NT Reading) or 'Arise, and go into the city, and it shall be told
thee what thou must do' (BCP)

Turned Around ...

Paul was converted, changed, turned around. From being the persecutor of the infant Church, he became its greatest missionary.
How much we owe to his penetrating and wide-ranging mind; he
was an educated and sophisticated man, some considerable contrast to many if not most of the early Christians. It was Paul who
took the first giant steps into the mysteries of redemption; many
have followed where he led, but Paul was the first to argue that
redemption is, on the one hand, from the bondage of sin, death
and the devil, and on the other from the curse of the Divine Law
and the wrath of God.

The Strategist

As well as theologian, Paul was the strategist who saw what was
needed to ensure the development of the primitive – mainly Jewish
– Church, into the all-embracing Church of All Nations. It was Paul
who enabled the Gospel message to break out from its confines in
the Hebrew people and in the Hebrew mind, and to reach out
with transforming and transformed power into every country and
every people of the world.

Alas, how that source of power has been blocked, and that vital energy has been dissipated; that reaching-out has been too often stultified and made of no effect. How has this happened? How has the freshness and the vigour been so lost? The answer, of course, is through our divisions, through the rivalries and hatreds between differing Christian bodies. Even in St Paul's time, there were already divisions and enmities, quarrels and disputes (1 Cor. 1, vv. 10–13 for example).

Joyful Remembrance, Painful Penitence

We keep today not only a joyful celebration of the Conversion of St Paul, and his gifts and powers, but also a day of penitence. For today we keep the last day of the Annual Week of Prayer for Christian Unity. Nearly all the Churches take part in this week, and share in a time of reflection, sorrow and penitence. It was started originally by some Anglicans in the 1920s and has spread gradually throughout most of the Christian world. It is a time when we compare what Christ would have us do and would have us be, with what we are and how we behave. 'Love one another as I have loved you,' said Jesus. 'Be united as the Father and I are united, so that the world may know that the Father sent me, and loves you as he has loved me.'

Prejudice, Unhappy Regulations, Hatreds

All these persist even in our own time, though the worst have been changed and we meet together, pray together and work together. We are still a long way from St Paul's words of hope: 'I appeal to you by the Name of our Lord Jesus Christ, that there be no dissensions among you, but be united in the same mind and the same judgement . . .' (1 Cor. 1,10) What can we do? The answers for us would seem to be first of all, prayer – a deep and heartfelt leaning upon God; and secondly, to increase the making of the fullest, closest and most open contacts with our neighbours of other Christian Churches. Only by knowing and understanding one another, and coming together in mutual love and care, can we lessen the divisions of Christendom, and help to bring nearer the conversion of the world.

> *Heavenly Father,*
> *you have called us*
> *in the Body of your Son Jesus Christ*
> *to continue his work of reconciliation*

and reveal you to the world.
Forgive us the sins which tear us apart;
Give us the courage to overcome our fears
and to seek that unity
which is your gift and your will;
through Jesus Christ our Lord.
    ASB (For the Unity of the Church)

Wednesday 19 March *St Joseph of Nazareth, Husband of Our Lady* A Good Man

'Joseph was the husband of Mary, of whom Jesus was born, who is called Christ.' Matthew 1,16 (ASB Gospel)

The Carpenter

Joseph was a pious Hebrew man, a descendant of David, and a carpenter. Most likely he was not just an individual craftsman, but had a workshop of his own, employing others; tradition and Christian artists depict him as an older man, of some importance and wealth, and certainly able to provide for Mary and the Child. Down the ages, he has been claimed as patron saint of carpenters and wood-workers, but there are surprisingly few churches dedicated to him, at least in this country. In mediaeval times he was treated with scant respect in the 'Mystery Plays', and even became something of a figure of fun. This is strange, and unfair; for certainly he is pictured in St Matthew's gospel as a man of deep devotion, receptive to his mystical experiences, faithful in his religious observances, considerate and compassionate, and one who accepted his God-given responsibilities with gentleness and humility.

The Guardian

How fully Joseph and Mary understood that they were guardians of a Child on whom the future of our world depended, we do not know; but certainly they must have been aware that in Jesus thy had a very great responsibility. Joseph took the child and mother away to Egypt, to escape the danger of Herod's murderous brutality; it must have been with considerable care and consideration that he brought them back and settled at Nazareth, and began to rear the boy as a faithful Hebrew. From incidents that Jesus brings into his parables ('Plank in your eye', 'My yoke is easy' for example) he must have had some experience of the workshop; and we may picture him with nails and hammer, little thinking of what part they would play in later years. Joseph would be, like most woodworkers, a calm man, ready to listen to the demands or ideas of his customers, always concerned with the quality and strength of the materials available. The workshop would be a place of meeting for farmers, stewards, local notabilities and others; and Jesus no doubt took notice of the gossip and stories, and in his parables we may discern echoes and reflections of local people and their tales. Above all, however, it was from Joseph that Jesus the child learnt what it means to call God 'Father'.

Farewell

The evangelists do not tell us the full story; Joseph drops quietly out of the picture. It is only Mary who appears at the wedding in Cana of Galilee; perhaps Joseph had died peacefully at Nazareth, busy till the last. His epitaph might well read: 'A Good Man, a man of principle, obedient to God's call' and we may fairly see him mirrored in the descriptions of a loving Father that Jesus gives – getting up in the night to provide for the hungry stranger; hard-working and upright, but generous and fair, like the owner of the vineyard who took on the men 'standing about idle in the market-place', unwilling to see them without any employment, and hence no wages.

The simple daily routine, the plain business of living, the duties laid upon us – all may seem dull and uninspiring at times. Yet if we look to the example of Joseph, we can see how a measure of sacrifice, of discipline, of self-denial, provide a key to true happiness in marriage as in life itself.

Monday 7 April   *The Annunciation of Our Lord*
(trans from Mar. 25)   God's Choice
'The Word was made flesh, and dwelt among us.' John 1,14

A Message from God

The Bible contains many stories of how God sent messages to human beings; indeed the Bible might be described as an extended communication from God to humanity. There are, however, some special features about the Annunciation which make it the most significant incident of its kind which Scripture describes to us. The fact that the Annunciation message was presented by an angel is not unique; other people besides Mary are described as having the experience. Gabriel was sent to Daniel to tell him of the restoration of Jerusalem; to Zacharias to announce the coming birth of the son who was to be John the Baptist. Numbered among the recipients are the old and the very young, like the child Samuel, humble people and great kings.

Mary, the Recipient

The first remarkable point is God's choice of Mary for the great, the fantastic responsibility of being the mother of the Redeemer, the Messiah, our Lord. Mary seems to have been a village girl, probably with only the very limited education given to such in those days; nevertheless, she must have had great faith, and as every Jewish girl must have hoped, the great and joyful task of bearing the Messiah and bringing the child up, would have been a sign and token of God's special care and love.

There is little in the New Testament about Mary after the birth of Jesus is recorded, but what there is, and the traditions of the Church, suggest she carried out her immense task with great courage, quiet dignity, and above all love.

A Message for Us

Mary is a type of believer for all times and all places, in her quietness and confidence, the believer's strength; in that receptiveness of soul which is our life, and in that entire self-yielding to God which is our reasonable service. For all of us here it is a declaration of God's purpose to reveal himself more fully to us, opening a way of salvation from our sins; we thank him for his mercy, his love and his goodness as shown to us in this great event, and what followed.

> Almighty God,
> who by your grace called the blessed Virgin Mary
> and opened for all the door
> of infinite mercy and eternal light:
> Fill us with your grace
> that, through our obedience and faith,
> the world may rejoice in your mercy
> and walk in your light;
> for the sake of Jesus Christ our Lord.
>
> *(PHG 91)*

Thursday 1 May   *SS Philip & James the Apostles*
Trust

'Do not let your hearts be troubled.' John 14.1

'The Lord's Brother'

James is described by St Paul as 'the Lord's brother' (Galatians 1.19) but he has also been identified as 'James, son of Alpheus' (Mark 3.18) and he certainly presided at the Council of Jerusalem (Acts 15). Philip was a native of Bethsaida (John 1,44); he speaks at the feeding of the multitude (John 6,7) and is accosted by 'certain Greeks' who wish to see Jesus (John 12,21) and in the Gospel for today he is the disciple asking Jesus 'Lord, let us see the Father . . .'

There seems to be no special connection between the two; the commemoration of them together seems to be due to the consecration of a church in Rome during the 6th century, on May 1st, with relics claimed to be from both apostles being enshrined – so this date was taken afterwards as their joint Festival.

'Following in His footsteps'

The readings seem to give us the theme of 'following in Christ's footsteps'. We are to walk in the way, the road, the life; we follow in the steps of the apostles who themselves are walking in the steps of Christ the Master, as the Collect tells us. The first reading tells us of the paths of righteousness and uprightness, and the way of wisdom; St Paul teaches about the mysterious fact that we have been chosen by God, chosen in Christ; even before the world was founded. This wondrous gift and blessing, however, does carry with it the joyful obligation of proclaiming the message of salvation.

The Apostles
We thank God for the examples and the work of the apostles, those whose efforts we know of and those whose proclamation of the gospel has passed into the limbo of human memory – though not forgotten by God. Certainly we can take both the saints remembered today as examples of faithfulness and love for the Lord. 'We wish to see Jesus' – are we willing and ready to bring strangers and visitors into the Church, into our churches, and making sure that they are welcomed and met with warmth and fellowship as in the days of the Apostles?

Wednesday 14 May *St Matthias the Apostle* (BCP Feb. 24) **Choice**
'You have not chosen me, I have chosen you, says the Lord.' John 15,16

The Young Church
What a fascinating picture we are given of the young Church, taking the first tentative exploring steps without the direction and leadership of the living Christ there, amongst them, to guide and counsel. In the 'Upper Room' are the leaders, the original 'Twelve' – now reduced to eleven, by the defection and suicide of Judas Iscariot. With them are a group of women, including Mary the mother of Jesus; and his brothers. (The word 'brother' in Greek and Semitic use covers varied degrees of blood relationship; and there is of course, the theory that Joseph – by a previous marriage – had children already before his marriage to Mary. Some scholars, however, prefer the simpler interpretation of the word.) Then there is the 'brotherhood' of about one hundred and twenty people assembled, to whom Peter addresses his oration.

Conditions and the Lottery

The apostles were convinced that a replacement for Judas must be from the group who had known Jesus and had been with the apostles from the earliest days. Peter agreed; we may conclude that Matthias was one of the 'Seventy' (Luke 10,1–16). The method of choosing was to be a solemn and prayerful use of the system known as 'Urim and Thummin', casting lots in a sacred tradition that goes right back to the days of the beginning of the Jewish worship (see 1 Samuel 14,41–42). The actual objects may have been stones, selected with black on one side and white on the other, or perhaps shaped bones or bone fragments. These would be thrown onto the ground, or onto a table, and the results carefully noted. The choice of Matthias was a solemn and profound action undertaken by the consent of the Body of Christ as a whole.

The Choice Today

The history of the Church shows many methods of selecting bishops – popular election, choice by Kings, Popes or lords, election by a group such as a Cathedral Chapter, to some extent representing the clergy, and so on. What is important is that the candidates should be clearly seen to be of godly life, and that in some way the opinion of the people over whom they will bear rule are consulted, and can express their opinions, the voice of the Body. Without this, those chosen will all too often be mere mouthpieces of whoever has the power to select them.

PRAYER

Father of light and God of all truth,
purge your Church on earth
from all errors, abuses, corruptions and sins;
let humility triumph over pride and ambition,
and may those in authority ever act
with unselfish love and fairness to all,
and, in the true light of the Gospel,
care for those in their charge;
for the sake of Jesus Christ our Lord.
(Percy Dearmer)

Thursday 5 June *St Boniface, Missionary and Martyr* **A European Indeed**

'You shall be called by a new name which the mouth of the Lord will give. You shall be a crown of beauty in the hand of the Lord.' Isaiah 62.2,3 (Of an Abbot – ASB)

Called to Europe

St Boniface was born at Crediton, among the hills of Devonshire. An Anglo-Saxon, his baptismal name was Winfrid; his mind was turned towards a missionary vocation while yet a child, over-hearing the adventures of some Celtic monks – how far reaching was the influence of those few Irish preachers who had sailed with St Columba to spread the Gospel, not only in the Scottish Isles but also in the Netherlands! From that time Winfrid's mind was set on fire – he would be a missionary himself. He began his training at Exeter, then at Nutshulling near Winchester, where he became head of the Abbey School, and was ordained priest in 710. In 716 he set out for Germany on his first missionary expedition, which proved a failure. In 718 he left England again, this time for Rome to get the Pope's blessing, and forthwith evangelized Bavaria, Hesse, Friesland, Thurungia and Franconia. In 723 Gregory II consecrated him bishop, when he changed his name to Boniface, with full jurisdiction over the Germans.

Help from Home

From the religious houses in Britain many monks and nuns went out to join in Boniface's evangelistic work among the devotees of Woden, Thor and Friya, the heathen gods, whose names we still pronounce when we say the days of the week. From the homeland, too, came gifts of money, books and vestments. The Abbess Ead-burga of Minster sent the Epistles of St Peter lettered in gold; many others sent food, clothing and altar vessels.

Many of St Boniface's letters and sermons have been preserved, and from them we can learn much of the wisdom, sanctity and humanity of the great missionary. To St Boniface and his English helpers must be credited the origins and first foundations of German civilization and culture. He founded the abbey of Fulda (where his body now rests) as the centre of German missionary and cultural activities. The schools he founded were staffed by bands of monks and nuns from England.

Europeans All

At the present time some people in this country are worried about 'loss of sovereignty' and an increase in 'foreign' influence. They forget what each nation owes to its neighbours over the years. We share a common European heritage; of course there are problems and difficulties that arise from time to time, but the aim of European Union is so important and so worth while, for all our futures, that surely we must make every effort to ensure its success. We need St Boniface to show us the fellowship of different nations and peoples, to break down barriers which divide and alienate neighbours, and instead bring us together as members of one community, supporting and sharing problems and successes. We as Christians, in particular, should not be afraid to step forward and demonstrate mutual respect, consideration and love. As between people, so also between nations.

The Martyr

St Boniface was martyred in his old age, with a number of companions who had gathered to celebrate Whitsun in a meadow where an altar had been erected. A band of heathen marauders murdered them all; Boniface is said to have died with a book of the Gospels in his hand, stained with blood and pierced by swords. His body rests in his abbey of Fulda, in a sacred shrine; he is greatly revered by Germans and is rightly styled the 'Apostle of Germany'. Among the apostles of all time, he stands on a par with St Paul and St Francis Xavier. Perhaps one day his native land will give St Boniface a better recognition.

His letters, in many respects, seem to be as apposite today as when written over 1200 years ago; here is a small part of one:

'In her voyage across the ocean of this world, the Church is like a great ship being pounded by the waves of life's different stresses. Our duty is not to abandon ship but to keep her on her course.

Let us stand fast in what is right and prepare our souls for trial. Let us wait upon God's strengthening aid, and say to him: "O Lord, you have been our refuge in all generations".

Let us trust in him who has placed this burden upon us. What we ourselves cannot bear, let us bear with the help of Christ. For he is all-powerful, and he tells us: "My yoke is easy and my burden is light".'

> *Almighty Father,*
> *who called your servant Boniface*
> *to carry the good news of your love to the Germans,*
> *and to yield up his life for the gospel:*
> *Grant to us and all your people*
> *grace to bear the yoke of Christ,*
> *and to find in his service rest for their souls;*
> *through Jesus Christ our Lord.*
>
> *(The Cloud of Witnesses)*

Wednesday 11 June   *St Barnabas the Apostle*
Son of Encouragement

'They sent Barnabas ... when he came and saw the grace of God, he was glad.' Acts 11,22 & 23

A Man of Generosity

'Joseph, a Levite born in Cyprus, whom the Apostles called Barnabas, meaning "Son of Encouragement", sold a field he owned, brought the money, and handed it over to the Apostles.' (Acts 4,36–37)

Barnabas is introduced to us as a generous farmer, a friend of St Paul, and like St Paul, a Hebrew of the Dispersion. When Paul came to Jerusalem after the tremendous experience of his Damascus Road conversion, the disciples were afraid – not without cause, having in mind the fierce anti-Christian campaign Paul – or rather, Saul – had been wreaking on the 'Followers of the Way'. But Barnabas, his old friend – perhaps of college days? – brought Paul to them and told them the whole story; how Paul had had that vision on the way, had completely changed his views, had preached Jesus in different places boldly and with faith, and how he (Barnabas) was completely converted to a belief in the change in Paul, and put him forward as a good man and someone to be trusted completely. 'I give you my word,' Barnabas must have said, and all who heard him accepted his account and rejoiced.

Missionary
Barnabas called Paul to join him in Antioch, then the pair were sent to take some relief funds to the Church in Jerusalem. After that, they were sent off on a missionary journey beginning at Cyprus; but the happy association between the two was disrupted by a squabble over Barnabas's cousin Mark. Paul was opposed to him (15,36–41) and there was a 'sharp contention' which ended in Barnabas sailing away from Cyprus with Mark. In Cyprus Barnabas is honoured as founder of the Church there, and it may be that he met a martyr's death at Salamis. Barnabas showed a grasp of the creative love of Christ – Christ who said 'You are my friends!' Christ sees us not just as we are, but as God meant us to be; to Christ we are not sinners, nor servants, but friends – his friends, and friends of one another. We are to love one another with the same creative love that the Lord displays to us.

> Lord God,
> the source of truth and love,
> keep us faithful to the apostles' teaching and fellowship,
> united in prayer and the breaking of bread,
> and one in joy and simplicity of heart,
> in Jesus Christ our Lord.
>
> *(Patterns for Worship 52.27)*

Tuesday 24 June   *Birth of St John the Baptist*
The Herald
'A voice cries "In the wilderness prepare the way of the Lord."' Isaiah 40.3

Children Together
The artists love to show John Baptist and Jesus, as children together, playing (as Leonardo da Vinci's fine depiction for instance has it) together around their parents – or at least their mothers, Mary and Elizabeth. John, we are told in the Bible, was

six months older than Jesus, and so the date of this festival is fixed by referring back to Christmas Day, the birthday of Jesus.

Why 'John'? The name in the Hebrew, we are told, means 'God is gracious'; and the surprise was the agreement between mother and father, independently, in choosing the same name – not a family name, as everyone expected, but something new. From his earliest days the child, therefore, was thought to be special. How special was to be seen as he grew up.

The One sent Ahead

John was chosen by the Lord to be the herald, to prepare people, to make a road smooth through the rough places of the desert; but he was by no means a smooth person nor a smooth character. Those who went out into the desert did not find a tactful, neat and trim, polished in speech, well-dressed person at all. Consider John's message in St Luke: 'Be ready to share: share your clothes, share your food, with those without. Do not swindle others in your financial dealings; no robbery, no violence, no false accusations; be content with your wages. Live as if God's judgement is about to fall upon you.'

A Message for Us

There's a message for today! With our financial trickery in high places (even the Queen's bankers were caught up in it) our big business-men's tax havens, property speculators and developers, our corrupt local governments, lotteries and scratchcards. Violence – no need to comment upon that with so much brutality, so many muggings on our streets, attacks and rapes even on the most elderly, children who attack their teachers, stabbings and bullying the order of the day, 'road rage' an excuse for killings and injuries, political violence and bombings. False accusations against the police, 'racism!' the continual cry, crooked lawyers using every trick of a weak and spineless law; and the police themselves not free of accusations which sometimes prove all too true – What would John say to our society today?

Thursday 3 July (BCP December 21) *St Thomas the Apostle* – 'My Lord and My God!'

'Have you believed because you have seen me? Blessed are those who have not seen, and yet believe!' John 20.29

Unfair?

The name was usually give to St Thomas – 'Doubting Thomas' – is quite wrong. Let us look at the eleventh chapter of St John's Gospel. The situation is quite a tricky one – Jesus is proposing to go to Bethany, where Lazarus, the brother of the well-beloved sisters Martha and Mary, is ill. (Now Jesus loved Martha and her sister and Lazarus' – v. 5.) Surprisingly, the Lord stays on two more days; *then* he says, 'Let us go into Judea again.' The disciples are dismayed, indeed terrified at the prospect. Bethany, the village where the sisters and brother live, is 'enemy territory', far too close to Jerusalem for safety; it is well known that the enemies of Jesus are busy plotting his death. Is he crazy, that he proposes to give them a perfect opportunity? In this tense moment, it is Thomas's brave voice alone saying, 'Let us also go, that we may die with him!'

The Last Supper

In the gospels nothing is recorded about Thomas, besides this brave and loyal cry, apart from the Resurrection scene, except that he questions Jesus at the Last Supper – 'Lord, we do not know where you are going, so how can we know the way?' Is this question put in his mouth as suggesting doubt; or is it simply a reflection of a plain straightforward character, that takes nothing for granted, and relies only on what can be seen or can be touched. In his reply, Jesus delivers the great title-sentence – 'I am the Way, the Truth and the Life.'

Proof

Maybe it was all for the best that one disciple, at least, was hard to convince, and obstinately refused to accept without further proof. This is the thought behind the Collect; God allowed the apostle to doubt until 'word and sight convinced him'.

Let us pray then, for the gift of faith without any cloud of doubt, that we may – as the Collect puts it – 'receive the fullness of Christ's blessing'.

Thursday 22 July *Mary Magdalen*
Adoring the Lord
'Now on the first day of the week Mary Magdalen came to the tomb early, while it was still dark . . .' John 20.1

Healed
Mary, called Magdalen, from whom seven demons had gone out' (Luke 8.2) Whatever the disease, whether moral, spiritual or physical, it was healed by our Lord; the devils went out at his word, the sickness disappeared, the wound – physical or spiritual or mental – was healed. Mary had received a great blessing and a complete change of life from Jesus, and henceforth she was his loving and devoted follower. She was one of the women who 'provided for him out of their means'. They shared the tasks of helping and caring for the Lord and his disciples, on the long and often wearying walks through the countryside on the dusty roads of Palestine. (Anyone who has seen the film 'Gandhi' will understand!)

She Loved Greatly
Mary watched in deepest sorrow and distress the great tragedy of Calvary; she was one of the last at the Cross. She was the first at the tomb; hers was a personal love for the Lord Jesus. Can our love for him be thus described? Have we a personal love for a personal Saviour? How cold we are; like children with coppers in a purse, we tend to eke out our little store of money – that is our love. We cannot, I suppose, help our characters. But there is a lesson to be learnt from Mary Magdalen.

She was so swept up by love and devotion that she could not care less for the formal boundaries of affection and behaviour. She was there, weeping and distraught at the foot of the cross; careless of the biting comments of the passers-by, careless of what the soldiers thought or said.

Her Reward
Her reward was the meeting on that Sunday morning very early, with the Love of her life.

Friday 25 July   *St James the Apostle*   Chosen
'He allowed no one to follow him except Peter and James and John the brother of James.' (Mark 5.37)

Companion of Jesus
St James was a close companion of Jesus; James and John, the sons of Zebedee the well-to-do fisherman, were with Jesus at the mysterious event of the Transfiguration, and were also with the Lord at the Garden of Gethsemane. Two of the three, Peter and John, lived to be leaders of the Church in its formative years; the third, St James, whom we commemorate today, was executed by Herod. Apart from the traitor Judas, James is the only apostle whose death is recorded in the New Testament, and the first of them to die.

Parallel
Probably most of us could recall, in our own experience, at least one or two parallels to the fate of St James, when we have known a life promising much to be useful and good, ending early before that promise was given effect. Less close, but parallel to the story of St James, are cases of men and women whose lives have not been cut short, but – anxious though they were to devote themselves to a special service to God or their fellow human beings, the opportunity has been somehow withheld, and they have had to devote themselves and their gifts to other and humbler tasks.

God's Will
When Peter asked Jesus about John's future (John 21.20–22) he was firmly put down for his very natural curiosity; a reminder to us that we are to accept God's plans for our lives. The same lesson is to be learnt from the story of James; he was specially close to Jesus, and might well look forward to being used on earth to pass on to others all he had learned. Instead, he was called to renew

more fully in heaven, the earthly fellowship he had with his Master.

> O God,
> by whose command the order of time runs its course;
> forgive our impatience, perfect our faith,
> and, while we wait for the fulfilment of your promises,
> grant us to have a good hope because of your word;
> through Jesus Christ our Lord.
>
> (Gregory Nazianzen)

Thursday 15 August   *The Falling-Asleep of St Mary*   The Mother of Jesus

'Blessed is she who believed.' Luke 1.45; or, 'A great portent appeared in heaven, a woman clothed with the sun, beneath her feet the moon, and on her head a crown of twelve stars.' Revelation 12.1; or, 'Mary kept all these things, pondering them in her heart.' Luke 2.19

Blessed Among Women

The respect and honour paid to Mary, the Mother of Jesus Christ, goes back to the earliest days of our faith. The angel's greeting (Luke 1.28) tells of God's favour and grace, and Mary's own words when visiting Elizabeth (Luke 1.48) give our warrant for calling her 'Blessed'.

In many lands, through many centuries, Christians have loved and honoured Mary, and kept her festival, sung her praises and asked her prayers. The painter, the sculptor, the poet have all brought their several skills to spread her fame and enhance her glory. The history of Christian art would be immensely the poorer without Mary. Today, she is honoured by members of differing denominations, and shrines such as Walsingham and Lourdes are centres of prayer and healing for all.

Challenge and Hope

Mary is both a challenge and a hope to this divided world of ours; for Mary is both mother of God and mother of Man. A picture which illustrates this double title is given to us by St John in his

Book of Revelations – 'A woman clothed with the sun, beneath her feet the moon, and on her head a crown of twelve stars.' This woman, about to bear a child, is confronted by a fierce dragon who stands before her, that he 'might devour her child when she brought it forth'. Mary is confronting evil – a world in the grip of the dragon; but a world to which she is about to give a Redeemer; a woman who with her Son, will crush the dragon's head.

Unity

Thus they become the hope and the joy of the world. Mary, since she is the mother of 'the Word made Flesh' is the means and the bond by which matter and spirit are joined in divine unity; our material world is transformed, and takes on a dignity and a greatness it did not have before. Therefore, Mary is rightly called 'Highly Favoured', 'Blessed of all ages'; and in her Festival we acclaim her ultimate vindication, and acknowledge her as 'the lowly who has indeed been lifted high'.

> God and Father of our Lord Jesus Christ,
> whose virgin Mother was blessed in bearing him,
> give the will to us,
> who honour the lifting up of her lowliness,
> to follow the example of her faith and obedience;
> through the same Jesus Christ our Lord.
>
> (PHG 92)

Monday 29 September   *St Michael and All Angels*   Doing and Being

'All the angels stood round the throne and round the elders and the four living creatures, and they fell on their faces before the throne and worshipped God.' Revelation 7.11

Practicalities

People of practical minds will ask about big churches: 'Why are they so big, so ergonomically inefficient, so cold in winter, so difficult to fill?' The reason has nothing to do with usefulness. The

251

vicar of a cold and remote Victorian church in the Pennines, used to tell with relish of an old priest who fought his way through the icy winds to conduct Evensong one winter's night, and found four parishioners waiting for him. His wife was distressed when he came home shivering and tired out, and she asked rather crossly why he bothered to go out to an empty church? 'Empty?' said the old priest. 'The church was full – full of angels and archangels, and all the company of heaven!'

Angels, like steeples and big churches, are not meant to be useful. Perhaps that is why Christians tend not to speak of them much. Earlier ages did: Dionysius the pseudo-Areopagite devised a wonderful scheme of three times three angelic ranks: Cherubim, Seraphim, Thrones; Dominations, Virtues, Powers; Principalities, Archangels, Angels. Only archangels and angels had anything to do with humanity. The rest waited upon God.

Not Necessary

Christians know that angels and archangels are not, so to speak, necessary. We know God as Father; we know Jesus as his Son and our brother; and we know that the Holy Spirit dwells and works in us. No matter how huge a gap there may be between us and God, God has filled that gap. No matter how many layers of being there may be above or beneath us, Jesus has sliced through them all. And no matter how active the hosts of heaven may be, Jesus shows us beyond all mistaking that God does the dirty work himself.

Having made us lower than the angels, God has exalted us far above them, since it is as human that he has chosen to reveal himself. It is that knowledge that makes us glad to be Christians. It is a knowledge that does rather rob angels of their usefulness.

Not to *Do* but to *Be*

But you don't have to be useful to be important or significant. The whole duty of the angels is not to *do* but to *be*. They are creatures who look not to themselves but to God. If God wills that they should be doers, that doing springs naturally out of what they are. This is the truth behind all creation. God doesn't *need* any of it; instead he chose to make it. Christians should know that better than anyone, not least because we know how fundamentally limited human beings are. Our creativity is not our own. Like everything else that is good in us, it is derived from a God who has no need of us, but who has chosen to make us in his image.

In Proportion

We live at a time when there seems to be lots to be done. That is particularly true in the life of the Church. The past couple of centuries have shown just how much humans can do if they put their minds to it. Christians have been to the forefront in that process, and that is where they should remain.

But we must keep our doing in proportion. God has set us a huge task. He calls us to join him in making and rescuing, in creating and redeeming. If we think our first duty is to *do*, either we shall be proud or we shall be overwhelmed. The truth lies elsewhere. Like the angels, like ergonomically inefficient churches, our first duty is not to *do* but to *be*. With the unseen hosts of heaven, we too have an appointed part in the great Dance of Creation that takes place before the face of God.

Wednesday 15 October *St Teresa of Avila*
Prayer and Faith

'I call to my God, I cry out toward him: I call to my God, and surely he will answer.' Ps 77.1

Reformer, Mystic and Writer

Teresa of Avila (1515–1582) is now regarded, in our day, as one of Spain's greatest Christians. She was not so regarded in her own lifetime, however; and her 'Life' shows the damage done to her by incompetent confessors and spiritual directors. It also shows the great inner determination she had to have, in order to do what she believed was right. It was by no means always what the authorities said was right!

She was a person of great organizing ability and shrewdness. She founded and re-founded Carmelite houses throughout Spain. She was a great reformer, and combined a life of contemplation with intense activity in many fields. She wrote forcefully and yet with great care, whether she was addressing Popes, kings or the most ordinary laypeople. But her real importance to us, who are part of a different tradition, lies somewhere else.

Mystical Prayer
St Teresa was the first person to make a serious analysis of the various stages of mystical prayer, at least as they applied to her own soul. And prayer did not come easily to her; she admitted that it cost her hard spiritual effort.

Perhaps the most illuminating thing she said on the subject, was that prayer is about knowing you are in God's presence and that he is watching you with love and care. That is a truth we can value whether we are inside a religious house, as Teresa was, or in the world outside, as most of us are.

SEEKING TO KNOW GOD

As I see it, we shall never succeed in knowing ourselves unless we seek to know God: let us think of his greatness and then come back to our own baseness; by looking at his purity we shall see our foulness; by meditating upon his humility, we shall see how far we are from being humble.

(The Interior Castle)

Saturday 18 October   *St Luke the Evangelist*
Beloved Physician
'I have no one with me but Luke.' 2 Timothy 4.11

What it means to be active
The readings for the Feast of St Luke should make us pause to think about what it means to be active. All these passages from the Scriptures have something to teach us about activity, about being busy – about our response to God, God the Creator, who is himself always active.

The Old Testament reading from Isaiah urges us to:

> Strengthen the weak hands,
> and make firm the feeble knees.
> *(Is. 35.3)*

That is what the Church's social action should be doing! Then there is the reading from the second letter to Timothy, from St Paul. Paul is older now, he is a grand old man calmly facing death – he knows he is going to be taken to Rome, he knows the result of the 'arranged' trial there long before he even starts on the journey. He looks back over a ministry packed with action – and he still would like to fit in some reading, and some further writing up of his memoirs – if only dear Timothy will bring the books and his notebooks he left in Troas. (And Paul's big winter cloak – it's more than a little chilly here, in the big city, waiting about for the lawyers . . .)

Instructions from Jesus
Above all the Gospel makes us conscious of activity in the service of God; Jesus is shown sending our thirty-five couples of disciples, telling them to prepare the way before him. Luke is the only evangelist who mentions this episode; it seems to go in with his special interest in activity. He is very strong on action: it is in Luke's gospel that we have the stories of the Good Samaritan – who was certainly active – Lazarus the beggar and the Rich Man – who was certainly not active at all – and little Zacchaeus, who so badly wanted to see Jesus that he was prepared to make a fool of himself and climb a tree.

And part two of Luke's Gospel is of course The *Acts* of the Apostles, which tells us everything by its name.

Theological
These are not just examples to follow. All three readings are deeply theological. That is, they give us the reason *why* we should be active. The reason is, that this is the way we respond to God, who is also active. It was best put by Teresa of Avila, who wrote:

> *'Christ has no body on earth but yours,*
> *no hands but yours,*
> *no feet but yours.*
> *Yours are the eyes through which he is to look out into the world;*
> *yours the feet with which he is to go about doing good,*
> *and yours are the hands with which he is to bless us now.'*

Maybe she was talking to a priest; but she might just as easily have been talking to any Christian man or woman.

Prayer

But when the writer of 2 Timothy says, 'Do all the duties of your calling' he means more than that. He means prayer – and I wonder whether we are slipping here. I know from bitter experience that when I am under pressure the first thing that goes is prayer. I say to myself that God will understand and forgive. So he does. But that is not the point: prayer is not for his benefit, it is for mine. The best definition of prayer I know, comes also from St Teresa:

> *Prayers is knowing, remembering, considering,*
> *that I am always in the presence of God,*
> *who is closer than breathing,*
> *closer than hands and feet.*

If we are too busy to lay that to heart, to busy to pray, we are letting go of the very thing that makes us Christian.

It is a most remarkable fact that Luke is the most 'active' and least theological of all the gospel writers. *But he is the one who is most bothered about prayer.* He is always showing us Jesus at prayer. And he is the one who gives us that amazing little cameo about Martha – who rushed around – and Mary who chose the better part and listened.

Prayer Life

Our prayer life is absolutely crucial. I earnestly beg each one of you to consider. Are you praying enough? at home? with your brothers and sisters in church? Will you come and pray more? It's for your sake and our sake and the sake of the work we are doing together.

J.C.T.

Saturday 1 November   *All Saints' Day*
The Victorious Ones

'These are they who have come through the great ordeal; they have washed their robes and made them white in the blood of the Lamb.' Rev. 7.14

All Saints

This festival is the festival of *all* saints. Today we do not think only of the great and noble heroes and heroines of the Faith, but also of those who make up the great, innumerable, vast company of the faithful ones, many indeed of whom are not known to their successors. Yet, if they are not known to us, their names are written in the Lamb's great Book of Life.

Grace

We believe that God gives power to face and overcome trials. The saints confirm our belief by their examples. We are convinced that a belief in the unseen – that is to say, God – truly gives men and women the power to face trial, to overcome cruelty, and to defeat the powers of this world. The saints show us that their faith in God and in the redeeming power of the blood of the Lamb, can make them conquerors over all the pains and ills and cruelties that this life can produce. So, if we are inclined to despond over failures, or to be depressed over our continued trials, All Saints' Day can say boldly to us: 'These have won the victory, they have overcome tribulations, and so can you.'

Power

In that innumerable company of the faithful, we can find examples of those who are like ourselves in our individual trials and difficulties. They come very close to our lives and to our own experiences. Tt may be that under trial, they felt despair, looked back in dread and expected the future in fear. Have we not done the same? Overwhelmed with sin and shame, perhaps afraid that we should never rise to the lowest level of Christian behaviour again . . . Yet in the end they conquered in the fight. Our Lord took them just as they were, with all their frailties and weaknesses, and gave them strength, sincerity and power. Through their weakness they were made strong. So All Saints' Day asks: 'Why should it be impossible for you to do the same?'

Grace

It is more than probable that we will never become great saints – yet the weakest of us may be granted a place in that great company, which cannot be numbered, by living our lives in the power of God's word to St Paul: 'My grace is sufficient for you.' Lord, give us grace so to follow your blessed saints in all godly living, that we may come to the joys prepared for those who love you; through Jesus Christ our Redeemer. Amen.

Monday 3 November (tr. from 2nd)
Commemoration of All Souls   Those who are Asleep

'We would not have you ignorant, brethren, concerning those who are asleep, that you may not grieve as others do who have no hope.'
1 Thessalonians 4.13

Sympathy

St Paul gives sympathetic and encouraging answers to the genuine, sorrowful, enquiries of the Christians at Thessalonica; he is both generous and sensible. He appreciates their sorrows and their fears, their pain and their needs. Bereavement is a profound emotional shock; and emotional wounds take so much longer to heal than physical ones. Their mourning of loved ones is not being discouraged, as such; but rather the Apostle wishes to clear away whatever ignorance there is about what happens after death.

Too often in the past, the impression may have been given that Christians should not weep or give way to emotion, even be sad, at death, because of the promise – and expectation – of resurrection of the dead and of life with Jesus afterward.

Unhelpful

But that is an unhelpful and unrealistic outlook, even unscriptural; and a wrong burden to be laid upon relatives and friends still in the shock of the death of a loved one.

Jesus himself wept at the grave of Lazarus, despite what was about to happen; so we have the best example of all to look to, when we ourselves meet the loss and the death of a near friend or relative.

What we can all struggle to do at funerals and in the months that follow, is to bring our faith and our emotions together. Grief is both natural and necessary. How is it that simple peasant communities can meet and accept the death of relatives and friends, with a simple and direct faith and trust, that we seem to have lost in our over-sophisticated lives? And they show the grief and pain that they feel, quite openly and frankly; where we button ourselves up, 'keep a straight face'. We smile at the Victorian black clothes, black-edged notepaper and all the rest – but how sensible to be able to *show* grief instead of pretending an impassivity that is false.

Our Comforter

Jesus is no academic spectator to our personal tragedies, but someone who knows about it all, from the inside. Hence his ability to come alongside us as we suffer, and to be our Comforter, bringing the presence of the Holy Spirit, to strengthen and uphold us in all our trials. Grief is natural; but hopeless grief is not so; our Christian hope is in Jesus who died and rose again.

The Focal Point

This eucharist is the focal point where all meet; they are with Christ and he is with us in this act of remembrance, where sorrow and love, faith and hope, are all mingled together. While we commend them in the Father's love, where they without doubt can have refreshment, light and peace, they will, as they grow in love, penitence, forgiveness and goodwill, with thankfulness pray that Christ's life given for all, may have its fruit in the salvation of all.

PRAYER FOR LIGHT AND PEACE

Almighty God,
give to all who mourn a sure confidence in
*   your loving care,*
that we may cast all our sorrow on you,
and know the consolation of your love.
Lord of mercy–
*   Lord hear us*
Give us grace to entrust N. to your unfailing love
which sustained him/her in this life

Lord of Mercy –
    Lord hear us
May all who have been made one with Christ
in his death and in his resurrection
die to sin and rise to newness of life.
Lord of mercy–
    Lord hear us

(Patterns for Worship 51.7)

(Another Sermon for All Souls' Tide, or at a Funeral or a Commemoration) **The Christian Hope**

'He is not a God of the dead, but of the living.' Mark 12.27

In Between

The Scriptures are clear about those who have confessed Jesus as Saviour and Lord, they will be saved – 'Through Jesus, God will bring with him those who have fallen asleep' (1 Thessslonians 14) But what of those 'in between' – not overt disbelievers nor believers? Concerning them, we should surely be hopeful, be realistic, be reassured of God's right but loving decisions. We can remember the words of Jesus (Mark 9.40), 'Whoever is not against us, is for us.' We cannot change our height by worrying about it; neither can we change God's judgement by worrying about it. Let us be reassured that the Judge of all the world will judge justly (Genesis 18, 25) God knows where a person's heart really is, whatever we ourselves may think; he knows all.

Here is a passage written by a great evangelical on this very point:

Our Hope

I am imbued with hope; I have never been able to conjure up – as some great Evangelical missionaries have – the appalling vision of the millions who are not only perishing but will inevitably perish. On the other hand, as I have said, I am not and cannot be a universalist. Between these extremes I cherish the hope that the majority of the human race will be saved. And I have a solid biblical basis for this belief. True, Jesus said that those who find the narrow road that leads to life were 'few' (was he referring to the little remnant of his own day within the nation of Israel?). We need to remember that God is the Creator of all humankind, and remains infinitely loving, patient and compassionate towards all whom he has made. Yes, and he is also everybody's 'Father', both in the sense that they 'live and move and have their being' in him, derive the richness of their human life from his generosity (Acts 17.25–28), and in the sense that he continues to yearn for his lost children, as in the parable of the Prodigal Son. (It is the intimacy of a father–child relationship, which according to the New Testament is given only to those whom God has reconciled to himself through Jesus Christ.)

Compassion

We have to remember too, that God does not *want* anybody to perish, but *wants* everybody to be saved (2 Peter 3.9; 1 Timothy 2.4); that Jesus expressed his compassion for society's outcasts – the publicans and sinners and the prostitutes – refused to reject them and deliberately made friends with them. His own forecast was that 'many' would come from the four points of the compass, and the four corners of the earth, to join the Jewish Patriarchs in God's kingdom (Luke 13.29) and that the final vision of the redeemed in the Book of Revelation is of 'a great multitude that no-one could count' (7.9), a huge international throng in whom God's promise to Abraham will at last be fulfilled – that his seed (his spiritual posterity) would be as innumerable as the stars in the sky, the dust of the earth, and the waves of the oceans.

('Essentials' – David L. Edwards & John Stott)

> *Jesus, the resurrection and the life*
> *we give you thanks for all*
> *who have lived and believed in you*
> *(and especially . . .)*
> *Raise us with them to eternal life.*
> *Jesus, Lord of life,*
> >   *in your mercy, hear us,*
> >   *accept our prayers,*
> >   *and be with us always. Amen.*
> >   *(Patterns for Worship 51.60)*

Remembrance Sunday (9 November 1997)
Remembrance and Resurrection

'Jesus said: "I am the resurrection, and I am the life."'   John 11.25

Worship
We meet together today, as we meet every Sunday, to worship God: to praise and honour him, to proclaim our love for him, and to celebrate his love for us. And it is within that worship, before God, that we offer our Remembrance of the evil days of war, with their suffering, their losses and their deaths. Some of us still have heavy hearts today; many families still hold sad memories. But for many here, war is something totally unreal, something to read about or to see on the TV.

Memories
I suppose I come somewhere in the middle, since I was born in the Second World War years. I can still remember the wail of the sirens which sent people rushing to the shelters. I can remember being carried at night into the crowded space under the stairs or the garden shelter with its iron ceiling. I remember the long journey away to Wales where I was evacuated with my mother and my baby brother, and the little cottage on the hillside with the cold stone floor, and the toilet that seemed miles away down the road – well, I was *very* small. And the bull that chased us when we went to pick mushrooms, and the goat that butted mother! But we were lucky. Our home lost just windows and ceilings. And my father came back home in 1945 – but my cousin's father did not.

The Poppies
And mingling now with those memories is a little red flame – the poppy, the symbol chosen for Remembrance. The poppies which spread themselves across the war-torn fields of Flanders, red as the blood shed there. Red and black, the colours of war and passion, of blood and death; symbol of the lives lost and wasted there. But it is also the symbol of hope, Green for Peace, and Red for Life.

The Message

But we have to understand their true message. We can't sit back and say 'They died to give us freedom and peace, and now everything is all right' because it is not. Wars go on: The Falklands, the Gulf War, War in the Holy Land, War in Liberia, in Africa, in Russia, in Serbia and so many places over the world. Peace is never secure. Those who lost their lives and those who survived, on the battlefields, in the bombings, in the hideous extermination camps, at sea and in the air – all links in the long chain of history, a chain being bitterly forged even now. To make sense of their sacrifices, we must carry on the struggle against evil, whenever it is found, wherever it is, and whatever shape it takes.

Not Alone

But we do not have to go it alone. We hold another symbol precious – the Cross of Christ. As the poppy symbolizes the blood shed in war, so the Cross symbolizes the blood of Jesus Christ, shed for us in the spiritual war against evil in all its forms. His blood poured out that we might be made whole. His death for our life; his Cross a sign of Hope; his Resurrection a triumph over sin and death.   J.M.Y.

Mothering Sunday   *(Fourth Sunday in Lent)*
Our Mothers

'Jerusalem, which is above, is free, which is the mother of us all.' Galatians 4,26 (BCP Epistle) or, 'Mary kept all these things in her heart.' Luke 2.19

Our Mothers' Day

Today is Mother's Day, if we go by the advertisements in our local paper shops, and card shops, and florists – Good luck to them all, for it is very right and proper to remember our mothers, to thank God for them, and bring some small present, a gift of flowers perhaps (we have flowers here today, so that every child can present Mum with a token of love and thanks, for all that we owe our Mothers). Or something made by the children themselves . . .

The Home

Some important person has said, remembering younger days, 'The true primary school of vital and vitalizing love – is the home.' A home means a family, and a family where parents and children share their experiences, their laughter and their tears, their energies and their adventures – plus a strong awareness of their sense of belonging. Added to this should be a strong awareness of their love and worship of God. For God should share the home; he should be a member of the family – a unifying love shown in a common allegiance.

Pressures

There are many adverse pressures which bear down on family life. There may be tensions arising from the 'generation gap' – when children begin to assert their individuality, often with ideas very different from those of their parents. But even here, there should be and can be, unity in diversity. For a home to survive there must be understanding and tolerance – children towards parents and parents towards children. The days when children were 'seen and not heard' are long gone. In a sensible family they are heard, and their ideas treated with respect, even though they may be disagreed with.

Tensions

Tensions, are of course, sometimes created through differences of temperament or conduct, but here again, they must be resolved in a spirit of love and not of anger. A home should radiate happiness among its members; and the centre of that happiness – who else? – should be the mother. It is the mother who can help to make happiness radiate in the home and through its members. The home fires of love and charity should never be allowed to burn out – and it is the mother who can see that the flame and warmth is not extinguished.

Two or Three Gathered Together

The Lord Jesus himself said that where two or three or more are gathered together in his Name, he is there in the midst of them. Jesus is the source of true love, true care, true happiness. Our families should gather round Jesus in the knowledge that he is the unifying force of their unity.

Another source of tension, of course, can arise when children grow older and wish to break away from home; parents must view what is a natural enough human urge as the young minds and bodies grow towards maturity. View this with tolerance but also with wisdom at the same time. Clearly circumstances must be taken into consideration, but possessiveness on the part of the parents should not be the deciding factor. Love must decide this, as indeed all our problems, even if sometimes it brings a sense of pain rather than joy.

Young and Old
So, Mothering Sunday is rightly regarded as a day which reminds our young people of the care and love their parents have given them – and are giving them still – and telling them to show their gratitude; while parents may well thank God for their children, think of their duties and problems as parents, and ask for God's help and guidance in them.

Harvest Thanksgiving
'O All Ye Green Things'

'O all ye Green Things upon the earth, bless ye the Lord; praise him and magnify him for ever.' Benedicite (v. 20 BCP)

Praise and Thanksgiving
In most of our churches, when Morning Prayer (Mattins) is used, the Canticle after the First Lesson is that fine hymn called 'Te Deum' – 'We Praise thee, O God . . .' It is only rarely we hear the lovely alternative Canticle 'Benedicite'. The trouble is, 'Benedicite' does go on rather – 'The Heavens, the Sun and Moon, the Stars, Showers and Dews, the Winds, Nights and Days' – right on to 'Seas, Whales, Fowls of the Air,' and at the very end 'Ye Children of Men' – all blessing the Lord, joyful in their creation and their life. What a wonderful hymn of thanksgiving, for life, for Harvest and the blessings of the crops and all the fruits of the earth, for the work of farmers and fishermen, and all who bring us our food and drink, the necessities of life. It seems right, therefore, for a preacher on Harvest to look to the 'Benedicite' and take verse 20 as text:

'O all ye Green Things upon the earth, bless ye the Lord: praise him and magnify him for ever.'

The Green Movement

I must admit I feel pretty green, addressing you at Harvest Time on Green Issues which you must know more about than I do – I confess I am pretty low down on the ladder of the Green Movement. But I am climbing that ladder and will continue to do so; I am convinced that the Church should be far greener in its thinking and in its actions. We are already green in outward show, since for most of the year green is the dominant colour of the Church hangings, curtains, frontals and vestments. Green may be a pretty common ordinary colour, but how we miss it when we have a long hot summer – the poet Blake described England as 'a green and pleasant land' and we rejoice to see that greenness restored, with our lawns and parks, fields and woods alive with fresh colour once again. But shocking that so many people have been without proper supplies of water for so long, and that our Water Boards have been so improvident in certain places and parts of our country, and caused so much distress.

Back to our Roots

The Green Movement for me is a movement or journey back to our roots – so that we learn again old lessons, journey back to our start, rediscover our origins. We have made ourselves too cold and calculating; we measure everything in terms of cash and power, and success is in those areas, not of the heart but of the mind, or rather, of the greedy and calculating urges of money and consumerism. We live in a society that has drastically narrowed our sensibility to moral and spiritual issues. But I am detecting a change. We are beginning to see that we cannot go on like this; we do not have all the answers, we are slowly realizing that humanity is more than a thinking, grabbing animal, we have a spiritual side. The Church has taught this from the beginning; Creation and Creatures are intense with Divinity, for nothing is excluded from the Mind of God. As that remarkable prophet of our own time – Simone Weil – commented, 'The Church can only call itself catholic, if the universe and the whole of Creation is included.' The Green Movement will only reach its full influence when it concerns itself not just with human activities but will all aspects of the whole world. St Francis of Assisi taught this eloquently with his love of Nature, of animals and birds and plants; indeed if what he taught, and the present debates teach us, it is that there is no clear-cut distinction between what we called 'the sacred' and 'the secular'. All is of God, and we must respect and honour Creation and the Creator. Yes, the Green Movement brings us back to our real and true roots.

Challenge
We need to step beyond the modern strait-jackets of mechanism, rationalism and materialism, and bring a return of the soul to wholeness, to let God back in once again. We need a value system that brings head and heart together again, in an ethic and programme of care, as part of our world view and part of our own process of healing. We cannot heal the cruel mess we humans have made, of our world and indeed of ourselves, without undergoing a spiritual healing process. The Green Movement is 'healing from within', getting ourselves right first, so that then we can be of enormous influence. We must grasp and keep that divine sense of life as a miracle, of the power of imagination, of the deep meanings of faith and hope, of dream and vision. The Green Movement is a challenge to us to find, once again, the sacredness within the world, to recover our lost souls and to root ourselves again in this tiny spaceship Earth. Then we can make our prayer again from the Benedicite, 'O all ye Green Things upon the earth, bless ye the Lord.'   T.D.J.

Tailpiece
'Spare us, good Lord, spare thy people, and be not angry with us for ever.' (Litany, the Book of Common Prayer 1662)

Anger
The story of a rather timid clergyman (which as you know isn't me!) who was told by one part of his flock to preach 'The Old-Fashioned Gospel'. By the rest he was told 'to be more broad-minded' . . .

On Sunday he got up to preach and ended his sermon by saying, 'Unless you repent (to a degree), and are saved (so to speak), you are – I'm sorry to say – in danger of hell-fire and damnation – to a certain extent.'

The words of Jesus don't give us that luxury: 'You have heard that it was said to the men of old, "You shall not kill; and whoever kills shall be liable to judgement." But I say to you, that everyone who is angry with his brother shall be liable to judgement; whoever insults his brother shall be liable to the council; and whoever says, "You fool!" shall be liable to the hell of fire.' (Matthew 5.21–23)

Question

We could ask ourselves here and now, why did Jesus make such far-reaching and definite statements? Being angry is not a sin in itself: it is what you can say and do when angry that may be sinful – not the anger itself. Firstly then, the severity of Jesus' verdict: the more we look at this verse, the clearer it becomes that it isn't getting *angry* that is being condemned, but when we call *people* 'good for nothing' – 'worthless fool', and so on.

It is when we 'write people off', that we are in danger of being written off ourselves. It is one thing to get angry with, say, the potholes in the road; but quite another to say the Council is completely useless, they never do anything worthwhile; all their workers are dead idle . . . The transition from a factual situation which may quite justifiably get us angry, to one where we make a personal attack, is in Jesus' view unacceptable – and even may call in question our own salvation.

Serious

This is a serious matter, so we had better check it out. Just think of the situations that have made you angry in the last month or so: maybe a lost ten minutes waiting for a bus; maybe, the children's behaviour; maybe, something to do with the Council – housing repairs not done, maybe the Government's tax on fuel. But do we ever cross over from getting angry about a decision, or a lack of action, or a change of some kind; and then make a comment about someone's personal worth. 'Your housing officer makes me sick!' 'Look at your children, they're out of control! You're useless as a parent!' 'You never do anything on time; what's the matter with you lot!'

How easy it seems, to change from a specific situation or incident, to a generalized comment which says something quite extreme.

That is when we are in danger of hell, because we are not showing self-control, kindness, understanding, forbearance. We know that if we don't forgive them, we won't be forgiven ourselves.

Begging the Question

So should we never get angry? No, indeed we are duty bound to get angry at injustice, and at evil; and to do something about them. We would all want to quote Jesus getting angry at the money-changers in the Temple.

Can we get angry with things going on around us? with people in church?

Notice that Jesus' words are addressed to *whoever* calls his brother (or sister) a fool; that's someone you know well, perhaps a fellow Christian. Yes, the problem will occur from time to time; we will annoy one another, even get angry *but* we are never allowed to write one another off.

Lastly Then . . .

Make sure that your anger is justified, not just a difference of opinion. Make sure you dissociate the *action* from the *person*. Not ever: 'You make me angry!' but 'I'm angry because you are making assumptions about what we should do; let's discuss things some more . . .' So let's stick to the issue concerned, don't bring in other things; don't annihilate the person, don't make your concern lead to grudges.

Let's end on a positive note; anger is an emotion that can be used constructively, it can result in a relationship being strengthened when you understand one another, *and* you may see how you come across to other people!

Above all, don't forget, if we don't forgive others, we won't be forgiven ourselves.   M.P.

INDEX OF SUBJECTS

INDEX OF TEXTS

Church Book & Desk Diary 1997

– a Reference book – a Year Planner – a Diary
Dark blue hardback, ribbon marker
size 240 × 148 mm (A5). 480pp. £11.25 (inc. VAT)

New English Hymnal

Since its introduction in 1986 this book has been adopted by nearly all the
CofE's cathedrals and some Roman Catholic cathedrals and over 1000
parish churches in England and abroad – over 500,000 copies in use.

Available in Words only, Words and Melody edition, Words and Full
Music edition, Presentation de-luxe edition, and Large Print edition.
Introductory cassette also available.

Hymns Ancient & Modern
New Standard

Since publication of this edition in 1983, over a million copies have been
sold. Available in Words only, Words and Melody edition, Words and
Full Music, Organ edition, Presentation de-luxe edition, Large Print and
Small Print editions. Three cassettes also available.

Worship Songs Ancient & Modern

Fills the gap between the classic hymn and the popular chorus.
Available now in Words and Melody edition; Words and Full Music
Edition; also a cassette featuring 20 of the songs in the collection.

'Highly recommended' – *Choir Schools Today*.

'Beautifully edited . . . one of the best collections I have seen'
– *Methodist Recorder*

*Generous grants are available to assist parishes wishing to introduce new hymn
books. Send for application form and catalogue.*

 The Canterbury Press Norwich

The book publishing imprint of Hymns Ancient and Modern Limited
ST MARY'S PLAIN, NORWICH, NORFOLK, NR3 3BH
Telephone: (0603) 616563 and 612914   Fax: (0603) 624483